# TRS-80
# Color Programs

**Programs for Color BASIC and
Extended Color BASIC on the
TRS-80 Color Computer,
and for Micro Color BASIC on the
TRS-80 MC-10 Micro Color Computer**

# TRS-80
# Color Programs

**Programs for Color BASIC and
Extended Color BASIC on the
TRS-80 Color Computer,
and for Micro Color BASIC on the
TRS-80 MC-10 Micro Color Computer**

## Tom Rugg and Phil Feldman

**dilithium Press**
Beaverton, Oregon

10    9    8    7    6    5    4    3

**Library of Congress Cataloging in Publication Data**

Rugg, Tom.
  TRS-80 color programs.

  Bibliography: p.
  1. TRS-80 (Computer) — Programming. 2. Basic (Computer program language) I. Feldman, Phil. II. Title.
QA76.8.T18R834          001.64'2          81-22121
ISBN 0-918398-61-4                        AACR2

Printed in the United States of America

Cover: Marty Urman

dilithium Press
8285 S.W. Nimbus
Suite 151
Beaverton, Oregon 97005

TRS-80 refers to the Radio Shack microcomputer and is a registered trademark of Tandy Corporation, Fort Worth, Texas.

# Acknowledgements

Our thanks to the following for their help and encouragement: Our wives and families, John Craig, Merl and Patti Miller, Asenatha McCauley, Herb Furth, Freddie, Jim Rugg (W6DVZ), and Wayne Green.

## AN IMPORTANT NOTE

The publisher and authors have made every effort to assure that the computer programs are accurate and complete. However, this publication is prepared for general readership, and neither the publisher nor the authors have any knowledge about or ability to control any third party's use of the programs and programming information. There is no warranty or representation by either the publisher or the authors that the programs or programming information in this book will enable the reader or user to achieve any particular result.

# Preface

You have bought yourself a Radio Shack TRS-80 Color Computer (or maybe you just have access to one at school or work). You will soon find that the most frequent question you are asked goes something like this: "Oh, you got a computer, eh? Uh...what are you going to do with it?"

Your answer, of course, depends on your own particular situation. Maybe you got it for mathematical work, or for your business, or for home usage, or to enable you to learn more about computers. Maybe you got it for a teaching/learning tool or for playing games.

Even if you got the computer specifically for only one of these reasons, you should not neglect the others. The computer is such a powerful tool that it can be used in many different ways. If it is not being used for its "intended" function right now, why not make use of it in some other way?

The Color Computer is so small and portable that you can, say, take it home from work over the weekend and let the kids play educational games. They will have fun *and* learn a lot. After they go to bed, you can use it to help plan your personal finances. Or, you can let your guests at a party try to outsmart the computer (or each other) at some fascinating games. The possibilities go on and on.

All these things can be done with the Color Computer, but it cannot do any of them without the key ingredient — a computer program. People with little or no exposure to computers may be in for a surprise when they learn this. A computer without a program is like a car without a driver. It just sits there.

So you ask, "Where can I get some programs to do the things I want my computer to do?" Glad you asked. There are several alternatives.

1. Hire a computer programmer. If you have a big budget, this is the way to go. Good programmers are expensive and hard to find (and you will not know for sure if they're really good until after the job is finished). Writing a couple of programs that are moderately complex will probably cost you more than you paid for the computer itself.

2. Learn to program yourself. This is a nice alternative, but it takes time. There are lots of programming books available—some are good, some are not so good. You can take courses at local colleges. If you can afford the time and you have a fair amount of common sense and inner drive, this is a good solution.

3. Buy the programs you want. This is cheaper than hiring your own programmer because all the buyers share the cost of writing the programs. You still will not find it very cheap, especially if you want to accumulate several dozen programs. Each program might cost anywhere from a few dollars to several hundred dollars. The main problem is that you cannot be sure how good the programs are, and, since they are generalized for all possible buyers, you may not be able to easily modify them to do exactly what *you* want. Also, they have to be written in a computer language that *your* computer understands. Even if you find a program written in the BASIC language, you will soon learn that Color and Extended Color BASIC are not the same as other versions. Variations between versions of the same language typically result in the program not working.

This book gives you the chance to take the third alternative at the lowest possible cost. If you divide the cost of the book by the number of programs in it (use your computer if you like), you will find that the cost per program is amazingly low. Even if there are only a few programs in the book that will be useful to you, the cost is pretty hard to beat.

Just as important is the fact that these programs are written specifically for your TRS-80 Color Computer. If you type them in exactly as shown, they will work! No changes are needed. In addition, we show you exactly what to change in order to make some simple modifications that may suit your taste or needs. Plus, if you have learned a little about BASIC, you can go even further and follow the suggestions about more extensive changes that can be made. This approach was used to try to make every program useful to you, whether you are a total beginner or an old hand with computers.

But enough of the sales pitch. Our main point is that we feel a computer is an incredibly flexible machine, and it is a shame to put it to only one or two limited uses and let it sit idle the rest of the time. We are giving you a pretty wide range of things to do with your computer, and we are really only scratching the surface.

So open your eyes and your mind! Play a mental game against the computer (WARI, JOT). Evaluate your next financial decision (LOAN, DECIDE). Expand your vocabulary or improve your reading speed (VOCAB, TACHIST). Solve mathematical equations (DIFFEQN, SIMEQN).

But please, don't leave your computer asleep in the corner too much. Give it some exercise.

# How to Use This Book

Each chapter of this book presents a computer program that runs on a 16K Radio Shack TRS-80 Color Computer. Most will also run on a 4K TRS-80 Color Computer or a 4K TRS-80 MC-10 Micro Color Computer (see the Appendix). All the programs work with either "standard" Color BASIC or Extended Color BASIC. Each chapter is made up of eight sections that serve the following functions:

1. **Purpose:** Explains what the program does and why you might want to use it.
2. **How To Use It:** Gives the details of what happens when you run the program. Explains your options and the meanings of any responses you might give. Provides details of any limitations of the program or errors that might occur.
3. **Sample Run:** Shows you what you will see on the screen when you run the program.
4. **Program Listing:** Provides a "listing" (or "print-out") of the BASIC program. These are the instructions to the computer that you must provide so it will know what to do. You must type them in extremely carefully for correct results.
5. **Easy Changes:** Shows you some very simple changes you can make to the program to cause it to work differently, if you wish. You do not have to understand how to program to make these changes.
6. **Main Routines:** Explains the general logic of the program, in case you want to figure out how it works. Gives the BASIC line numbers and a brief explanation of what each major portion of the program accomplishes.

7. **Main Variables:** Explains what each of the key variables in the program is used for, in case you want to figure out how it works.

8. **Suggested Projects:** Provides a few ideas for major changes you might want to make to the program. To try any of these, you will need to understand BASIC and use the information provided in the previous two sections (Main Routines and Main Variables).

To use any of these programs on your Color Computer, you need only use the first four sections. The last four sections are there to give you supplementary information if you want to tinker with the program.

## RECOMMENDED PROCEDURE

Here is our recommendation of how to try any of the programs in this book:

1. Read through the documentation that came with the Color Computer to learn the fundamentals of communication with the computer. This will teach you how to turn the computer on, enter a program, correct mistakes, run a program, etc.

2. Pick a chapter and read Section 1 ("Purpose") to see if the program sounds interesting or useful to you. If not, move on to the next chapter until you find one that is. If you are a beginner you might want to try one of the short "Miscellaneous Programs" first.

3. Read Sections 2 and 3 of the chapter ("How To Use It" and "Sample Run") to learn the details of what the program does.

4. Enter the NEW command to eliminate any existing program that might already be in your computer's memory. Using Section 4 of the chapter ("Program Listing"), *carefully* enter the program into the computer. Be particularly careful to get all the punctuation characters right (i.e., commas, semicolons, colons, quotation marks, etc.).

5. After the entire program is entered into the computer's memory, use the LIST command to display what you have entered so you can double check for typographical errors, omitted lines, etc. Don't mistake a semicolon for a colon, or

an alphabetic I or O for a numeric 1 or 0 (zero). *Take a min-*
*ute to note the differences in these characters before you*
*begin.*

6. Before trying to RUN the program, use the CSAVE command to save the program temporarily on cassette. This
could prevent a lot of wasted effort in case something goes
wrong (power failure, computer malfunction, etc.). If the
computer "hangs up" when you enter RUN, you can simply
reset it, reload the program from cassette, and look for typing errors.

7. Now RUN the program. Is the same thing happening that is
shown in the Sample Run? If so, accept our congratulations
and go on to step 9. If not, stay cool and go to step 8.

8. If you got a SYNTAX ERROR in a line, LIST that line and
look at it closely. Something is not right. Maybe you inter-
changed a colon and a semicolon. Maybe you typed a
numeric 1 or 0 instead of an alphabetic I or O. Maybe you
misspelled a word or omitted one. Keep looking until you
find it, then correct the error and go back to step 7.

If you got some other kind of error message, consult the
computer's documentation for an explanation. Keep in
mind that the error might not be in the line that is pointed to
by the error message. It is not unusual for the mistake to be
in a line immediately preceding the error message line.
Another possibility is that one or more lines were omitted
entirely. In any event, fix the problem and go back to step 7.

If there are no error messages, but the program is not doing the same thing as the Sample Run, there are two possibilities. First, maybe the program isn't *supposed* to do exactly the same thing. Some of the programs are designed to
do unpredictable things to avoid repetition (primarily the
game programs and graphic displays). They should be doing
the same *types* of things as the Sample Run, however.

The second possibility is that you made a typing error that
did not cause an error message to be displayed, but simply
changed the meaning of one or more lines in the program.
This can be a little tricky to find, but you can usually narrow
it down to the general area of the problem by noting the
point at which the error takes place. Is the first thing displayed correct? If so, the error is probably after the PRINT

statement that caused the first thing to be displayed. Look for the same types of things mentioned before. Make the corrections and go back to step 7.

9. Continue running the program, trying to duplicate the Sample Run. If you find a variation that cannot be accounted for in the "How To Use It" section of the chapter, go to step 8. Otherwise, if it seems to be running properly, CSAVE the program on cassette.

10. Read Section 5 of the chapter ("Easy Changes"). Try any of the changes that look interesting. If you think the changed version is better, CSAVE it on cassette, too. You will probably want to give it a slightly different title in the first REM statement to avoid future confusion.

## A NOTE ON THE PROGRAM LISTINGS

A line on the screen of the Color Computer is 32 characters wide. However, the printer that was used to create the Program Listing section of each chapter prints lines up to 80 characters long. When typing into your computer a line longer than 32 characters, simply type the entire line as shown in the listing followed by the **ENTER** key. Don't be fooled by the fact that the cursor on your Color Computer jumps down to the next line after you enter the 32nd character — it's just one long line until you press **ENTER**.

# Contents

## Section 3 — GAME PROGRAMS \
*Match wits with the computer or a friend.*

## Section 4 — GRAPHICS DISPLAY PROGRAMS
*Dazzling visual diversions.*

# Section 5 — MATHEMATICS PROGRAMS
*For math, engineering, and statistical uses.*

# Section 6 — MISCELLANEOUS PROGRAMS
*Short programs that do interesting things.*

# Section 1

# Applications Programs

## INTRODUCTION TO APPLICATIONS PROGRAMS

Good practical applications are certainly a prime use of personal computers. There are a myriad of ways the TRS-80 Color Computer can help us to do useful work. Here are eight programs for use around the home or business.

Financial considerations are always important. LOAN will calculate interest, payment schedules etc. for mortgages, car loans, or any such business loan. Do you ever have trouble balancing your checkbook(s)? CHECKBOOK will enable you to rectify your monthly statements and help you find the cause of any errors. With the many types of investments available today, there is often confusion about their true annual yields. ANNUAL will make sure you don't have this problem any more.

Perhaps you find yourself compiling various lists at home or work. These could be lists of names, words, phrases, etc. The chore of alphabetizing such a list is duck soup for SORTLIST.

Fuel usage is a constant concern for those of us who drive. MILEAGE will determine and keep track of a motor vehicle's general operating efficiency.

The tedium of analyzing questionnaires and examinations can be greatly relieved with the aid of your computer. In particular, teachers and market researchers should find QUEST/EXAM useful.

Often we are faced with difficult decisions. DECIDE transforms the Color Computer into a trusty advisor. Help will be at hand for any decision involving the selection of one alternative from several choices.

Before anything else, you might want to consult BIO-RHYTHM each day. Some major airlines, and other industries, are placing credence on biorhythm theory. If you agree, or "just in case," simply turn on your computer and load this program.

# ANNUAL

## PURPOSE

Suppose you put $1000.00 into an investment that pays ten percent interest. How much interest will you earn by the end of one year?

Generally the answer is *not* simply $100.00 (the interest rate times the principal). The amount of interest earned per year depends on how often the interest is compounded (calculated) and paid. If it is done only once at the end of the year, you really do earn only ten percent. But if it is done more often (each month, for example) you earn more. This is because the interest after the first month begins earning interest too.

This program shows you the annual yield of any interest rate for various compounding techniques, assuming that the interest is added to the principal as it is calculated. Be aware that some savings institutions use different techniques for calculating annual yield. Their published figures may differ from the ones calculated here.

## HOW TO USE IT

Simply enter the interest rate you want to evaluate. The program shows the annual yield for annual, semi-annual, quarterly, monthly, weekly, and daily compounding. Then it asks you for another interest rate to evaluate. If you have no more, enter zero to end the program.

Due to the way numbers are represented inside the computer, you may occasionally notice the last significant digit to be inaccurate. Fortunately, there is seldom any need to know the annual yield beyond two or three decimal places, so this should be no problem.

The calculated answers come out almost instantaneously for most compounding techniques, but daily compounding takes a little longer to compute (about 3 or 4 seconds).

The Easy Changes section below shows how to send the output to a printer, if you have one. It also shows how to add other compounding techniques to the program.

**SAMPLE RUN**

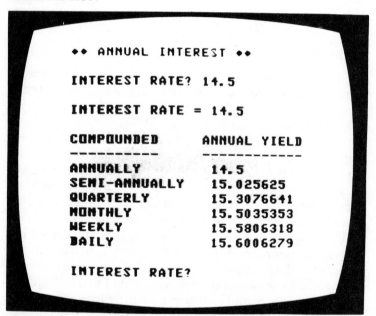

The program asks what interest rate should be evaluated. The operator provides it, and the program shows the annual yield for six different compounding techniques.

**PROGRAM LISTING**

```
100 REM: ANNUAL INTEREST
110 REM: (C) 1981, TOM RUGG AND PHIL
    FELDMAN
130 CLEAR 200:CLS
140 P=0
```

```
150 PRINT"** ANNUAL INTEREST **"
160 PRINT
170 INPUT"INTEREST RATE";R
180 PRINT:IF R=0 THEN END
190 PRINT#P,"INTEREST RATE =";R
200 PRINT#P
210 PRINT#P,"COMPOUNDED";TAB(15);
220 PRINT#P,"ANNUAL YIELD"
230 PRINT#P,"------------";TAB(15);
240 PRINT#P,"------------"
250 RESTORE
260 READ N$,N
270 IF N$="END" THEN 400
280 PRINT#P,N$;TAB(15);
290 T=R/100:W=T/N:S=1
300 FOR J=1 TO N
310 S=S+S*W:NEXT
320 S=(S-1)*100
330 PRINT#P,S
340 GOTO 260
400 PRINT#P
410 GOTO 170
800 END
900 DATA ANNUALLY,1
910 DATA SEMI-ANNUALLY,2
920 DATA QUARTERLY,4
930 DATA MONTHLY,12
940 DATA WEEKLY,52
950 DATA DAILY,365
960 DATA END,999
```

**EASY CHANGES**

1. If you have a printer, you can send the output to it very easily. Just change this line:

$$140 \ P = -2$$

2. Adding another compounding technique is done by inserting another DATA statement between lines 900-950. For example, bimonthly compounding would mean once every two months, or six times per year. To include it, add this statement:

$$925 \ DATA \ BIMONTHLY,6$$

3. The program can be changed to make calculations for a whole series of interest rates without stopping. If you have a printer, you may want to create your own reference tables. To do so for, say, interest rates from 10 to 12 percent in increments of one-quarter percent, make these changes:

170 FOR R = 10 TO 12 STEP .25
410 NEXT

## MAIN ROUTINES

| | |
|---|---|
| 130-140 | Initializes variables. |
| 150-160 | Displays title. |
| 170-180 | Gets interest rate. Ends program if zero. |
| 190-240 | Displays rate and column headings. |
| 250-410 | Makes calculation and displays result for each compounding technique. |
| 900-960 | DATA statements for each compounding technique. |

## MAIN VARIABLES

| | |
|---|---|
| P | Pointer to where output will be sent (0 = video, − 2 = printer). |
| R | Interest rate supplied by operator (as percentage). |
| N$ | Name of compounding technique. |
| N | Number of times per year to compound. |
| T | Interest rate (as decimal). |
| W | Interest rate per compounding period. |
| S | Sum of interest earned for the year. |
| J | Loop variable. |

## SUGGESTED PROJECTS

1. Take inflation and taxes into account and show the "real" gain or loss of the investment. For example, a person in a 50 percent tax bracket during a year of nine percent inflation needs to make about an 18 percent annual yield just to break even at the end of the year.
2. Change the program to display (or print) a table of annual yields. Show a column for each compounding technique, and a row for each interest rate.

# BIORHYTHM

## PURPOSE

Did you ever have one of those days when nothing seemed to go right? All of us seem to have days when we are clumsy, feel depressed, or just cannot seem to force ourselves to concentrate as well as usual. Sometimes we know why this occurs. It may result from the onset of a cold or because of an argument with a relative. Sometimes, however, we find no such reason. Why can't we perform up to par on some of those days when nothing is known to be wrong?

Biorhythm theory says that all of us have cycles, beginning with the moment of birth, that influence our physical, emotional, and intellectual states. We will not go into a lot of detail about how biorhythm theory was developed (your local library probably has some books about this if you want to find out more), but we will summarize how it supposedly affects you.

The physical cycle is twenty-three days long. For the first 11½ days, you are in the positive half of the cycle. This means you should have a feeling of physical well-being, strength, and endurance. During the second 11½ days, you are in the negative half of the cycle. This results in less endurance and a tendency toward a general feeling of fatigue.

The emotional cycle lasts for twenty-eight days. During the positive half (the first fourteen days), you should feel more cheerful, optimistic, and cooperative. During the negative half, you will tend to be more moody, pessimistic, and irritable.

The third cycle is the intellectual cycle, which lasts for thirty-three days. The first half is a period in which you should have greater success in learning new material and pursuing creative, intellectual activities. During the second half, you are supposedly better off reviewing old material rather than attempting to learn difficult new concepts.

The ups and downs of these cycles are relative to each individual. For example, if you are a very self-controlled, unemotional person to begin with, your emotional highs and lows may not be very noticeable. Similarly, your physical and intellectual fluctuations depend upon your physical condition and intellectual capacity.

The day that any of these three cycles changes from the plus side to the minus side (or vice versa) is called a "critical day." Biorhythm theory says that you are more accident-prone on critical days in your physical or emotional cycles. Critical days in the intellectual cycle aren't considered as dangerous, but if they coincide with a critical day in one of the other cycles, the potential problem can increase. As you might expect, a triple critical day is one on which you are recommended to be especially careful.

Please note that there is quite a bit of controversy about biorhythms. Most scientists feel that there is not nearly enough evidence to conclude that biorhythms can tell you anything meaningful. Others believe that biorhythm cycles exist, but that they are not as simple and inflexible as the 23, 28, and 33 day cycles mentioned here.

Whether biorhythms are good, bad, true, false, or anything else is not our concern here. We are just presenting the idea to you as an interesting theory that you can investigate with the help of your TRS-80 Color Computer.

**HOW TO USE IT**

The program first asks for the birth date of the person whose biorhythm cycles are to be charted. You provide the month and day as you might expect. For the year, you only need to enter the last two digits if it is between 1900 and 1999. Otherwise, enter all four digits.

Next the program asks you for the start date for the biorhythm chart. Enter it in the same way. Of course, this date cannot be earlier than the birth date.

After a delay of about a second, the program clears the screen and begins plotting the biorhythm chart, one day at a time. The left side of the screen displays the date, while the right side displays the chart. The left half of the chart is the "down" (negative) side of each cycle. The right half is the "up" (positive) side. The center line shows the critical days when you are at a zero point (neither positive nor negative).

Each of the three curves is plotted with an identifying letter — P for physical, E for emotional, and I for intellectual. When the curves cross, an asterisk is displayed instead of either of the two (or three) letters.

Twelve days of the chart are displayed on one screen, and then the program waits for you to press a key. If you press the E key, the current chart ends and the program starts over again. If you press the **SPACE** key (or any other key except **BREAK** or **SHIFT**), the program clears the screen and displays the next twelve days of the chart.

The program will allow you to enter dates from the year 100 A.D. and on. We make no guarantees about any extreme future dates, however, such as entering a year greater than 3000. We sincerely hope that these limitations do not prove to be too confining for you.

**SAMPLE RUN**

```
   ♦♦ BIORHYTHM ♦♦

ENTER BIRTH DATE

MONTH(1 TO 12)? 3
DAY (1 TO 31)? 4
YEAR? 47
 1947 ASSUMED.
ENTER START DATE FOR CHART

MONTH(1 TO 12)? 11
DAY (1 TO 31)? 1
YEAR? 81
 1981 ASSUMED.
```

The operator enters his or her birth date and the date for the beginning of the chart.

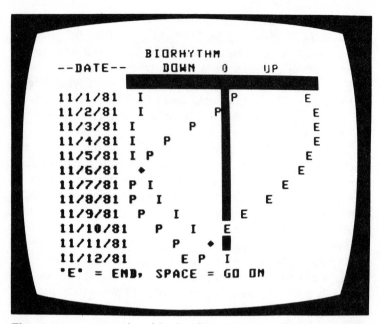

The program responds with the first 12 days of the operator's biorhythm chart, then waits for a key to be pressed.

## PROGRAM LISTING

```
100 REM: BIORHYTHM
110 REM: (C) 1981, TOM RUGG AND PHIL
    FELDMAN
120 CLEAR 200:CLS
130 L=0:T=11:P=3.14159265
140 PRINT"** BIORHYTHM **":PRINT
150 PRINT"ENTER BIRTH DATE"
160 GOSUB 500:GOSUB 600:JB=JD
190 PRINT"ENTER START DATE FOR CHART"
200 GOSUB 500:GOSUB 600:JC=JD
230 IF JC>=JB THEN 270
240 PRINT"CHART DATE CAN'T BE EARLIER"
250 PRINT"THAN BIRTH DATE."
260 SOUND 8,8:PRINT:GOTO 150
270 FOR K=1 TO 1000:NEXT
280 GOSUB 700
300 N=JC-JB
310 V=23:GOSUB 800
320 V=28:GOSUB 800
```

```
330 V=33:GOSUB 800
340 GOSUB 1000
350 PRINT C$;TAB(8);L$
360 JC=JC+1:L=L+1:IF L<12 THEN 300
370 PRINT"'E' = END, SPACE = GO ON";
380 R$=INKEY$:IF R$="" THEN 380
390 IF R$="E" THEN 120
400 L=0:GOTO 280
500 PRINT
505 INPUT"MONTH(1 TO 12)";M
510 M=INT(M):IF M<1 OR M>12 THEN 505
520 INPUT"DAY (1 TO 31)";D
530 D=INT(D):IF D<1 OR D>31 THEN 520
540 INPUT"YEAR";Y
550 Y=INT(Y):IF Y<0 THEN 540
560 IF Y>99 THEN 580
570 Y=Y+1900:PRINT Y;"ASSUMED."
580 RETURN
600 W=0:IF M<3 THEN W=-1
610 JD=INT(1461*(Y+4800+W)/4)
620 B=INT(367*(M-2-W*12)/12)
630 IF B<0 THEN B=B+1
640 JD=JD+B
650 B=INT(INT(3*(Y+4900+W)/100)/4)
660 JD=JD+D-32075-B
670 RETURN
700 CLS
710 PRINT TAB(10);"BIORHYTHM"
720 PRINT"--DATE--";TAB(12);
730 PRINT"DOWN";TAB(19);"0";TAB(24);"UP"
740 PRINT TAB(8);
750 FOR K=1 TO T+T+1:PRINT CHR$(175);
760 NEXT:PRINT:RETURN
800 W=INT(N/V):R=N-(W*V)
850 IF V<>23 THEN 900
860 L$=CHR$(32):FOR K=1 TO 4
870 L$=L$+L$:NEXT
880 L$=LEFT$(L$,T)+CHR$(175)+LEFT$(L$,T)
890 IF V=23 THEN C$="P"
900 IF V=28 THEN C$="E"
910 IF V=33 THEN C$="I"
920 W=R/V:W=W*2*P
930 W=T*SIN(W):W=W+T+1,5
940 W=INT(W):A$=MID$(L$,W,1)
```

```
950 IF A$="F" OR A$="E" OR A$="*" THEN
    C$="*"
955 IF W=1 THEN 980
957 IF W=T+T+1 THEN 990
960 L$=LEFT$(L$,W-1)+C$+RIGHT$(L$,T+T+1-W)
970 RETURN
980 L$=C$+RIGHT$(L$,T+T):RETURN
990 L$=LEFT$(L$,T+T)+C$:RETURN
1000 W=JC+68569:R=INT(4*W/146097)
1010 W=W-INT((146097*R+3)/4)
1020 Y=INT(4000*(W+1)/1461001)
1030 W=W-INT(1461*Y/4)+31
1040 M=INT(80*W/2447)
1050 D=W-INT(2447*M/80)
1060 W=INT(M/11):M=M+2-12*W
1070 Y=100*(R-49)+Y+W
1080 A$=STR$(M):W=LEN(A$)-1
1090 C$=MID$(A$,2,W)+"/"
1100 A$=STR$(D):W=LEN(A$)-1
1110 C$=C$+MID$(A$,2,W)+"/"
1120 A$=STR$(Y):W=LEN(A$)-1
1130 C$=C$+MID$(A$,W,2)
1140 RETURN
```

## EASY CHANGES

1. Want to see the number of days between any two dates? Insert this line:

   305 PRINT "DAYS = ";N: END

   Then enter the earlier date as the birth date, and the later date as the start date for the chart. This will cause the program to display the difference in days and then end.

2. To alter the number of days of the chart shown on each screen, alter the 12 in line 360.

## MAIN ROUTINES

120- 140 Initializes variables. Displays titles.

150- 160 Asks for birth date and converts to Julian date format (i.e., the number of days since January 1, 4713 B.C.

190- 200 Asks for start date for chart and converts to Julian date format.

| | |
|---|---|
| 230- 260 | Checks that chart date is not sooner than birth date. |
| 270 | Delays about one second before displaying chart. |
| 280 | Displays heading at top of screen. |
| 300 | Determines number of days between birth date and current chart date. |
| 310- 330 | Plots points in L$ string for each of the three cycles. |
| 340 | Converts Julian date back into month-day-year format. |
| 350 | Displays one line on the chart. |
| 360- 400 | Adds one to chart date. Checks to see if the screen is full. |
| 500- 580 | Subroutine to ask operator for month, day, and year. Edits replies. |
| 600- 670 | Subroutine to convert month, day, and year into Julian date format. |
| 700- 760 | Subroutine to clear screen and display headings. |
| 800- 990 | Subroutine to calculate remainder R of N/V, and plot a point in L$ based on V and R. |
| 1000-1140 | Subroutine to convert Julian date JC back into month-day-year format. |

## MAIN VARIABLES

| | |
|---|---|
| L | Counter of number of lines on screen. |
| T | Number of characters on one side of the center of the chart. |
| P | Pi. |
| JB | Birth date in Julian format. |
| JD | Julian date calculated in subroutine. |
| JC | Chart start date in Julian format. |
| K | Loop and work variable. |
| N | Number of days between birth and current chart date. |
| V | Number of days in present biorhythm cycle (23, 28, or 33). |
| C$ | String with date in month/day/year format. |
| L$ | String with one line of the biorhythm chart. |
| R$ | Reply from operator after screen fills up. |
| M | Month (1-12) |
| D | Day (1-31) |
| Y | Year (100 or greater) |

W, B        Work variables.
R           Remainder of N/V (number of days into cycle).
A$          Work variable.

## SUGGESTED PROJECTS

1. Investigate the biorhythms of some famous historical or athletic personalities. For example, are track and field athletes usually in the positive side of the physical cycle on the days that they set world records? Where was Lincoln in his emotional and intellectual cycles when he wrote "The Gettysburg Address"? Do a significant percentage of accidents befall people on critical days?
2. Modify the program to print the chart on a line printer. (Be sure to print the name and/or birthdate on the chart, too.)

# CHECKBOOK

**PURPOSE**

Many people consider the monthly ritual of balancing the checkbook to be an irritating and error-prone activity. Some people get confused and simply give up after the first try, while others give up the first time they cannot reconcile the bank statement with the checkbook. Fortunately, you have an advantage — your computer. This program takes you through the necessary steps to balance your checkbook, doing the arithmetic for you, of course.

**HOW TO USE IT**

The program starts off by giving you instructions to verify that the amount of each check and deposit are the same on the statement as they are in your checkbook. Sometimes the bank will make an error in reading the amount that you wrote on a check (especially if your handwriting is not too clear), and sometimes you will copy the amount incorrectly into your checkbook. While you are comparing these figures, make a check mark in your checkbook next to each check and deposit listed on the statement. A good system is to alternate the marks you use each month (maybe an "x" one month and a check mark the next) so you can easily see which checks and deposits came through on which statement.

Next, the program asks for the ending balance shown on the bank statement. You are then asked for the *check number* (not the amount) of the most recent check shown on the statement. This will generally be the highest numbered check the bank has processed, unless you like to write checks out of sequence. Your account balance after this most recent check will be reconciled with the statement balance, so that is what the program asks for next—your checkbook balance after the most recent check.

The program must compensate for any differences between what your checkbook has in it prior to the most recent check and what the statement has on it. First, if you have any deposits that are not shown on the statement before the most recent check, you must enter them. Generally, there are none, so you just enter "END."

Next you have to enter the amounts of any checks that have not yet "cleared" the bank and that are prior to the most recent check. Look in your checkbook for any checks that do not have your check mark next to them. Remember that some of these could be several months old.

Next you enter the amount of any service charges or debit memos that are on the statement, but which have not been shown in your checkbook prior to the most recent check. Typically, this is just a monthly service charge, but there might also be charges for printing new checks for you or some other adjustment that takes money away from you. Credit memos (which give money back to you) are not entered until later. Be sure to make an entry in your checkbook for any of these adjustments so that next month's statement will balance.

Finally, you are asked for any recent deposits or credit memos that were *not* entered in your checkbook prior to the most recent check, but that *are* listed on the bank statement. It is not unusual to have one or two of these, since deposits are generally processed by banks sooner than checks.

Now comes the moment of truth. The program tells you whether or not you are in balance and displays the totals. If so, pack things up until next month's statement arrives.

If not, you have to figure out what is wrong. The best thing to do first is to make sure you entered all the data correctly. You can verify that the outstanding checks were entered correctly with this command:

FOR J = 1 TO NC:PRINT C(J);:NEXT

Then, to review the balancing summary, you can enter:

GOTO 810

To verify that you entered everything else correctly, simply RUN the program again and compare results.

If you entered everything correctly, the most likely cause of the out of balance condition is an arithmetic error in your checkbook. Look for errors in your addition and subtraction, with subtraction being the most likely culprit. This is especially likely if the amount of the error is a nice even number like one dollar or ten cents.

Another common error is accidentally adding the amount of a check in your checkbook instead of subtracting it. If you did this, your error will be twice the amount of the check (which makes it easy to find).

If this still does not explain the error, check to be sure you subtracted *last* month's service charge when you balanced your checkbook with the previous statement. And, of course, if you did not balance your checkbook last month, you cannot expect it to come out right this month.

The program has limitations of how many outstanding checks you can enter, but this can be changed easily. See "Easy Changes" below.

With a 4K computer, you will need to enter the command CLEAR50 before you enter this program from the keyboard or from cassette.

**SAMPLE RUN**

```
  ••  CHECKBOOK  ••

FIRST, BE SURE YOUR BANK
STATEMENT AND CHECKBOOK SHOW
THE SAME FIGURES FOR EACH CHECK
AND DEPOSIT LISTED ON THE
STATEMENT.

WHAT'S THE ENDING BALANCE SHOWN
ON THE STATEMENT?
? 520.16
NOW FIND THE MOST RECENT CHECK
THAT IS ON THE STATEMENT.
WHAT IS THE CHECK NUMBER OF IT?
? 1652
```

The program displays an introduction, and the operator begins providing the necessary information.

```
? 520.16
NOW FIND THE MOST RECENT CHECK
THAT IS ON THE STATEMENT.
WHAT IS THE CHECK NUMBER OF IT?
? 1652

WHAT BALANCE IS SHOWN IN YOUR
CHECKBOOK AFTER CHECK NO. 1652
? 480.12

ENTER THE AMOUNT OF ANY DEPOSIT
SHOWN IN YOUR CHECKBOOK PRIOR
TO CHECK 1652 THAT IS NOT
ON THE STATEMENT.
ENTER 'END' WHEN DONE
? END
```

The operator continues by entering the checkbook balance, followed
by END to indicate no outstanding deposits.

```
TOTAL = 0

NOW ENTER THE AMOUNTS OF ANY
CHECKS IN THE CHECKBOOK PRIOR
TO CHECK 1652 THAT HAVE NOT
YET BEEN SHOWN ON A STATEMENT.
ENTER 'END' WHEN DONE
? 35.04
? 10
? END
TOTAL = 45.04

NOW ENTER THE AMOUNTS OF ANY
SERVICE CHARGES OR DEBIT MEMOS.
ENTER 'END' WHEN DONE
?
```

The operator enters the outstanding checks, and prepares to enter service charges.

```
TOTAL = 45.04

NOW ENTER THE AMOUNTS OF ANY
SERVICE CHARGES OR DEBIT MEMOS.
ENTER 'END' WHEN DONE
? 2.35
? 2.65
? END
TOTAL = 5

ENTER THE AMOUNT OF ANY DEPOSIT
SHOWN IN YOUR CHECKBOOK AFTER
CHECK NO. 1652 THAT IS ALSO
LISTED IN THE STATEMENT.
ENTER 'END' WHEN DONE
? END
```

After the service charges are entered, the operator indicates no late deposits.

```
TOTAL = 0

IT BALANCES!

STATEMENT BALANCE +
DEPOSITS OUTSTANDING +
SERVICE CHARGES = 525.16

CHECKBOOK BALANCE +
CHECKS OUTSTANDING +
RECENT DEPOSITS = 525.16

DIFFERENCE = 0

OK
```

Finally, the program displays balancing information and ends.

## PROGRAM LISTING

```
100 REM: CHECKBOOK
110 REM: (C) 1981, TOM RUGG AND PHIL
    FELDMAN
120 CLEAR 50:CLS
130 PRINT"** CHECKBOOK **":PRINT
150 MC=10
160 DIM C(MC)
180 E$="ERROR. RE-ENTER."
190 PRINT"FIRST, BE SURE YOUR BANK"
200 PRINT"STATEMENT AND CHECKBOOK SHOW"
210 PRINT"THE SAME FIGURES FOR EACH CHECK"
220 PRINT"AND DEPOSIT LISTED ON THE"
230 PRINT"STATEMENT.":PRINT
280 PRINT"WHAT'S THE ENDING BALANCE SHOWN"
290 PRINT"ON THE STATEMENT?":INPUT SB
300 PRINT"NOW FIND THE MOST RECENT CHECK"
310 PRINT"THAT IS ON THE STATEMENT."
330 PRINT"WHAT IS THE CHECK NUMBER OF IT?"
340 INPUT LC
350 L$="NO MORE ROOM."
```

```
380 PRINT
390 PRINT"WHAT BALANCE IS SHOWN IN YOUR"
400 PRINT"CHECKBOOK AFTER CHECK NO.";LC
410 INPUT CB:PRINT
430 PRINT"ENTER THE AMOUNT OF ANY DEPOSIT"
440 PRINT"SHOWN IN YOUR CHECKBOOK PRIOR"
450 PRINT"TO CHECK";LC;"THAT IS NOT"
460 PRINT"ON THE STATEMENT."
470 A$="ENTER 'END' WHEN DONE":PRINT A$
480 INPUT R$:IF R$="END" THEN 540
500 IF VAL(R$)>0 THEN 520
510 PRINT E$:GOTO 470
520 ND=ND+1:TD=TD+VAL(R$)
530 GOTO 480
540 PRINT"TOTAL =";TD:PRINT
550 PRINT"NOW ENTER THE AMOUNTS OF ANY"
560 PRINT"CHECKS IN THE CHECKBOOK PRIOR"
570 PRINT"TO CHECK";LC;"THAT HAVE NOT"
580 PRINT"YET BEEN SHOWN ON A STATEMENT."
600 PRINT A$
610 INPUT R$
620 IF R$="END" THEN 690
630 IF VAL(R$)>0 THEN 660
640 PRINT E$:GOTO 600
660 NC=NC+1:C(NC)=VAL(R$):TC=TC+C(NC)
670 IF NC<MC THEN 610
680 PRINT L$
690 PRINT"TOTAL =";TC:PRINT
700 PRINT"NOW ENTER THE AMOUNTS OF ANY"
710 PRINT"SERVICE CHARGES OR DEBIT MEMOS."
720 PRINT A$
730 INPUT R$
740 IF R$="END" THEN 790
750 IF VAL(R$)>0 THEN 770
760 PRINT E$:GOTO 720
770 NS=NS+1:TS=TS+VAL(R$)
780 GOTO 730
790 PRINT"TOTAL =";TS:PRINT
800 GOSUB 2000
810 W=SB+TD+TS-CB-TC-TR:W=ABS(W)
815 IF W>.001 THEN 840
820 W=0:PRINT"IT BALANCES!"
830 GOTO 850
840 PRINT"SORRY, IT'S OUT OF BALANCE."
```

```
850 PRINT:PRINT"STATEMENT BALANCE +"
860 PRINT"DEPOSITS OUTSTANDING +"
870 PRINT"SERVICE CHARGES =";SE+TD+TS
880 PRINT:PRINT"CHECKBOOK BALANCE +"
890 PRINT"CHECKS OUTSTANDING +"
900 PRINT"RECENT DEPOSITS =";CB+TC+TR
910 PRINT:PRINT"DIFFERENCE =";W
920 PRINT
930 END
2000 PRINT"ENTER THE AMOUNT OF ANY DEPOSIT"
2010 PRINT"SHOWN IN YOUR CHECKBOOK AFTER"
2020 PRINT"CHECK NO.";LC;"THAT IS ALSO"
2030 PRINT"LISTED IN THE STATEMENT."
2050 PRINT A$
2060 INPUT R$
2070 IF R$="END" THEN 2130
2080 IF VAL(R$)>0 THEN 2100
2090 PRINT E$:GOTO 2050
2100 NR=NR+1:TR=TR+VAL(R$)
2110 GOTO 2060
2130 PRINT"TOTAL =";TR:PRINT
2140 RETURN
```

## EASY CHANGES

Change the limitation of how many outstanding checks you can enter. Line 150 establishes this limit. If you have more than 10 checks outstanding at some time, change the value of MC to 100, for example. You will need to have a 16K (or larger) computer to make MC larger than about 40.

## MAIN ROUTINES

120- 290 Initializes variables and displays first instructions.
300- 340 Gets most recent check number.
380- 410 Gets checkbook balance after most recent check number.
430- 540 Gets outstanding deposits.
550- 690 Gets outstanding checks.
700- 790 Gets service charges and debit memos.
800       Gets recent deposits and credit memos.
810- 930 Does balancing calculation. Displays it. Ends program.
2000-2140 Subroutine to get recent deposits.

## MAIN VARIABLES

| | |
|---|---|
| MC | Maximum number of checks outstanding. |
| C | Array for checks outstanding. |
| TC | Total of checks outstanding. |
| TD | Total of deposits outstanding. |
| TS | Total of service charges and debit memos. |
| TR | Total of recent deposits and credit memos. |
| NC | Number of checks outstanding. |
| ND | Number of deposits outstanding. |
| NS | Number of service charges and debit memos. |
| NR | Number of recent deposits and credit memos. |
| E$ | Error message. |
| SB | Statement balance. |
| LC | Number of last check on statement. |
| CB | Checkbook balance after last check on statement. |
| R$ | Reply from operator. |
| W | Amount by which checkbook is out of balance. |
| A$ | Message showing how to indicate no more data. |
| L$ | Message indicating no more room for data. |

## SUGGESTED PROJECTS

1. Add more informative messages and a more complete introduction to make the program a tutorial for someone who has never balanced a checkbook before.
2. Save all entries from the operator and allow any of them to be reviewed and/or modified if found to be incorrect.
3. If the checkbook is out of balance, have the program do an analysis (as suggested in the "How To Use It" section) and suggest the most likely errors that might have caused the condition.
4. Allow the operator to find arithmetic errors in the checkbook. Ask for the starting balance, then ask for each check or deposit amount. Add or subtract, depending on which type the operator indicates. Display the new balance after each entry so the operator can compare with the checkbook entry.

# DECIDE

## PURPOSE

"Decisions, decisions!" How many times have you uttered this lament when confronted by a difficult choice? Wouldn't a trusty advisor be helpful on such occasions? Well, you now have one—your TRS-80 Color Computer of course.

This program can help you make decisions involving the selection of one alternative from several choices. It works by prying relevant information from you and then organizing it in a meaningful, quantitative manner. Your best choice will be indicated and all of the possibilities given a relative rating.

You can use the program for a wide variety of decisions. It can help with things like choosing the best stereo system, saying yes or no to a job or business offer, or selecting the best course of action for the future. Everything is personalized to your individual decision.

## HOW TO USE IT

The first thing the program does is ask you to categorize the decision at hand into one of these three categories:

1) Choosing an item (or thing),
2) Choosing a course of action, or
3) Making a yes or no decision.

You simply press 1, 2, or 3 followed by the **ENTER** key to indicate which type of decision is facing you. If you are choosing an item, you will be asked what type of item it is.

If the decision is either of the first two types, you must next enter a list of all the possibilities under consideration. A question mark will prompt you for each one. When the list is complete, type "END" in response to the last question mark. You must, of course, enter at least two possibilities. (We hope you don't have trouble making decisions from only one possibility!) After the list is finished, it will be re-displayed so that you can verify that it is correct. If not, you must re-enter it.

Now you must think of the different factors that are important to you in making your decision. For example, location, cost, and quality of education might govern the decision of which college to attend. For a refrigerator purchase, the factors might be things like price, size, reliability, and warranty. In any case, you will be prompted for your list with a succession of question marks. Each factor is to be entered one at a time with the word "END" used to terminate the list. When complete, the list will be re-displayed. You must now decide which single factor is the most important and input its number. (You can enter 0 if you wish to change the list of factors.)

The program now asks you to rate the importance of each of the other factors relative to the most important one. This is done by first assigning a value of 10 to the main factor. Then you must assign a value from 0-10 to each of the other factors. These numbers reflect your assessment of each factor's relative importance as compared to the main one. A value of 10 means it is just as important; lesser values indicate how much less importance you place on it.

Now you must rate the decision possibilities with respect to each of the importance factors. Each importance factor will be treated separately. Considering *only* that importance factor, you must rate how each decision possibility stacks up. The program first assigns a value of 10 to one of the decision possibilities. Then you must assign a relative number (lower, higher, or equal to 10) to each of the other decision possibilities.

An example might alleviate possible confusion here. Suppose you are trying to decide whether to get a dog, cat, or canary for a pet. Affection is one of your importance factors. The program assigns a value of 10 to the cat. Considering *only* affection, you might assign a value of 20 to the dog and 6.5 to the canary. This means *you* consider a dog twice as affectionate as a cat but a canary only about two thirds as affectionate as a cat. (No slighting of bird lovers is intended here, of course. Your actual ratings may be entirely different.)

Armed with all this information, the program will now determine which choice seems best for you. The various possibilities are listed in order of ranking. Alongside each one is a relative rating with the best choice being normalized to a value of 100.

Of course, DECIDE should not be used as a substitute for good, clear thinking. However, it can often provide valuable insights. You might find one alternative coming out surprisingly low or high. A trend may become obvious when the program is re-run with improved data. At least, it may help you think about decisions systematically and honestly.

**SAMPLE RUN**

```
                DECIDE
   I CAN HELP YOU MAKE A
DECISION. ALL I NEED TO DO IS
ASK SOME QUESTIONS AND THEN
ANALYZE YOUR RESPONSES.
-------------------------------
WHICH OF THESE BEST DESCRIBES
THE DECISION FACING YOU?
   1) CHOOSING AN ITEM FROM
      VARIOUS ALTERNATIVES.
   2) CHOOSING A COURSE OF ACTION
      FROM VARIOUS ALTERNATIVES.
   3) DECIDING 'YES' OR 'NO'.

WHICH ONE (1,2,OR 3)? 1

WHAT TYPE OF ITEM IS IT
? VACATION

   I NEED TO HAVE A LIST OF EACH
VACATION UNDER
CONSIDERATION.

   INPUT THEM ONE AT A TIME IN
RESPONSE TO EACH QUESTION MARK.

   TYPE THE WORD 'END' TO
INDICATE THAT THE WHOLE LIST
HAS BEEN ENTERED.
```

```
? CAMPING
? SAFARI
? TRIP TO D.C.
? END

OK. HERE'S YOUR LIST:

  1) CAMPING
  2) SAFARI
  3) TRIP TO D.C.

IS THE LIST CORRECT (Y OR N)? Y

  NOW, THINK OF THE FACTORS THAT
ARE IMPORTANT IN CHOOSING THE
BEST VACATION.

  INPUT THEM ONE AT A TIME IN
RESPONSE TO EACH QUESTION MARK.

  TYPE THE WORD 'END' TO
TERMINATE THE LIST.

? RELAXATION
? AFFORDABILITY
? CHANGE OF PACE
? END

HERE'S YOUR LIST OF FACTORS:
  1) RELAXATION
  2) AFFORDABILITY
  3) CHANGE OF PACE
DECIDE WHICH FACTOR ON THE
LIST IS THE MOST IMPORTANT AND
INPUT ITS NUMBER. (TYPE 0 IF
THE LIST NEEDS CHANGING.)
? 2

  NOW LET'S SUPPOSE WE HAVE A
SCALE OF IMPORTANCE RANGING
FROM 0-10. WE'LL GIVE
AFFORDABILITY A VALUE OF
10 SINCE AFFORDABILITY
WAS RATED THE MOST IMPORTANT.

  ON THIS SCALE, WHAT VALUE OF
IMPORTANCE WOULD THE OTHER
FACTORS HAVE?
```

RELAXATION
? 5.5

CHANGE OF PACE
? 9

   EACH VACATION MUST NOW
BE COMPARED WITH RESPECT TO
EACH IMPORTANCE FACTOR.
   WE'LL CONSIDER EACH FACTOR
SEPARATELY AND THEN RATE
EACH VACATION IN TERMS
OF THAT FACTOR ONLY.

*** (HIT ANY KEY TO CONTINUE)

(A key is pressed)

   LET'S GIVE CAMPING
A VALUE OF 10 ON EVERY SCALE.
   EVERY OTHER VACATION
WILL BE ASSIGNED A VALUE HIGHER
OR LOWER THAN 10. THIS VALUE
DEPENDS ON HOW MUCH YOU THINK
IT IS BETTER OR WORSE THAN
CAMPING.
   ------------------
   CONSIDERING ONLY RELAXATION
AND ASSIGNING 10 TO
CAMPING,
WHAT VALUE WOULD YOU ASSIGN TO
SAFARI? 3
TRIP TO D.C.? 9
   ------------------
   CONSIDERING ONLY AFFORDABILITY
AND ASSIGNING 10 TO
CAMPING,
WHAT VALUE WOULD YOU ASSIGN TO
SAFARI? 1
TRIP TO D.C.? 8
   ------------------
   CONSIDERING ONLY CHANGE OF PACE
AND ASSIGNING 10 TO
CAMPING,
WHAT VALUE WOULD YOU ASSIGN TO
SAFARI? 60
TRIP TO D.C.? 25

```
TRIP TO D.C. IS BEST
BUT IT'S VERY CLOSE.
  HERE'S THE FINAL LIST IN
ORDER. TRIP TO D.C.
HAS BEEN GIVEN A VALUE OF 100
AND THE OTHERS RATED
ACCORDINGLY.

  HIT ANY KEY TO SEE THE LIST.
(A key is pressed)
  100              TRIP TO D.C.
  98.6587184       CAMPING
  78.8375559       SAFARI
OK
```

## PROGRAM LISTING

```
100 REM: DECIDE - 16K
110 REM: (C) 1981, PHIL FELDMAN AND TOM
    RUGG
150 CLEAR 500
160 MD=10
170 DIM L$(MD),F$(MD),V(MD)
180 DIM C(MD,MD),D(MD),Z(MD)
190 E$="END"
200 GOSUB 5000
210 PRINT"  I CAN HELP YOU MAKE A"
220 PRINT"DECISION.  ALL I NEED TO DO IS"
230 PRINT"ASK SOME QUESTIONS AND THEN"
240 PRINT"ANALYZE YOUR RESPONSES."
250 FOR J=1 TO 30:PRINT"-";:NEXT
260 PRINT
270 PRINT"WHICH OF THESE BEST DESCRIBES"
280 PRINT"THE DECISION FACING YOU?"
290 PRINT" 1) CHOOSING AN ITEM FROM"
300 PRINT"     VARIOUS ALTERNATIVES."
310 PRINT" 2) CHOOSING A COURSE OF ACTION"
320 PRINT"     FROM VARIOUS ALTERNATIVES."
330 PRINT" 3) DECIDING 'YES' OR 'NO'."
340 PRINT
350 INPUT"WHICH ONE (1,2,OR 3)";T
360 IF T<1 OR T>3 THEN 200
400 GOSUB 5000
410 ON T GOTO 420,440,460
420 PRINT"WHAT TYPE OF ITEM IS IT"
430 INPUT T$:GOTO 500
```

```
440 T$="COURSE OF ACTION"
450 GOTO 500
460 T$="'YES' OR 'NO'":NI=2
470 L$(1)="DECIDING YES"
480 L$(2)="DECIDING NO"
490 GOTO 900
500 GOSUB 5000:NI=0
510 PRINT"  I NEED TO HAVE A LIST OF EACH"
520 PRINT T$;" UNDER"
530 PRINT"CONSIDERATION.":PRINT
540 PRINT"  INPUT THEM ONE AT A TIME IN"
550 PRINT"RESPONSE TO EACH QUESTION MARK."
560 PRINT
570 PRINT"  TYPE THE WORD '";E$;"' TO"
580 PRINT"INDICATE THAT THE WHOLE LIST"
590 PRINT"HAS BEEN ENTERED.":PRINT
600 IF NI<MD THEN 620
610 PRINT"-LIST FULL-":GOTO 650
620 NI=NI+1:INPUT L$(NI)
630 IF L$(NI)<>E$ THEN 600
640 NI=NI-1
650 IF NI>=2 THEN 700
660 PRINT
670 PRINT"YOU NEED AT LEAST 2 CHOICES!"
680 PRINT:PRINT"TRY AGAIN"
690 GOSUB 5200:GOTO 500
700 GOSUB 5000
710 PRINT"OK. HERE'S YOUR LIST:"
720 PRINT:FOR J=1 TO NI
730 PRINT J;CHR$(8);") ";L$(J)
740 NEXT:PRINT
750 FOR J=1 TO 9:R$=INKEY$:NEXT
760 INPUT"IS THE LIST CORRECT (Y OR N)";R$
770 IF R$="Y" THEN 900
780 IF R$<>"N" GOTO 700
790 PRINT
800 PRINT"THE LIST MUST BE RE-ENTERED"
810 GOSUB 5200:GOTO 500
900 GOSUB 5000:R$=INKEY$
910 PRINT"  NOW, THINK OF THE FACTORS THAT"
920 IF T<3 THEN PRINT"ARE IMPORTANT IN
    CHOOSING THE"
930 IF T<3 THEN PRINT"BEST ";T$;"."
940 IF T=3 THEN PRINT"ARE IMPORTANT TO
    YOU IN"
```

```
950 IF T=3 THEN PRINT"DECIDING ";T$;","
960 PRINT:PRINT" INPUT THEM ONE AT A TIME
    IN"
970 PRINT"RESPONSE TO EACH QUESTION MARK,"
980 PRINT:PRINT" TYPE THE WORD '";E$;"'/ TO"
990 PRINT"TERMINATE THE LIST,"
1000 PRINT:NF=0
1010 IF NF>=MD THEN PRINT"-- LIST FULL --"
     :PRINT
1020 IF NF>=MD THEN GOTO 1060
1030 NF=NF+1:INPUT F$(NF)
1040 IF F$(NF)<>E$ THEN 1010
1050 NF=NF-1:PRINT
1060 IF NF<1 THEN PRINT"YOU NEED AT
     LEAST 1 - REDO IT !"
1070 IF NF<1 THEN GOSUB 5200
1080 IF NF<1 THEN 900
1100 GOSUB 5000
1110 PRINT"HERE'S YOUR LIST OF FACTORS:"
1130 FOR J=1 TO NF
1140 PRINT J;CHR$(8);") ";F$(J)
1150 NEXT
1160 PRINT"DECIDE WHICH FACTOR ON THE"
1170 PRINT"LIST IS THE MOST IMPORTANT AND"
1180 PRINT"INPUT ITS NUMBER, (TYPE 0 IF"
1190 PRINT"THE LIST NEEDS CHANGING,)"
1200 INPUT A:A=INT(A)
1210 IF A=0 THEN 900
1220 IF A>NF OR A<0 THEN 1100
1300 GOSUB 5000
1310 IF NF=1 THEN 1500
1320 PRINT" NOW LET'S SUPPOSE WE HAVE A"
1330 PRINT"SCALE OF IMPORTANCE RANGING"
1340 PRINT"FROM 0-10, WE'LL GIVE"
1350 PRINT F$(A);" A VALUE OF"
1360 PRINT"10 SINCE ";F$(A)
1370 PRINT"WAS RATED THE MOST IMPORTANT,"
1380 PRINT:PRINT" ON THIS SCALE, WHAT
     VALUE OF"
1390 PRINT"IMPORTANCE WOULD THE OTHER"
1400 PRINT"FACTORS HAVE?"
1410 FOR J=1 TO NF
1420 IF J=A THEN 1490
1430 PRINT:PRINT F$(J)
1440 INPUT V(J)
```

```
1450 IF V(J)<0 THEN 1480
1460 IF V(J)>10 THEN 1480
1470 GOTO 1490
1480 PRINT" IMPOSSIBLE VALUE - TRY AGAIN"
     :GOTO 1430
1490 NEXT
1500 V(A)=10:Q=0:FOR J=1 TO NF
1510 Q=Q+V(J):NEXT:FOR J=1 TO NF
1520 V(J)=V(J)/Q:NEXT:GOSUB 5000
1530 IF T<>3 THEN PRINT" EACH ";T$;" MUST
     NOW"
1540 IF T=3 THEN PRINT" DECIDING 'YES' OR
     DECIDING"
1550 IF T=3 THEN PRINT"'NO' MUST NOW"
1560 PRINT"BE COMPARED WITH RESPECT TO"
1570 PRINT"EACH IMPORTANCE FACTOR."
1580 PRINT" WE'LL CONSIDER EACH FACTOR"
1590 PRINT"SEPARATELY AND THEN RATE"
1600 IF T<>3 THEN PRINT"EACH ";T$;" IN
     TERMS"
1610 IF T=3 THEN PRINT"DECIDING 'YES' OR
     DECIDING"
1620 IF T=3 THEN PRINT"'NO' IN TERMS"
1630 PRINT"OF THAT FACTOR ONLY."
1634 PRINT:PRINT"*** (HIT ANY KEY TO
     CONTINUE)"
1638 R$=INKEY$:IF R$="" THEN1638
1640 PRINT:PRINT" LET'S GIVE ";L$(1)
1650 PRINT"A VALUE OF 10 ON EVERY SCALE."
1660 IF T<>3 THEN PRINT" EVERY OTHER ";T$
1670 IF T=3 THEN PRINT" THEN DECIDING 'NO'"
1680 PRINT"WILL BE ASSIGNED A VALUE HIGHER"
1690 PRINT"OR LOWER THAN 10. THIS VALUE"
1700 PRINT"DEPENDS ON HOW MUCH YOU THINK"
1710 PRINT"IT IS BETTER OR WORSE THAN"
1720 PRINT L$(1);"."
1800 FOR J=1 TO NF
1810 PRINT" --------------------------"
1820 PRINT" CONSIDERING ONLY ";F$(J)
1830 PRINT"AND ASSIGNING 10 TO"
1835 PRINT L$(1);","
1840 PRINT"WHAT VALUE WOULD YOU ASSIGN TO"
1850 FOR K=2 TO NI
1860 PRINT L$(K);:INPUT C(K,J)
1870 IF C(K,J)>=0 THEN 1900
```

```
1880 PRINT" -- NEGATIVE VALUES ILLEGAL --"
1890 GOTO 1860
1900 NEXT:PRINT:C(1,J)=10:NEXT
2000 FOR J=1 TO NF:Q=0
2010 FOR K=1 TO NI
2020 Q=Q+C(K,J):NEXT
2030 FOR K=1 TO NI
2040 C(K,J)=C(K,J)/Q:NEXT:NEXT
2050 FOR K=1 TO NI:D(K)=0
2060 FOR J=1 TO NF
2070 D(K)=D(K)+C(K,J)*V(J):NEXT
2080 NEXT:MX=0:FOR K=1 TO NI
2090 IF D(K)>MX THEN MX=D(K)
2100 NEXT:FOR K=1 TO NI
2110 D(K)=D(K)*100/MX:NEXT
2200 FOR K=1 TO NI:Z(K)=K:NEXT
2210 NM=NI-1:FOR K=1 TO NI
2220 FOR J=1 TO NM:N1=Z(J)
2230 N2=Z(J+1)
2240 IF D(N1)>D(N2) THEN 2260
2250 Z(J+1)=N1:Z(J)=N2
2260 NEXT:NEXT:J1=Z(1):J2=Z(2)
2270 DF=D(J1)-D(J2):GOSUB 5000
2300 PRINT L$(J1);" IS BEST"
2310 IF DF<5 THEN PRINT"BUT IT'S VERY
     CLOSE."
2320 IF DF<5 THEN 2380
2330 IF DF<10 THEN PRINT"BUT IT'S FAIRLY
     CLOSE."
2340 IF DF<10 THEN 2380
2350 IF DF<20 THEN PRINT"BY A FAIR AMOUNT."
2360 IF DF<20 THEN 2380
2370 PRINT"QUITE DECISIVELY."
2380 PRINT"  HERE'S THE FINAL LIST IN"
2390 PRINT"ORDER. ";L$(J1)
2400 PRINT"HAS BEEN GIVEN A VALUE OF 100"
2410 PRINT"AND THE OTHERS RATED"
2420 PRINT"ACCORDINGLY."
2430 PRINT
2440 PRINT"  HIT ANY KEY TO SEE THE LIST."
2450 R$=INKEY$
2460 IF R$="" THEN 2450
2470 PRINT
2480 FOR J=1 TO NI:Q=Z(J)
```

```
2490 PRINT D(Q),L$(Q):NEXT
3000 END
5000 FOR J=1 TO 500:NEXT
5010 CLS:PRINT@12,"DECIDE"
5020 PRINT:RETURN
5200 FOR J=1 TO 1500:NEXT:RETURN
```

## EASY CHANGES

1. The word "END" is used to flag the termination of various input lists. If you wish to use something else (because of conflicts with items on the list), change the definition of E$ in line 190. For example, to use the word "DONE," change line 190 to

   190 E$ = "DONE"

2. Line 5200 contains a timing delay used regularly in the program. If things seem to change too fast, you can make the number 1500 larger. Try

   5200 FOR J = 1 TO 3000:NEXT: RETURN

3. The program can currently accept up to ten decision alternatives and/or ten importance factors. If you need more, increase the value of MD in line 160. Thus, to use 15 values, line 160 should be

   160 MD = 15

## MAIN ROUTINES

150- 190   Initializes and dimensions variables.
200- 360   Determines category of decision.
400- 490   Gets or sets T$.
500- 810   Gets list of possible alternatives from user.
900-1220   Gets list of importance factors from user.
1300-1490  User rates each importance factor.
1500-1900  User rates the decision alternatives with respect to each importance factor.
2000-2110  Evaluates the various alternatives.
2200-2270  Sorts alternatives into their relative ranking.
2300-3000  Displays results.
5000-5020  Subroutine to clear screen and display header.
5200       Time wasting subroutine.

## MAIN VARIABLES

| | |
|---|---|
| MD | Maximum number of decision alternatives. |
| NI | Number of decision alternatives. |
| NM | NI − 1. |
| L$ | String array of the decision alternatives. |
| NF | Number of importance factors. |
| F$ | String array of the importance factors. |
| V | Array of the relative values of each importance factor. |
| A | Index number of most important factor. |
| C | Array of relative values of each alternative with respect to each importance factor. |
| T | Decision category (1 = item, 2 = course of action, 3 = yes or no). |
| T$ | String name of decision category. |
| E$ | String to signal the end of an input data list. |
| J,K | Loop indices. |
| R$ | User reply string. |
| Q,N1,N2 | Work variables. |
| D | Array of each alternative's value. |
| MX | Maximum value of all alternatives. |
| DF | Rating difference between best two alternatives. |
| Z | Array of the relative rankings of each alternative. |

## SUGGESTED PROJECTS

1. Allow the user to review his numerical input and modify it if desired.
2. Insights into a decision can often be gained by a sensitivity analysis. This involves running the program a number of times for the same decision. Each time, one input value is changed (usually the one you are least confident about). By seeing how the results change, you can determine which factors are the most important. Currently, this requires a complete rerunning of the program each time. Modify the program to allow a change of input after the regular output is produced. Then recalculate the results based on the new values. (Note that many input arrays are clobbered once all the input is given. This modification will require saving the original input in new arrays so that it can be reviewed later.)

# LOAN

## PURPOSE

One of the most frustrating things about borrowing money from a bank (or credit union or Savings and Loan) is that it's not easy to fully evaluate your options. When you are borrowing from a credit union to buy a new car, you might have the choice of a thirty-six or a forty-eight month repayment period. When buying a house, you can sometimes get a slightly lower interest rate for your loan if you can come up with a larger down payment. Which option is best for you? How will the monthly payment be affected? Will there be much difference in how fast the principal of the loan decreases? How much of each payment will be for interest, which is tax-deductible?

You need to know the answers to all these questions to make the best decision. This program gives you the information you need.

## HOW TO USE IT

The program first asks you the size of the loan you are considering. Only whole dollar amounts are allowed—no pennies. Loans of one million dollars or more are rejected (you can afford to hire an investment counselor if you want to borrow that much). Then you are asked the yearly interest rate for the loan. Enter this number as a percentage, such as "10.8." Next, you are asked to give the period of the loan in months. For a five year loan, enter 60. For a thirty year mortgage, enter 360. The program then displays this information for you and calculates the monthly payment that will cause the loan to be paid off with equal payments each month over the life of the loan.

At this point you have four options. First, you can show a monthly analysis. This displays a month-by-month breakdown, showing the state of the loan after each payment. The four columns of data shown for each month are the payment number (or month number) of the loan, the remaining balance of the loan after that payment, the amount of that payment that was interest, and the accumulated interest paid to date. Twelve lines of data are displayed on the screen, and then you can either press the T key to get the final totals for the loan, or any other key to get the data for the next twelve months of the loan.

The second option is overriding the monthly payment. It is a common practice with second mortgage loans to make smaller monthly payments each month with a large "balloon" payment as the final payment. You can use this second option to try various monthly payments to see how they affect that big payment at the end. After overriding the monthly payment, you will want to use the first option next to get a monthly analysis and final totals using the new monthly payment.

The third option is to simply start over. You will generally use this option if you are just comparing what the different monthly payments would be for different loan possibilities.

The fourth option ends the program.

By the way, there is a chance that the monthly payment calculated by your lender will differ from the one calculated here by a penny or two. We like to think that this is because we are making a more accurate calculation.

NOTE: SEE DISCLAIMER IN FRONT PART OF BOOK

**SAMPLE RUN**

```
LOAN CALCULATOR

LOAN AMOUNT? 62000
INTEREST RATE? 15.5
LENGTH OF LOAN (MONTHS)? 360
```

The operator enters the three necessary pieces of information about his or her loan.

```
   62000 FOR 360 MO. AT 15.5 %
MONTHLY PAYMENT IS 809.81

NEXT ACTION:
1 - MONTHLY ANALYSIS
2 - OVERRIDE PAYMENT
3 - START OVER
4 - END
? 1
```

The program responds with the monthly payment that will pay off the loan with equal payments over its life, then asks the operator what to do next. The operator asks for the monthly analysis.

```
   62000 FOR 360 MO. AT 15.5 %
          REMAINING      ---INTEREST---
   MO.    BALANCE    MONTH    TO-DATE
   1      61992.02   800.83    800.83
   2      61983.94   800.73   1601.56
   3      61975.76   800.63   2402.19
   4      61967.47   800.52   3202.71
   5      61959.07   800.41   4003.12
   6      61950.56   800.30   4803.42
   7      61941.94   800.19   5603.61
   8      61933.21   800.08   6403.69
   9      61924.37   799.97   7203.66
   10     61915.42   799.86   8003.52
   11     61906.35   799.74   8803.26
   12     61897.16   799.62   9602.88
   PRESS KEY TO GO ON (T=TOTALS)
```

The program responds with information about the first twelve months of the loan, then waits.

```
   62000 FOR 360 MO. AT 15.5 %
          REMAINING      ---INTEREST---
   MO.    BALANCE    MONTH    TO-DATE

   CALCULATING TOTALS..

   LAST PAYMENT = 731.38

   TOTAL PAYMENTS = 291094.17

   MONTHLY PAYMENT WAS 808.81

   PRESS KEY TO GO ON
```

The operator presses "T", and after a few seconds the program displays totalling information about the loan.

## PROGRAM LISTING

```
100 REM: LOAN CALCULATOR
110 REM: (C) 1981, TOM RUGG AND PHIL
    FELDMAN
120 CLEAR 200:CLS:BL$="          "
130 PRINT"LOAN CALCULATOR"
140 PRINT
150 INPUT"LOAN AMOUNT";A
155 GOSUB 1000:IF A=0 THEN 150
160 INPUT"INTEREST RATE";R
170 INPUT"LENGTH OF LOAN (MONTHS)";N
180 R=ABS(R):M=R/1200
190 GOSUB 800:W=1
200 FOR J=1 TO N:W=W*(1+M):NEXT
210 P=(A*M*W)/(W-1)
220 P=INT(P*100+.99):P=P/100
230 PRINT"MONTHLY PAYMENT IS";P
240 FP=P:PRINT
250 PRINT"NEXT ACTION:"
270 PRINT"1 - MONTHLY ANALYSIS"
280 PRINT"2 - OVERRIDE PAYMENT"
290 PRINT"3 - START OVER"
300 PRINT"4 - END"
310 INPUT C
320 ON C GOTO 440,400,120,370
330 PRINT"CHOICES ARE 1,2,3,4"
340 GOTO 250
370 END
400 PRINT
410 INPUT"MONTHLY PAYMENT";P
420 GOTO 240
440 GOSUB 450:GOTO 510
450 GOSUB 800
460 PRINT TAB(5);"REMAINING";
470 PRINT TAB(17);"----INTEREST----"
480 PRINT"MO.    BALANCE";TAB(16);
490 PRINT"MONTH    TO-DATE"
500 RETURN
510 B=A*100:TT=0:TP=0:L=0
520 P=P*100:R$="":FOR J=1 TO N
530 T=M*B:T=INT(T+.5)
540 IF J=N THEN P=B+T
550 TP=TP+P:B=B-P+T:TT=TT+T
560 IF B<0 THEN GOSUB 2000
```

```
570 IF R$="T" THEN 690
580 W=B:GOSUB 900:B$=S$
590 W=T:GOSUB 900:T$=RIGHT$(S$,8)
600 W=TT:GOSUB 900:TT$=" "+S$
605 J$=STR$(J):J$=RIGHT$(J$,LEN(J$)-1)
610 PRINT J$;TAB(4);B$;T$;TT$
620 L=L+1:IF L<12 THEN 690
630 PRINT"PRESS KEY TO GO ON";
640 PRINT" (T=TOTALS)";
650 R$=INKEY$:IF R$="" THEN 650
660 L=0:GOSUB 450
670 IF R$<>"T" THEN 690
675 PRINT
680 PRINT"CALCULATING TOTALS.."
690 NEXT
700 PRINT:PRINT"LAST PAYMENT =";
710 PRINT P/100
720 PRINT:PRINT"TOTAL PAYMENTS =";
730 PRINT TP/100
740 PRINT:PRINT"MONTHLY PAYMENT WAS";FP
750 PRINT
760 PRINT"PRESS KEY TO GO ON"
770 IF LEN(INKEY$)=0 THEN 770
780 P=FP:GOTO 240
800 CLS:PRINT A;"FOR";N;
810 PRINT"MO. AT";R;"%"
820 RETURN
900 W=INT(W):S$=STR$(W)
910 K=LEN(S$)-1:S$=MID$(S$,2,K)
920 IF K=1 THEN S$=BL$+".0"+S$:RETURN
930 IF K=2 THEN S$=BL$+"."+S$:RETURN
940 D$=","+RIGHT$(S$,2)
950 S$=LEFT$(S$,K-2)+D$
960 S$=LEFT$(BL$,8-K)+S$
970 RETURN
1000 A=ABS(A):A=INT(A)
1010 IF A<1000000 THEN RETURN
1020 PRINT"TOO LARGE"
1030 A=0:RETURN
2000 P=P+B:TP=TP+B:B=0:RETURN
```

## EASY CHANGES

1. The number of lines of data displayed on each screen when getting a monthly analysis can be changed by altering the constant 12 in statement 620.

2. To include the monthly payment in the heading at the top of each screen of the monthly analysis, insert the following line:

815 IF FP < >0 THEN PRINT"MONTHLY PAYMENT IS";FP

**MAIN ROUTINES**

120- 170 Displays title. Gets loan information.
200- 230 Calculates and displays monthly payment.
250- 370 Asks for next action. Goes to corresponding routine.
400- 410 Gets override for monthly payment.
440- 780 Calculates and displays monthly analysis.
800- 820 Subroutine to clear screen and display data about the loan at the top.
900- 970 Subroutine to convert integer amount to fixed-length string with aligned decimal point.
1000-1030 Edits loan amount (size and whole dollar).
2000 Subroutine to handle early payoff of loan.

**MAIN VARIABLES**

| | |
|---|---|
| BL$ | String of 6 blank spaces. |
| A | Amount of loan. |
| R | Interest rate (percentage). |
| N | Length of loan (number of months). |
| M | Monthly interest rate (not percentage). |
| W | Work variable. |
| P | Monthly payment (times 100). |
| FP | First monthly payment. |
| C | Choice of next action. |
| B | Remaining balance of loan (times 100). |
| TT | Total interest to date (times 100). |
| TP | Total payments to date. |
| L | Number of lines of data on screen. |
| R$ | Reply from operator at keyboard. |
| J | Work variable for loops. |
| T | Monthly interest. |
| B$ | Remaining balance to be displayed (two decimal places). |
| T$ | Monthly interest to be displayed (two decimal places). |
| TT$ | Total interest to be displayed (two decimal places). |
| S$,D$ | Work strings. |
| K | Work variable. |

**SUGGESTED PROJECTS**

1. Display a more comprehensive analysis of the loan along with the final totals. Show the ratio of total payments to the amount of the loan (TP divided by A), for example.

2. Modify the program to show an analysis of resulting monthly payments for a range of interest rates and/or loan lengths near those provided by the operator. For example, if an interest rate of 9.5 percent was entered, display the monthly payments for 8.5, 9, 9.5, 10, and 10.5 percent.

# MILEAGE

## PURPOSE

For many of us, automobile operating efficiency is a continual concern. This program can help by keeping track of gasoline consumption, miles driven, and fuel mileage for a motor vehicle. It allows reading and writing data files with the cassette unit. Thus, a master data file may be retained and updated. The program computes mileage (miles per gallon or MPG) obtained after each gasoline fill-up. A running log of all information is maintained. This enables trends in vehicle operation efficiency to be easily checked.

## HOW TO USE IT

The program requests the following data from the operator as a record of each gasoline fill-up: date, odometer reading, and number of gallons purchased. The most useful results will be obtained if entries are chronological and complete, with each entry representing a full gasoline fill-up.

In order to use the cassette features, the operator must be able to position the tape correctly for both reading and writing. The simplest way to do this is to only record files at the beginning of a tape. One tape could certainly be used this way, with each file writing over the previous one. However, we suggest alternating between two physical tapes. This will insure a reasonably up-to-date back-up tape in case of any failure.

The program operates from a central command mode. The operator requests branching to any one of five available subroutines. When a subroutine completes execution, control returns to the command mode for any additional requests. A brief description of each subroutine now follows:

   1) READ OLD MASTER FILE

   This reads previously stored data from the cassette. Any data already in memory is deleted. During the read, the name of the data file and the total number of records read are displayed.

   2) INPUT FROM TERMINAL

   This allows data records to be entered directly from the terminal. This mode is used to provide additional information after a cassette read and to enter data for the first time. The program will prompt the operator for the required information and then let him verify that it was entered correctly. A response of "D" to the verification request signals that no more data is to be entered.

   3) WRITE NEW MASTER FILE

   This command causes the current data to be written on cassette. The program requests a name for the file. When later read, this name will be displayed, allowing verification of the correct data file.

   4) DISPLAY MILEAGE DATA

   This subroutine computes mileage (miles per gallon) from the available data. It formats all information and displays it in tabular form. Numerical values are rounded to the nearest tenth. When data fills the screen, the user is prompted to hit any key to continue the listing. When all data is displayed, hitting any key will re-enter command mode.

   5) TERMINATE PROGRAM

   Ends execution and returns the computer to BASIC.

## SAMPLE RUN

```
                MILEAGE

COMMAND LIST
1) READ OLD MASTER FILE
2) INPUT DATA FROM TERMINAL
3) WRITE NEW MASTER FILE
4) DISPLAY MILEAGE DATA
5) TERMINATE PROGRAM

ENTER COMMAND BY NUMBER? 2
```

The program's menu is displayed and the operator chooses option #2.
This allows data to be entered directly from the terminal.

```
ENTER THE FOLLOWING DATA
- DATE (E.G. 1/23/82)
- ODOMETER READING (MILES)
- # GALLONS BOUGHT

DATE? 9/28/81
ODOMETER? 51051.1
# GALLONS? 14.6

  INPUT      DATE: 9/28/81
  CHECK      ODOMETER: 51051.1
             GALLONS: 14.6

  - IS INPUT OK ? -
  (Y=YES, N=NO, D=YES AND DONE)? Y
```

The first data record is input and the operator confirms it is correct.

```
DATE       ODOMETER   GALLONS  MPG
9/28/81    51051.1    14.6      0
10/6/81    51299.7    13.8     18
10/17/81   51553.8    13.1     19.4
10/29/81   51798      13.7     17.8
11/5/81    52041.9    13.3     18.3
11/15/81   52304.9    14       18.8
11/26/81   52570.8    13.7     19.4
12/1/81    52842.5    14.6     18.6
12/9/81    53048.4    11.8     17.4
12/15/81   53359.7    14.7     21.2
12/23/81   53601.2    13.3     18.2

HIT ANY KEY FOR COMMAND MODE
```

After ten more data records are input, the operator selects option #4 from the command menu. This formats and displays the data along with the fuel MPG obtained. The program will re-enter command mode when a key is hit.

```
5) TERMINATE PROGRAM

ENTER COMMAND BY NUMBER? 3

1-POSITION THE TAPE FOR WRITING
2-PRESS THE RECORD AND PLAY
  KEYS ON THE RECORDER

NAME FOR FILE? VOLVO81
WRITING FILE: VOLVO81
   RECORDS # 1  2  3  4  5  6  7
   8  9  10  11

3-PRESS THE RECORDER'S STOP KEY
4-PRESS A KEYBOARD KEY
```

The operator now selects option #3 and writes the data to a file called VOLVO81 on cassette tape.

```
5) TERMINATE PROGRAM

ENTER COMMAND BY NUMBER? 1

1-POSITION THE TAPE FOR READING
2-PRESS THE PLAY KEY ON THE
  RECORDER
3-PRESS A KEYBOARD KEY

READING FILE: VOLVO81
READING RECORDS # 1  2  3  4  5
         6  7  8  9  10  11

4-PRESS THE RECORDER'S STOP KEY
5-PRESS A KEYBOARD KEY
```

By selecting option #1 in a subsequent run, the file VOLVO81 is retrieved from cassette tape to begin a new session.

## PROGRAM LISTING

```
100 REM: MILEAGE - 16K
110 REM: (C) 1981, PHIL FELDMAN AND TOM
    RUGG
140 CLEAR 300
150 MW=15
160 MR=20
170 N=0
180 DIM D$(MR),D(MR),G(MR),M(MR)
200 CLS:PRINT TAB(12);"MILEAGE"
210 PRINT:R=0
220 PRINT"COMMAND LIST"
230 PRINT"1) READ OLD MASTER FILE"
240 PRINT"2) INPUT DATA FROM TERMINAL"
250 PRINT"3) WRITE NEW MASTER FILE"
260 PRINT"4) DISPLAY MILEAGE DATA"
270 PRINT"5) TERMINATE PROGRAM"
280 PRINT
290 INPUT"ENTER COMMAND BY NUMBER";R
300 R=INT(R)
310 IF R=5 THEN 1800
320 ON R GOTO 1500,400,800,1100
```

```
330 GOTO 200
400 IF N<MR THEN 440
410 PRINT
420 PRINT"** NO MORE DATA ALLOWED **"
430 GOSUB 2000:GOTO 200
440 PRINT
450 PRINT"ENTER THE FOLLOWING DATA"
460 PRINT"- DATE (E.G. 1/23/82)"
470 PRINT"- ODOMETER READING (MILES)"
480 PRINT"- # GALLONS BOUGHT"
490 N=N+1:PRINT:INPUT"DATE";R$
500 R$=LEFT$(R$,8):D$(N)=R$
510 INPUT"ODOMETER";R:D(N)=R
520 IF R<0 THEN 510
530 INPUT"# GALLONS";R:G(N)=R
540 IF R<0 THEN 530
550 PRINT
560 PRINT" INPUT     DATE: ";D$(N)
570 PRINT" CHECK     ODOMETER:";D(N)
580 PRINT TAB(10);"GALLONS:";G(N)
590 PRINT:PRINT" - IS INPUT OK ? -"
600 INPUT" (Y=YES,N=NO,D=YES AND DONE)";R$
610 R$=LEFT$(R$,1)
620 IF R$<>"N" THEN 660
630 N=N-1:PRINT
640 PRINT" REDO LAST DATA"
650 GOTO 490
660 IF R$="D" THEN 200
670 IF R$<>"Y" THEN 590
680 IF N=MR THEN 410
690 GOTO 490
800 IF N>0 THEN 830
810 PRINT:PRINT"** NO DATA TO WRITE **"
820 GOSUB 2000:GOTO 200
830 R$="WRITING":GOSUB 3000
840 PRINT"2-PRESS THE RECORD AND PLAY"
850 PRINT" KEYS ON THE RECORDER"
860 PRINT
870 INPUT"NAME FOR FILE";T$
880 K=N:IF N>MW THEN K=MW
890 OPEN "O",#-1,"MILEAGE"
900 PRINT#-1,T$:PRINT#-1,K
910 K=1:L=N:IF N<=MW THEN 950
920 PRINT" - ONLY THE LAST";MW;"VALUES"
930 PRINT"    WILL BE WRITTEN"
```

```
940 K=N-MW+1
950 PRINT"WRITING FILE: ";T$
960 PRINT"  RECORDS #";
970 FOR J=K TO L
980 PRINT#-1,D$(J),D(J),G(J)
990 PRINT J;:NEXT:PRINT
1000 CLOSE #-1:P$="3":R$="4"
1010 PRINT:GOSUB 3200:GOTO 200
1100 IF N>0 THEN 1130
1110 PRINT:PRINT"** NOT ENOUGH DATA **"
1120 GOSUB 2000:GOTO 200
1130 M(1)=0:FOR J=2 TO N
1150 IF G(J)>0 THEN 1170
1160 M(J)=0:GOTO 1190
1170 R=(D(J)-D(J-1))/G(J)
1180 M(J)=R:IF R<0 THEN M(J)=0
1190 NEXT:K=-11:L=0
1200 K=K+12:L=L+12
1210 IF L>N THEN L=N
1220 CLS
1230 PRINT"DATE    ODOMETER";
1240 PRINT TAB(18);"GALLONS MPG"
1250 FOR J=K TO L:Q=D(J)
1260 GOSUB 4000
1270 IF Q>99999 THEN Q=99999
1280 GOSUB 4100
1290 PRINT D$(J);TAB(13-T);Q;
1300 Q=G(J):GOSUB 4000
1310 IF Q>999 THEN Q=999
1320 GOSUB 4100
1330 PRINT TAB(20-T);Q;
1340 Q=M(J):GOSUB 4000
1350 IF Q>999 THEN Q=999
1360 GOSUB 4100
1370 PRINT TAB(27-T);Q:NEXT
1380 PRINT:IF L<N THEN 1410
1390 PRINT"HIT ANY KEY FOR COMMAND MODE"
1400 GOSUB 3220:GOTO 200
1410 PRINT"HIT ANY KEY TO CONTINUE"
1420 GOSUB 3220:GOTO 1200
1500 R$="READING":GOSUB 3000
1510 PRINT"2-PRESS THE PLAY KEY ON THE"
1520 PRINT"  RECORDER"
1530 PRINT"3-PRESS A KEYBOARD KEY"
1540 R$=INKEY$
```

```
1550 IF R$="" THEN 1540
1560 OPEN "I",#-1,"MILEAGE"
1570 PRINT:INPUT#-1,T$
1580 PRINT"READING FILE: ";T$
1590 INPUT#-1,N
1600 IF N<=MR THEN 1640
1610 PRINT
1620 PRINT"** TOO MANY RECORDS ON TAPE **"
1630 GOSUB 2000:END
1640 PRINT"READING RECORDS # ";
1650 FOR J=1 TO N
1660 INPUT#-1,D$(J),D(J),G(J)
1670 PRINT J;:NEXT:CLOSE #-1
1680 PRINT:PRINT:P$="4":R$="5"
1690 GOSUB 3200:GOTO 200
1800 END
2000 SOUND 100,10
2500 FOR Q=1 TO 2000:NEXT:RETURN
3000 PRINT
3010 PRINT"1-POSITION THE TAPE FOR ";R$
3020 RETURN
3200 PRINT P$;"-PRESS THE RECORDER'S STOP
     KEY"
3210 PRINT R$;"-PRESS A KEYBOARD KEY"
3220 R$=INKEY$
3230 IF R$="" THEN 3220
3240 RETURN
4000 Q=Q*10+0.5:Q=INT(Q)/10
4010 RETURN
4100 IF Q>9999 THEN T=5:RETURN
4110 IF Q>999 THEN T=4:RETURN
4120 IF Q>99 THEN T=3:RETURN
4130 IF Q>9 THEN T=2:RETURN
4140 T=1:RETURN
```

## EASY CHANGES

1. Changing the value of MR in line 160 alters the maximum
   number of data records that the program allows. You may
   need to make MR larger to accommodate additional data.
   For typical data (such as in the sample run), a 16K TRS-80
   Color Computer will allow well over 300 data records. To
   adjust MR, simply change its value in line 160 from its current value of 20 to whatever you choose. If you increase the
   value of MR past 30, you should also change the argument

of the CLEAR in line 140. Make this argument ten times the value used for MR in line 160.

2. Currently, the program will write a maximum of fifteen data records during the cassette write operation. This number can be altered by changing the value of MW in line 150 from its value of fifteen to whatever you choose. Only the most recent MW records will be written to tape if MW is less than the number of available records when a cassette write is issued. If the number of available records is less than MW, then all the records will be written. The value of MW should not be larger than the value of MR.

3. If you do not care about seeing the dates, they can be removed easily. This saves a little typing on data entry. To remove this feature, delete line 460 entirely and change line 490 to read

$$490 \ N = N + 1:PRINT:R\$ = \text{"-----"}$$

## MAIN ROUTINES

| | |
|---|---|
| 140- 180 | Dimensioning and variable initialization. |
| 200- 330 | Command mode. Displays available subroutines. |
| 400- 690 | Accepts terminal input. |
| 800-1010 | Writes data to the cassette unit. |
| 1100-1420 | Calculates mileage and displays all information. |
| 1500-1690 | Reads data from the cassette unit. |
| 1800 | Terminates execution. |
| 2000 | Sounds warning for error messages. |
| 2500 | Delay loop. |
| 3000-3240 | Displays messages for cassette operation. |
| 4000-4010 | Numerical rounding subroutine. |
| 4100-4140 | Sets TAB arguments for printing. |

## MAIN VARIABLES

| | |
|---|---|
| MW | Maximum number of data records to write. |
| MR | Maximum number of data records in memory. |
| N | Current number of data records in memory. |
| D$ | Array of dates. |
| D | Array of odometer readings. |
| G | Array of gallons per fill-up. |
| M | Array of mileage per fill-up. |
| R | Command mode input. |

| P$,R$ | Temporary string variables. |
|---|---|
| T$ | Data file name used in reading or writing with cassette. |
| J | Work variable, loop index. |
| K,L | Loop bounds. |
| Q | Work variable. |
| T | TAB argument decrement. |

## SUGGESTED PROJECTS

1. Calculate and print the average MPG over the whole data file. The total miles driven is $D(N) - D(1)$. The total gallons used is the sum of $G(J)$ for $J = 2$ to N. This calculation can be done at the end of the DISPLAY MILEAGE subroutine. Programming should be done between lines 1370 and 1380.
2. Allow the user the option to write to cassette only the entries since a certain date. Ask which date and search the D$ array for it. Then set MW to the appropriate number of records to write. These changes are to be made at and after line 800 at the beginning of the subroutine to write on cassette.
3. Add a new command option to verify a data file just written to cassette. It would read the tape and compare it to the data already in memory.
4. Add an option to do statistical calculations over a given subset of the data. The operator inputs a beginning and ending date. He is then shown things like average MPG, total miles driven, total gallons purchased, etc.; all computed only over the range requested.
5. Write a subroutine to graphically display MPG. A bar graph might work well.
6. Add a new parameter in each data record — the cost of each fill-up. Then compute things like the total cost of gasoline, miles/dollar, etc.

# QUEST/EXAM

## PURPOSE

If you've ever had to analyze the results of a questionnaire, or grade a multiple-choice examination, you know what a tedious and time-consuming process it can be. This is particularly true if you need to accumulate statistics for each question showing how many people responded with each possible answer.

With this program, you provide the data, and the computer does the work.

## HOW TO USE IT

As currently set up, the program assumes that the questionnaire or exam has 15 questions, that there are four choices per question, and that there are no more than 20 entries (exam papers). If you have more than 4K of RAM, these limits can be increased. See the Easy Changes section for details.

To start off, the program asks you for the answer key. If you are scoring an exam, provide the correct answers. The program displays "guide numbers" to help you keep track of which answers you are providing. If you are analyzing a questionnaire, you have no answer key, so just press the **ENTER** key.

Now the program asks you to begin providing the answers for each entry. Again, guide numbers are displayed above the area where you are to enter the data so you can more easily provide the proper answer for the proper question number. If no answer was given for a particular question, leave a blank space. However, if the first question was left blank, you will have to enclose the entire string of answers within quotation marks. This will cause a small problem in keeping your alignment straight with the guide numbers, but you'll get used to it.

If you make a mistake when entering the data, the program will tell you and ask you to re-enter it. This is most commonly caused by either failing to enter the correct number of answers or entering an invalid character instead of an acceptable answer number. Remember that each answer must be either a blank or a number from one to the number of choices allowed per question.

By the way, you can avoid entering blanks for unanswered questions. Suppose you have a maximum of 5 possible answers per question. Simply tell the program there are 6 choices per question. Then, when a question is unanswered, you can enter a 6 instead of leaving it blank.

If you provided an answer key, the program displays the number and percentage correct after each entry before going on to ask for the next one. When you have no more entries, press the **ENTER** key instead of entering a string of answers.

At this point, the program displays four options from which you choose your next action. Here are brief explanations. You can experiment to verify how they work.

Option one lets you analyze each question, to see how many people responded with each answer. The percentage of people who responded with each answer is also shown. In the case of an exam, the correct answer is indicated with the letter "C" to the right.

Option two allows you to go back and provide more entries. This allows you to pause after entering part of the data, do some analysis of what you have entered so far, and then go back and continue entering data.

Option three lets you review what you have entered, including the answer key. This permits you to check for duplicate, omitted, or erroneous entries.

Option four ends the program.

**SAMPLE RUN**

```
QUESTIONNAIRE/EXAM ANALYZER

ENTER ANSWER KEY OR PRESS ENTER
           1
    1234567890 12345
?  123313244121134

ENTRY NUMBER 1
           1
    1234567890 12345
?
```

The operator provides the answer key for the examination being
scored. The program waits for the data from the first examination
paper.

```
ENTER ANSWER KEY OR PRESS ENTER
           1
    1234567890 12345
?  123313244121134

ENTRY NUMBER 1
           1
    1234567890 12345
?  123313243121144
   13 CORRECT, 86.6666667 PERCENT

ENTRY NUMBER 2
           1
    1234567890 12345
?
```

The answers are entered for the first student. The program responds
with the number and percentage correct.

```
    123456789012345
?  123323344122134
  12 CORRECT, 80 PERCENT

ENTRY NUMBER 9
         1
  123456789012345
?
AVERAGE = 84.1666667 PERCENT

NEXT ACTION:
1 - ANALYZE QUESTIONS
2 - ADD MORE ENTRIES
3 - REVIEW DATA ENTERED
4 - END PROGRAM
? 1
```

Later, instead of providing data for a ninth student, the operator
presses the ENTER key, indicating no more entries. The program
displays the overall percentage correct, and displays a "menu" of
choice of actions. The operator picks number one.

```
NEXT ACTION:
1 - ANALYZE QUESTIONS
2 - ADD MORE ENTRIES
3 - REVIEW DATA ENTERED
4 - END PROGRAM
? 1

ANALYSIS FOR QUESTION NO. 1
RESPONSE   COUNT   PERCENT
   1         7      87.5 C
   2         1      12.5
   3         0      0
   4         0      0
BLANK        0      0
PRESS A KEY
```

The program provides an analysis of the responses for question
number one, then waits for a key to be pressed. Note that seven
students answered with number 1, the correct answer.

```
   3 - REVIEW DATA ENTERED
   4 - END PROGRAM
   ? 3
                  1
      1234567890123+5
      12331324+4121134--KEY
      12331324+3121144--NO. 1
      12331324+4121134--NO. 2
      12331334+4111133--NO. 3
      22331324+4121134--NO. +
      12232324+4121134--NO. 5
      1234123+4+122134--NO. 6
      123312234112134--NO. 7
      1233233+4+122134--NO. 8
   PRESS A KEY
```

Later, the operator asks for option number 3, which lists the data
entered for each of the students.

## PROGRAM LISTING

```
100 REM: QUESTIONNAIRE/EXAM
110 REM: (C) 1981, TOM RUGG AND PHIL
    FELDMAN
120 CLEAR 340:CLS
130 PRINT"QUESTIONNAIRE/EXAM ANALYZER"
140 E$="ERROR. RE-ENTER.":P$="PRESS A KEY"
150 Q=15:C=4:N=20
160 DIM Q$(N),C(C)
250 PRINT
260 PRINT"ENTER ANSWER KEY OR PRESS ENTER"
270 GOSUB 900:C$=RIGHT$(STR$(C),1)
310 INPUT A$:IF LEN(A$)=0 THEN 340
320 IF LEN(A$)<>Q THEN PRINT E$:GOTO 250
330 T$=A$:GOSUB 850
335 IF T$="B" THEN PRINT E$:GOTO 250
340 K=1
350 R=0:PRINT:PRINT"ENTRY NUMBER";K
360 GOSUB 900
370 INPUT Q$(K):W=LEN(Q$(K))
380 IF W=0 THEN 500
```

```
390 IF W<>Q THEN PRINT E$:GOTO 350
400 T$=Q$(K):GOSUB 850
405 IF T$="B" THEN PRINT E$:GOTO 350
430 IF LEN(A$)=0 THEN 480
440 FOR J=1 TO Q
450 IF MID$(A$,J,1)=MID$(Q$(K),J,1)
    THEN R=R+1
460 NEXT
470 TR=TR+R:PRINT R;"CORRECT,";
475 PRINT R*100/Q;"PERCENT"
480 K=K+1:IF K<=N THEN 350
500 K=K-1:IF LEN(A$)=0 THEN 520
510 PRINT"AVERAGE =";TR*100/(Q*K);"PERCENT"
520 GOTO 960
530 FOR J=1 TO Q:R=0:PRINT
540 PRINT"ANALYSIS FOR QUESTION NO.";J
545 PRINT"RESPONSE   COUNT   PERCENT"
550 FOR L=0 TO C:C(L)=0:NEXT:M=0
560 FOR L=1 TO K:T$=MID$(Q$(L),J,1)
570 W=VAL(T$):C(W)=C(W)+1:NEXT
610 FOR L=1 TO C:PRINT L;TAB(11);
620 PRINT C(L);TAB(18);C(L)*100/K;
630 IF LEN(A$)=0 THEN PRINT:GOTO 660
640 T$=RIGHT$(STR$(L),1)
650 IF T$=MID$(A$,J,1) THEN PRINT"C":GOTO
    660
655 PRINT
660 NEXT:PRINT"BLANK";TAB(11);C(0);TAB(18);
670 PRINT C(0)*100/K:PRINT P$
680 IF LEN(INKEY$)=0 THEN 680
690 NEXT J:GOTO 960
700 L=0:GOSUB 900:IF LEN(A$)=0 THEN 720
710 PRINT TAB(2);A$;"--KEY"
720 FOR J=1 TO K
730 PRINT TAB(2);Q$(J);"--NO.";J;
740 PRINT
750 L=L+1:IF L<10 THEN 780
760 L=0:PRINT P$
770 IF LEN(INKEY$)=0 THEN 770
780 NEXT:PRINT P$
790 IF LEN(INKEY$)=0 THEN 790
800 GOTO 960
850 FOR J=1 TO LEN(T$):IF MID$(T$,J,1)=
    " " THEN 870
```

```
860 IF MID$(T$,J,1)<"1" OR MID$(T$,J,1)>C$
    THEN 880
870 NEXT:RETURN
880 T$="E":RETURN
900 W=Q/10:IF W<1 THEN 920
910 FOR J=1 TO W:PRINT TAB(J*10);J;:NEXT
    :PRINT
920 PRINT TAB(2);
930 FOR J=1 TO Q:T$=STR$(J)
940 PRINT MID$(T$,LEN(T$),1);:NEXT:PRINT
    :RETURN
960 PRINT:PRINT"NEXT ACTION:"
970 PRINT"1 - ANALYZE QUESTIONS"
980 PRINT"2 - ADD MORE ENTRIES"
990 PRINT"3 - REVIEW DATA ENTERED"
1000 PRINT"4 - END PROGRAM"
1040 INPUT T$:T$=LEFT$(T$,1)
1050 IF T$<"1" OR T$>"4" THEN 1070
1060 ON VAL(T$) GOTO 530,480,700,1100
1070 PRINT E$:GOTO 960
1100 END
```

## EASY CHANGES

1. As shown, the program will fit in a 4K Color Computer. With a 16K computer, you can allow for more questions per exam, more choices per question, and more students (or questionnaire respondents). For example, to allow for 25 questions, five choices per question, and 40 students, make these changes:

   120 CLEAR 2000:CLS
   150 Q = 25:C = 5:N = 40

## MAIN ROUTINES

120- 140 Initializes variables.
150- 160 Sets limits for questions, choices, and entries. Allocates arrays.
250- 320 Gets answer key (if any) from operator.
330- 335 Checks legality of answer key.
350- 400 Gets exam data for Kth entry.
430- 475 Scores Kth exam, if applicable.
500- 510 Displays average score, if an exam.

530- 690  Analyzes responses to each question.
700- 800  Displays data entered.
850- 880  Subroutine to check legality of input data.
900- 940  Subroutine to display guide numbers over input data area.
960-1100  Displays choices for next action. Gets response and goes to appropriate routine.

## MAIN VARIABLES

| | |
|---|---|
| E$ | Error message. |
| P$ | Message about pressing a key to continue. |
| Q | Number of questions. |
| C | Number of choices per question. |
| C | Array for tallying number of people responding with each choice. |
| N | Maximum number of entries. |
| Q$ | Array of N strings of entries. |
| A$ | Answer key string (null if not an exam). |
| C$ | String value of highest legal answer choice. |
| K | Counter of number of exams scored. |
| R | Number of questions answered right (if exam). |
| W | Work variable. |
| J,L,M | Loop variables. |
| TR | Total right for all entries. |
| T$ | Temporary work string variable. |

## SUGGESTED PROJECTS

1. Add an option to change the answer key after the data for the exams is entered. This would be useful in case a mistake is found when reviewing the data.
2. Add an option to allow the operator to re-score each of the exams after all are entered, in case some were overlooked at the time of entry.
3. Combine some of the capabilities of the STATS program with this one.
4. Allow the operator to enter a name for each exam paper. This will make it easier to review which person's exam has been entered when option three is used.

# SORTLIST

## PURPOSE

This program sorts a list of items (words or phrases) into alphabetical order. This is a tedious task to do manually, but your computer can do it in seconds. All you need to do is type in the list of items that need to be sorted.

## HOW TO USE IT

Simply type in the list of items that you want sorted, pressing **ENTER** after each one. An item does not have to be single word. You can have embedded spaces, but not commas or colons (unless the entire item is enclosed in quotation marks).

When done with your list, type the word END and press **ENTER**. The program then tells you how many items were entered and begins displaying them in sorted (alphabetical) order. If you have more than 14 items, you will want to use the Color Computer's capability to stop scrolling the display by pressing the SHIFT and "@" keys at the same time. This will stop the program before the first items disappear from the screen. Then you can let the list continue by pressing any key. If you do not stop the list quickly enough, you can type GOTO 500 after the program ends to display the list again. You may also want to try the Easy Change below that puts more than one item on each line of the display.

This program sorts string data. This means that you can also enter numeric data, but it will not sort numerically the way you probably would want. For example, if you entered the numbers 1, 2, 13, and 20, they would be sorted into the sequence 1, 13, 2, 20. The number 13 is sorted ahead of 2 because the first position gets sorted "alphabetically," and 1 comes ahead of 2.

You may find this program useful as shown, or you may want to make use of the technique it uses as part of a larger program. The sorting technique used is called a *straight selection* sort (see the book by Knuth in the bibliography). It has the advantages of being very simply programmed and executing quite quickly for small lists—no more than 30 to 50 or so. This program typically takes about four to seven seconds to sort 30 items, and about eight to thirteen seconds for 40 items, depending on the length and initial sequence of the items.

**SAMPLE RUN**

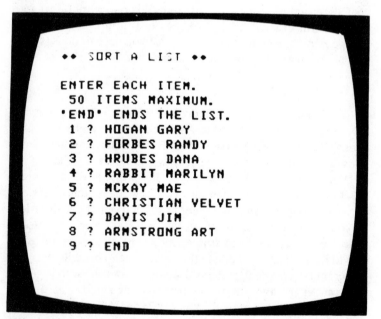

```
   ••  SORT A LIST ••

ENTER EACH ITEM.
  50 ITEMS MAXIMUM.
 'END' ENDS THE LIST.
  1 ?  HOGAN GARY
  2 ?  FORBES RANDY
  3 ?  HRUBES DANA
  4 ?  RABBIT MARILYN
  5 ?  MCKAY MAE
  6 ?  CHRISTIAN VELVET
  7 ?  DAVIS JIM
  8 ?  ARMSTRONG ART
  9 ?  END
```

The operator enters eight names, and END to end the data entry.

```
 5 ? MCKAY MAE
 6 ? CHRISTIAN VELVET
 7 ? DAVIS JIM
 8 ? ARMSTRONG ART
 9 ? END
 8 ITEMS ENTERED.
 1   ARMSTRONG ART
 2   CHRISTIAN VELVET
 3   DAVIS JIM
 4   FORBES RANDY
 5   HOGAN GARY
 6   HRUBES DANA
 7   MCKAY MAE
 8   RABBIT MARILYN
OK
```

The program displays the alphabetized list, and then ends.

## PROGRAM LISTING

```
100 REM: SORT A LIST
110 REM: (C) 1981, TOM RUGG AND PHIL
    FELDMAN
130 CLEAR 800
140 N=50:E$="END"
150 DIM A$(N):GOSUB 600
160 K=1
170 IF K>N THEN 250
180 PRINT K;:INPUT R$:IF R$=E$ THEN 250
190 IF R$="" THEN 180
200 A$(K)=R$:K=K+1:GOTO 170
250 K=K-1:IF K>0 THEN 300
260 PRINT"** NO INPUT **"
270 GOTO 160
300 PRINT K;"ITEMS ENTERED."
350 IF K=1 THEN 500
360 FOR J=K TO 2 STEP -1
370 R$=A$(1):F=1
380 FOR L=2 TO J
```

```
390 IF A$(L)>R$ THEN R$=A$(L):F=L
400 NEXT:A$(F)=A$(J):A$(J)=R$
410 NEXT
500 FOR J=1 TO K
510 PRINT J;TAB(4);A$(J)
520 NEXT
550 END
600 CLS
610 PRINT"** SORT A LIST **"
620 PRINT
630 PRINT"ENTER EACH ITEM."
640 PRINT N;"ITEMS MAXIMUM."
650 PRINT"'";E$;"'  ENDS THE LIST."
660 RETURN
```

## EASY CHANGES

1. Some simple changes can allow the program to handle more data. In a 4K computer, you can allow for up to 100 items, where the average item is no more than nine or ten characters long, by making these changes:

   130 CLEAR 1000
   140 N = 100:E$ = "END"

   With a 16K computer, you can have up to about 800 items of the same length with:

   130 CLEAR 8000
   140 N = 800:E$ = "END"

   Be aware that 100 items may take 40 to 60 seconds or more to sort, and 800 will take more than simply eight times that.

2. If you want to sort numbers instead of alphabetic data, make these changes:
   a. Delete the dollar signs in lines 150, 200, 370, 390, 400, and 510.
   b. Insert this line:
      195 R = VAL(R$)
   c. Change the title, if you wish. For example, replace "ITEM" in line 630 with "NUMBER," and "ITEMS" in 640 with "NUMBERS."

3. To reduce the problem of getting only 14 to 16 items on the screen at once, you can try one of these changes:

510 PRINT J;A$(J);"/";

or

510 PRINT A$(J);"/";

This will print multiple items separated by slashes on each line. The second change will also eliminate the item number from the display. Of course, you can separate the items with some character other than a slash if you like.

4. To use some word other than END to indicate the end of the list of items, change line 140. For example, to use DONE:

140 N = 50:E$ = "DONE"

5. To slow down the display of the sorted list, you can insert:

515 FOR L = 1 TO 200:NEXT

## MAIN ROUTINES

| | |
|---|---|
| 130-150 | Initializes variables. Displays instructions. |
| 160-300 | Inputs items to be sorted. |
| 350-410 | Sorts items alphabetically. |
| 500-550 | Displays sorted items and ends program. |
| 600-660 | Subroutine to display title and instructions. |

## MAIN VARIABLES

| | |
|---|---|
| N | Maximum number of items that can be entered. |
| E$ | Word to end entry of items. |
| A$ | Array of items to be sorted (in place). |
| K | Count of number of items actually entered. |
| R$ | Reply from operator. Also a work string variable. |
| J,L,F | Work and subscript variables. |

## SUGGESTED PROJECTS

1. Replace the sorting technique with one that is more efficient for large numbers of items. Knuth's and Gruenberger's books (see bibliography) both have discussions of alternatives.
2. Give the program the capability to add or change some items after the list has been sorted.
3. Add an option to allow the sorted list to be saved on cassette so it can be loaded into another program when needed.

# Section 2

# Educational Programs

## INTRODUCTION TO EDUCATION PROGRAMS

Education is one area where computers are certain to have more and more impact. Though a computer cannot completely replace a human teacher, the machine does have certain advantages. It is ready anytime you are, allows you to go at your own pace, handles rote drill effortlessly, and is devoid of any personality conflicts.

With a good software library, the Color Computer can be a valuable learning center in the school or at home. Here are seven programs to get you started.

Mathematics is certainly a "natural" subject for computers. NUMBERS is designed for pre-school children. While familiarizing youngsters with computers, it provides an entertaining way for them to learn numbers and elementary counting. ARITHMETIC is aimed at older, grade school students. It provides drill in various kinds of math problems. The child can adjust the difficulty factors, allowing the program to be useful for several years.

By no means is the TRS-80 Color Computer restricted to mathematical disciplines. We include two programs designed to improve your word skills. VOCAB will help you expand your vocabulary. TACHIST turns the computer into a reading clinic, helping you to improve your reading speed.

With the proper programs, the computer can teach you specific subjects. If you've ever wanted to learn International Radio Code, HAMCODE will instruct and then drill you. Many of us feel uncomfortable becoming familiar with the increasingly prevalent metric system. METRIC is the answer to this.

But, what about software that you can customize to help you learn a subject of your choice? FLASHCARD allows you to create your own "computer flashcards." Then you can drill yourself until you get it right.

# ARITHMETIC

## PURPOSE

ARITHMETIC provides mathematics drills for grade school children. The student can request problems in addition, subtraction, or multiplication from the program. Also, he or she may ask that the problems be easy, medium, or hard. The program should be useful to a child over an extended period of time. He can progress naturally to a harder category of problems when he begins to regularly perform well at one level. The difficulty and types of problems encompass those normally encountered by school children between the ages of six and ten.

The problems are constructed randomly within the constraints imposed by the degree of difficulty selected. This gives the student fresh practice each time the program is used. After entering answers, he is told whether he was right or wrong. The correct answers are also displayed.

## HOW TO USE IT

First, in order to initialize its random number generator, the program requests that any key (except **BREAK** or **SHIFT**) be hit.

Next, the student must indicate what type of problem he wishes to do. The program requests an input of **1, 2,** or **3** to indicate addition, subtraction, or multiplication, respectively. It then asks whether easy, medium, or hard problems are desired. Again an input of **1, 2,** or **3** is required.

Now the screen will clear and four problems of the desired type will be displayed. The user now begins to enter his answers to each problem.

A question mark is used to prompt the user for each digit of the answer, one digit at a time. This is done moving right to left, the way arithmetic problems are naturally solved.

To start each problem, the question mark will appear in the spot for the rightmost (or units column) digit of the answer. When the key for a digit from 0-9 is pressed, that digit will replace the question mark on the screen. The question mark moves to the immediate left waiting for a digit for the "tens" column.

Digits are entered in this right to left manner until the complete answer has been input. Then the **ENTER** key must be pressed. This will end the answer to the current problem and move the question mark to begin the answer for the next question.

If the **ENTER** key is pressed to begin a problem, an answer of zero is assumed intended. No problems created by this program have answers of more than three digits. If a four-digit answer is given, the program will accept the answer, but then go immediately to the next problem. Answers to the problems are never negative.

The program will display the correct answers to the four problems on the screen after the student has entered his four answers. The message "RIGHT" or "WRONG" will also be displayed below each problem. If all four problems are answered correctly, a cheerful high-pitched beeping will be sounded. If any problems are missed, a lower pitched monotone will be generated instead.

Then the message "HIT ANY KEY TO CONTINUE" will be displayed. After the key is pressed, a new set of four problems of the same type will be presented.

This continues until twenty problems have been worked. The program then shows what the student's performance has been. This is expressed as the number of problems solved correctly and also as the percentage of problems solved correctly.

The program then asks whether or not the student would like to do more problems. Simply hit "Y" or "N" to answer this question.

**SAMPLE RUN**

```
              A R I T H M E T I C

    WHAT TYPE PROBLEM SHALL WE DO?
      1 - ADDITION
      2 - SUBTRACTION
      3 - MULTIPLICATION
    WHICH TYPE (1, 2, OR 3) - 1
    ================================
    WHAT KIND SHALL WE DO?
      1 - EASY PROBLEMS
      2 - MEDIUM PROBLEMS
      3 - HARD PROBLEMS
    WHAT KIND (1, 2, OR 3) - 3
```

The operator chooses to do hard addition problems.

```
              A R I T H M E T I C


        60        88        25        88
      + 55      + 25      + 67      + 48
      ----      ----      ----      ----
        ?
```

The initial set of 4 problems is presented. With a question mark, the program prompts the operator for the answer to the first problem.

```
          A  R  I  T  H  M  E  T  I  C


         60        88        25        88
       + 55      + 25      + 67      + 48
       ----      ----      ----      ----
        115       103        92       136

             A  N  S  W  E  R  S


        115       113        92       136
       RIGHT     WRONG     RIGHT     RIGHT


       HIT ANY KEY TO CONTINUE
```

The operator has entered his or her four answers. The program displays the correct answers and indicates whether or not each problem was solved correctly. The program waits for the operator to hit any key in order to continue with the next set of four problems.

## PROGRAM LISTING

```
100 REM: ARITHMETIC - 16K
110 REM: (C) 1981, PHIL FELDMAN AND TOM
    RUGG
130 CLEAR 200
140 DIM A(4),B(4),C(4),G(4)
150 ND=0:A$=CHR$(32)
160 NP=20
200 GOSUB 2000:GOSUB 2600
210 PRINT:PRINT"WHAT TYPE ";
220 PRINT"PROBLEM SHALL WE DO?"
230 PRINT" 1 - ADDITION"
240 PRINT" 2 - SUBTRACTION"
250 PRINT" 3 - MULTIPLICATION"
260 PRINT"WHICH TYPE";
270 PRINT" (1, 2, OR 3) ?";
280 R$=INKEY$:T=VAL(R$)
290 IF T<1 OR T>3 THEN 280
300 PRINT CHR$(8);"-";T
```

```
310 GOSUB 2300:FOR J=1 TO 30
320 PRINT"=";:NEXT:PRINT
330 PRINT"WHAT KIND";
340 PRINT" SHALL WE DO?"
350 PRINT" 1 - EASY PROBLEMS"
360 PRINT" 2 - MEDIUM PROBLEMS"
370 PRINT" 3 - HARD PROBLEMS"
380 PRINT"WHAT KIND ";
390 PRINT"(1, 2, OR 3) ?";
400 R$=INKEY$:D=VAL(R$)
410 IF D<1 OR D>3 THEN 400
420 PRINT CHR$(8);"-";D
500 ON D GOTO 510,530,590
510 GOSUB 1700:GOSUB 1500
520 GOSUB 1600:GOTO 630
530 GOSUB 1700:GOSUB 1600
540 IF T=3 THEN 570
550 GOSUB 1710:GOSUB 1500
560 GOTO 630
570 GOSUB 1720:GOSUB 1500
580 GOTO 630
590 GOSUB 1710:GOSUB 1500
600 GOSUB 1600
610 IF T=3 THEN GOSUB 1700
620 IF T=3 THEN GOSUB 1600
630 IF T<>2 THEN 680
640 FOR J=1 TO 4
650 IF B(J)<=C(J) THEN 670
660 R=C(J):C(J)=B(J):B(J)=R
670 NEXT
680 GOSUB 2100:GOSUB 2000
700 FOR J=1 TO 4:GOSUB 2200:NEXT
710 FOR K=1 TO 4:P=223+7*K
720 GOSUB 1200:G(K)=N:NEXT
730 PRINT@297,"A N S W E R S"
740 FOR J=1 TO 4:P=347+J*7
750 GOSUB 2400:NEXT
760 F=1:FOR J=1 TO 4:P=379+J*7
770 IF A(J)=G(J) THEN 800
780 PRINT@P,"WRONG";:F=0
790 GOTO 810
800 PRINT@P,"RIGHT";:NR=NR+1
810 NEXT:FOR K=1 TO 9:R$=INKEY$
820 NEXT:IF F=1 THEN 840
830 SOUND 8,20:GOTO 860
```

```
840 FOR K=1 TO 14:SOUND 180,1
850 NEXT
860 PRINT@452,"HIT ANY KEY TO"
870 PRINT@467,"CONTINUE"
880 R$=INKEY$:IF R$="" THEN 880
890 ND=ND+4
900 IF ND>=NP THEN 920
910 GOSUB 2000:GOTO 500
920 GOSUB 2500:PRINT
930 PRINT"WANT MORE PROBLEMS";
940 PRINT" (Y OR N) ?"
950 R$=INKEY$:IF R$="" THEN 950
960 IF R$="N" THEN CLS:END
970 IF R$<>"Y" THEN 950
980 ND=0:NR=0:GOSUB 2000
990 GOTO 210
1200 N=0:M=1:FOR J=1 TO 10
1210 R$=INKEY$:NEXT
1220 PRINT@P,"?";
1230 R$=INKEY$
1240 IF R$="" THEN 1230
1250 A=ASC(R$)
1260 IF A<>13 OR M<>1 THEN 1280
1270 PRINT@P,"0";:RETURN
1280 IF A<>13 THEN 1300
1290 PRINT@P,A$;:RETURN
1300 V=VAL(R$)
1310 IF V=0 AND A<>48 THEN 1230
1320 PN=48+V:PRINT@P,CHR$(PN);
1330 N=N+M*V:M=M*10
1340 IF M>1000 THEN RETURN
1350 P=P-1:GOTO 1220
1500 FOR K=1 TO 4
1510 C(K)=L+RND(H-L+1)-1
1520 NEXT:RETURN
1600 FOR K=1 TO 4
1610 B(K)=L+RND(H-L+1)-1
1620 NEXT:RETURN
1700 H=9:L=0:RETURN
1710 H=99:L=0:RETURN
1720 H=25:L=1:RETURN
2000 CLS:PRINT@38,"A R I T H M"
2010 PRINT@50,"E T I C":RETURN
2100 ON T GOTO 2110,2140,2170
2110 FOR J=1 TO 4
```

```
2120 A(J)=B(J)+C(J)
2130 NEXT:RETURN
2140 FOR J=1 TO 4
2150 A(J)=C(J)-B(J)
2160 NEXT:RETURN
2170 FOR J=1 TO 4
2180 A(J)=B(J)*C(J)
2190 NEXT:RETURN
2200 B$="":IF C(J)<10 THEN B$=A$
2210 P=125+J*7:PRINT@P,B$;C(J)
2220 P=156+J*7:PRINT@P,C$;
2230 B$="":IF B(J)<10 THEN B$=A$
2240 P=157+J*7:PRINT@P,B$;B(J)
2250 P=188+J*7:PRINT@P,"-----"
2260 RETURN
2300 ON T GOTO 2310,2320,2330
2310 C$="+":RETURN
2320 C$="-":RETURN
2330 C$="X":RETURN
2400 B$=A$
2410 IF A(J)<1000 THEN 2430
2420 PRINT@P,A(J);:RETURN
2430 IF A(J)<100 THEN 2450
2440 PRINT@P,B$;A(J);:RETURN
2450 IF A(J)<10 THEN 2470
2460 PRINT@P,B$;B$;A(J);:RETURN
2470 PRINT@P,B$;B$;B$;A(J);
2480 RETURN
2500 GOSUB 2000:PRINT
2510 PRINT"YOU GOT";NR;"RIGHT"
2520 PRINT"OUT OF";NP;"PROBLEMS"
2530 P=NR/NP*100:PRINT
2540 PRINT"THAT'S";P
2550 PRINT" PERCENT CORRECT"
2560 RETURN
2600 PRINT:J=0
2610 PRINT"HIT ANY KEY TO BEGIN"
2620 J=J+1:R$=INKEY$
2630 IF R$="" THEN 2620
2640 R=RND(-J):GOSUB 2000:RETURN
```

## EASY CHANGES

1. The program currently does twenty problems per session.
   you can change this number by altering the variable NP in
   line 160. For example,

$$160 \ NP = 12$$

will cause the program to do only twelve problems per session. The value of NP should be kept a positive multiple of four.

2.  Zero is currently allowed as a possible problem operand. If you do not wish to allow this, change lines 1700 and 1710 to read as follows:

$$1700 \ H = 9:L = 1:RETURN$$
$$1710 \ H = 99:L = 1:RETURN$$

## MAIN ROUTINES

130- 160   Initializes constants.
200- 420   Asks operator for type of problems desired.
500- 680   Sets A, B, C arrays, clears screen.
700- 990   Mainline routine—displays problems, gets operator's answers, displays correct answers and user's performance.
1200-1350  Subroutine to get and display user's answers.
1500-1520  Subroutine to set B array.
1600-1620  Subroutine to set C array.
1700-1720  Subroutines to set L, H.
2000-2010  Subroutine to clear screen and display title.
2100-2190  Subroutine to calculate array A from arrays B, C.
2200-2260  Subroutine to display problems.
2300-2330  Subroutine to set C$.
2400-2480  Subroutine to display the correct answers.
2500-2560  Subroutine to display operator's performance.
2600-2640  Subroutine to initialize RND function.

## MAIN VARIABLES

| | |
|---|---|
| NP | Number of problems to do in the session. |
| ND | Number of problems done. |
| NR | Number of correct answers given. |
| C,B,A | Arrays of top operand, bottom operand, and correct answer to each problem. |
| N | Operator's answer to current problem. |
| G | Array of operator's answers. |
| T | Type of problems requested (1 = addition, 2 = subtraction, 3 = multiplication). |

| D | Kind of problem requested (1 = easy, 2 = medium, 3 = hard). |
| --- | --- |
| H,L | Highest, lowest integers to allow as problem operands. |
| M | Answer column being worked on. |
| R$ | Operator's input character. |
| V | Value of R$. |
| A | Ascii value of R$. |
| PN | CHR$ argument. |
| B$ | Character spacing string. |
| C$ | Operation symbol string. |
| A$ | String of one blank character. |
| R | Work variable. |
| J,K | Loop indices. |
| P | Screen position, also percentage correct. |
| F | Flag on operator's answers (1 = all correct, 0 = some wrong). |

## SUGGESTED PROJECTS

1. Keep track of problems missed and repeat them quickly for additional practice.
2. No negative operands or answers are currently allowed. Rewrite the problem generation routines and the operator's answer routines to allow the possibility of negative answers.
3. The answers are now restricted to three-digit numbers. However, the program will work fine for four-digit numbers if the operands of the problems are allowed to be large enough. Dig into the routines at lines 500-680 and 1700-1720. See how they work and then modify them to allow possible four-digit answers.
4. The operator cannot currently correct any mistakes he makes while typing in his answers. Modify the program to allow him to do so.
5. Modify the program to allow problems in division.

# FLASHCARD

## PURPOSE

There are certain things that the human mind is capable of learning only through repetition. Not many people can remember the multiplication tables after their first exposure, for example. The same applies to learning the vocabulary of a foreign language, the capital cities of the fifty states, or famous dates in history. The best way to learn them is to simply review them over and over until you have them memorized.

A common technique for doing this involves the use of flashcards. You write one half of the two related pieces of information on one side of a card, and the other half on the other side. After creating a set of these cards, you can drill yourself on them over and over until you always remember what's on the other side of each card.

But why waste precious natural resources by using cards? Use your computer instead. This program lets you create flashcards, drill using them, and save them on cassette tape for later review.

## HOW TO USE IT

The program gives you six options. The first time you run it, you'll want to enter new flashcards, so you should reply with number 1.

To create the cards, the program asks you for each side of each flashcard, one at a time. First enter side one of the first card, and so on. As you enter the data, be careful not to use any commas or colons unless the entire expression is enclosed in quotation marks.

At any time, you can enter the keyword "*BACK" instead of side one to correct an erroneous entry. This causes the program to back up and ask you for the previous card again.

As the program is currently written, you must enter at least three flashcards, and no more than ten. We will show you how to change these limits in the "Easy Changes" section.

When you have entered all the flashcards you want, enter "*END" instead of side one of the next card. This puts the program back into "command" mode to ask you what to do next. If you want to quiz yourself on the cards you just entered, respond with the number 4.

The program flashes one side of one card on the screen for you. Both are chosen at random—the side and the card. Your job is to respond with the other side. If you enter it correctly, the program says "RIGHT!" If not, it tells you the correct response. In either event, the program continues by picking another side and card at random. This continues until you respond with "*END", which tells the program you do not want to drill any more. It will then tell you how many you got right out of the number you attempted, as well as the percentage, and then return to command mode.

During the drill sequence, by the way, the program will not repeat a card that was used in the previous two questions (i.e., one less than the minimum number of cards you can enter).

To save a set of flashcards on cassette, use option number 3. The program will tell you to put the cassette into position and then enter a name for the file. You should give it a good descriptive name in order to remember what kind of flashcards they are in the future. Be sure to write the name on the cassette, too. After the flashcards have been copied to the cassette, the program will say "DONE" and return to the command mode.

The other commands are easily understood, so we will just explain them briefly. A little experimentation will show you how they work.

Command number 2 is used to load a flashcard tape that has been previously saved. The program asks for the name of the file, so it can scan the cassette until it finds the one you asked for. If you don't care or don't know the name of the file, you

can load the first file that is found on the cassette by entering a
null string for the name (two consecutive double quote marks).
 Command number 5 allows you to add more flashcards to
those currently in memory.
 Command number 6 ends the program.


**SAMPLE RUN**


```
FLASHCARD

**OPTIONS**
1 ENTER NEW FLASHCARDS
2 LOAD A FLASHCARD TAPE
3 SAVE CURRENT SET ON TAPE
4 DRILL ON CURRENT SET
5 ADD TO CURRENT CARDS
6 END PROGRAM
? 1

SIDE 1 OF CARD 1
? THE PEN
SIDE 2
? LA PLUMA

SIDE 1 OF CARD 2
? THE DOOR
SIDE 2
? LA PUERTA

SIDE 1 OF CARD 3
? THE SCHOOL
SIDE 2
? LA ESCUELA

SIDE 1 OF CARD 4
? THE FLOOR
SIDE 2
? EL SUELO
```

```
SIDE 1 OF CARD 5
? THE STORE
SIDE 2
? LA TIENDRA

SIDE 1 OF CARD 6
? *END

**OPTIONS**
1 ENTER NEW FLASHCARDS
2 LOAD A FLASHCARD TAPE
3 SAVE CURRENT SET ON TAPE
4 DRILL ON CURRENT SET
5 ADD TO CURRENT CARDS
6 END PROGRAM
? 4

*CARD DRILL*

THE DOOR
? LA PUERTA

RIGHT!

LA PLUMA
? THE PEN

RIGHT!

THE FLOOR
? LA ESCUELA

NO, THE CORRECT RESPONSE IS
EL SUELO

THE SCHOOL
? LA ESCUELA

RIGHT!
```

```
LA TIENDRA
? *END

3 RIGHT OUT OF 4
75%
```

## PROGRAM LISTING

```
100 REM: FLASHCARD
110 REM: (C) 1981, TOM RUGG AND PHIL
    FELDMAN
120 CLEAR 170:N=-1
130 L=10:M=3
140 DIM F$(L),B$(L),P(M-1)
150 CLS:E$="*ERROR*"
160 W$="*STOP RECORDER*"
170 PRINT"FLASHCARD"
180 PRINT:GOTO 2000
190 K=1:W=0:C=0:PRINT
200 F$(K)="":PRINT"SIDE 1 OF CARD";K
210 INPUT F$(K)
215 IF LEFT$(F$(K),4)="*END" THEN 280
220 IF LEFT$(F$(K),5)<>"*BACK" THEN 230
222 K=K-1:IF K<1 THEN K=1
225 PRINT:PRINT"BACKING UP":GOTO 200
230 B$(K)="":PRINT"SIDE 2":INPUT B$(K)
250 PRINT
260 K=K+1:IF K<=L THEN 200
270 PRINT"THAT'S THE";L;"CARD LIMIT."
280 PRINT:K=K-1:GOTO 2000
290 IF K>=M THEN 310
300 PRINT E$;" MINIMUM IS";M;"CARDS."
    :GOTO 2000
310 PRINT:PRINT"*CARD DRILL*"
330 PRINT
340 R=RND(K):FOR J=0 TO M-2
350 IF P(J)=R THEN 340
390 NEXT:J=RND(2):IF J=2 THEN 420
400 PRINT F$(R):C$=B$(R):GOTO 430
420 PRINT B$(R):C$=F$(R)
430 R$="":INPUT R$
440 IF LEFT$(R$,4)="*END" THEN 600
450 PRINT
```

```
460 IF R$=C$ THEN 500
470 PRINT"NO, THE CORRECT RESPONSE IS"
480 PRINT C$
490 W=W+1:GOTO 520
500 PRINT"RIGHT!"
510 C=C+1
520 FOR J=1 TO M-2:P(J-1)=P(J)
530 NEXT:P(M-2)=R:PRINT
560 GOTO 340
600 GOSUB 1500:GOTO 2000
700 IF K<1 THEN 1800
710 GOSUB 1600
720 PRINT"PRESS RECORD AND PLAY BUTTONS,"
730 PRINT"THEN ENTER NAME FOR FILE."
735 INPUT N$:PRINT"WRITING ";N$
737 OPEN"O",N,N$:REM ALPHA O
740 PRINT#N,N$:PRINT#N,STR$(K)
750 FOR J=1 TO K:PRINT#N,F$(J),B$(J)
760 PRINT J;:NEXT
770 PRINT#N,"*END"
780 CLOSE N
790 PRINT:PRINT"DONE"
800 PRINT W$:GOTO 2000
1150 INPUT"NAME OF FILE";N$
1160 GOSUB 1600:PRINT"PRESS PLAY,"
1170 PRINT"THEN PRESS A KEY."
1180 R$=INKEY$:IF R$="" THEN 1180
1185 PRINT"SEARCHING FOR ";N$
1190 OPEN"I",N,N$
1200 PRINT"FOUND ";N$
1210 INPUT#N,R$:INPUT#N,R$:K=VAL(R$)
1220 IF K<=L THEN 1250
1230 PRINT E$;" FILE HAS";K;"CARDS."
1240 PRINT"LIMIT =";L:GOTO 2000
1250 FOR J=1 TO K:INPUT#N,F$(J),B$(J)
1260 PRINT F$(J),B$(J)
1270 NEXT:CLOSE N
1300 PRINT"LOADED";K;"CARDS."
1310 PRINT W$:GOTO 2000
1500 PRINT:IF C+W=0 THEN RETURN
1510 PRINT C;"RIGHT OUT OF";C+W
1520 PRINT C*100/(C+W);"%"
1530 PRINT:RETURN
1600 PRINT
```

```
1610 PRINT"POSITION CASSETTE,"
1620 PRINT"THEN PRESS A KEY."
1630 IF INKEY$="" THEN 1630
1640 RETURN
1800 PRINT:PRINT E$
1810 PRINT"NO CARDS YET."
2000 R$="":PRINT:PRINT"**OPTIONS**"
2010 PRINT"1 ENTER NEW FLASHCARDS"
2020 PRINT"2 LOAD A FLASHCARD TAPE"
2030 PRINT"3 SAVE CURRENT SET ON TAPE"
2040 PRINT"4 DRILL ON CURRENT SET"
2050 PRINT"5 ADD TO CURRENT CARDS"
2060 PRINT"6 END PROGRAM"
2080 INPUT R:IF R<1 OR R>6 THEN 2100
2090 ON R GOTO 190,1150,700,290,260,2140
2100 PRINT:PRINT E$:GOTO 2000
2140 END
```

## EASY CHANGES

1. Change the limits of the number of flashcards that can be entered by altering line 130. L is the upper limit and M is the minimum. The current upper limit of ten will fit in a TRS-80 Color Computer with 4K of memory if each side of each flashcard averages no more than about eight characters in length. In a 16K TRS-80 Color Computer, you can make L as large as about five hundred for flashcards this size. You will also need to change line 120 to CLEAR 5000 or more instead of 170. Do not make M much larger than about ten or so, or you will slow down the program and use more memory than you might want.

2. If you want to use some keywords other than "*END" and "*BACK", substitute whatever you like in lines 215, 220, and 440. Be sure you use expressions that are the same length as these two, however. If not, you will also need to change the last number just before each occurrence of the expression to correspond with the length.

3. To cause the program to always display side one of the flashcards (and ask you to respond with side two), change line 390 to:

390 NEXT

To cause it to always display side two, change it this way:

390 NEXT:GOTO 420

4. To eliminate the "echoing" on the screen of a tape file being loaded, remove line 1260.

## MAIN ROUTINES

| | |
|---|---|
| 130- 180 | Initializes variables. Creates arrays. Displays title and options. |
| 190- 280 | Accepts flashcards entered by operator. |
| 290- 600 | Drills operator on flashcards in memory. |
| 700- 800 | Saves flashcards on cassette file. |
| 1150-1310 | Loads flashcards from cassette file into memory. |
| 1500-1530 | Subroutine to display number right and attempted during drill. |
| 1600-1640 | Subroutine to wait for cassette to be positioned until a key is held down. |
| 1800-1810 | Displays error message if operator tries to save flashcards on cassette before any are entered. |
| 2000-2140 | Displays options and analyzes response. Branches to appropriate routine. |

## MAIN VARIABLES

| | |
|---|---|
| N | Cassette number for cassette files. |
| L | Upper limit of number of flashcards that can be entered. |
| M | Minimum number of flashcards that can be entered. |
| E$ | Error message. |
| R | Subscript of random flashcard chosen during drill. |
| K | Number of flashcards entered. |
| W | Number of wrong responses. |
| C | Number of correct responses. |
| F$ | Array containing front side of flashcards (side 1). |
| B$ | Array containing back side of flashcards (side 2). |
| P | Array containing subscripts of $M-1$ previous flashcards during drill. |
| J | Loop and subscript variable. |
| C$ | The correct response during drill. |
| R$ | Response from operator. Also temporary string variable. |
| N$ | Name of cassette file. |
| W$ | Message to stop cassette recorder. |

## SUGGESTED PROJECTS

1. Modify the program for use in a classroom environment. You might want to allow only command 2 to be used (to load a cassette tape), and then immediately go into "drill" mode for some fixed number of questions (maybe 20 or 50).

# HAMCODE

## PURPOSE

At some time in your life you have undoubtedly heard the sound of "Morse Code." The familiar sound of dots and dashes is one that we have nearly all come in contact with at some time or other. Amateur radio operators ("hams") have to learn Morse code to obtain a license to operate an amateur radio station.

This program helps teach you what is officially called Continental Code, or sometimes referred to (ambiguously) as the International Morse Code, as used for ham radio. This is a little confusing, since the so-called *International* Morse Code, although similar, is *not* the same as Morse Code, which is still in use only for some types of land line transmissions. The code that nearly everyone uses anymore is Continental Code, so we picked the name HAMCODE for this chapter to try to be most descriptive of its use.

## HOW TO USE IT

The program begins by displaying its title and sounding it in code for you. It then shows you five options to choose from. To learn the code, you will be selecting different options to enable you to learn each character and become proficient at understanding groups of characters.

The first option teaches you each character. All you do is press any key on the computer's keyboard, and the program sounds the code of that character for you. As the code is sounded, the dots and dashes for it are displayed to help you both visualize and hear the code together. Be sure you have the sound on your TV set at a comfortable volume for hearing the code.

It's up to you to decide which characters you want to learn first. Most people will find it easiest to learn only a few each day (maybe three or four), and drill on them until they can be recognized immediately. Then add a few more characters the next day. Start with the alphabet, then move on to the numbers and punctuation characters. Keeping each session short is a good idea—half an hour is about right. Doing two or three short sessions each day is better than doing one long one.

Some keys on the computer keyboard do not have a code assigned to them. If you press one of the "illegal" keys, a distinctive low beep is sounded to let you know. To end the character-learning option, press the **CLEAR** key. This causes the five options to be displayed for you again.

After you have learned a few letters of the alphabet, you may want to try listening to groups of letters (words or phrases). This is done with option two. Simply enter one or more characters and press the **ENTER** key. The program will respond by sounding the code of the entire phrase at a rate of about 12 words per minute (five characters comprise an average word). The Easy Changes section shows how to change the speed, either faster or slower.

If the phrase has multiple words, they are separated by blue blocks on the color video display. As the program is currently written, you should limit the length of your phrases to no more than 40 characters. If you want to include any colons or commas in the phrase, you have to enclose the phrase in quotation marks. To hear a phrase a second time, simply press **ENTER** and it will be repeated.

To end option two, enter the word END as your phrase. Once again, this causes the five options to be displayed.

Once you have learned all the characters, you should try option three to quiz yourself on them. Option three randomly picks a character, sounds it for you, and waits for you to press the key of that character. There is no need to press the **ENTER** key. If you press the right key, the program tells you so and picks another random character.

If you press the wrong key, the program tells you what character it was and then sounds it for you again. You have to respond with the right answer before the program will pick a new character. This helps reinforce the correct answers. To end option three, press the **CLEAR** key.

Option four quizzes you on groups of characters which have been chosen at random. As currently written, groups of five characters are used, but the Easy Changes section shows how to make the program use other lengths.

After the five characters are sounded, enter the corresponding five characters and press the **ENTER** key. As with option three, the program tells you if you were right or wrong. If wrong, it tells you the correct answer and sounds the same characters for you again to make you enter them correctly. As with option two, if there are any colons or commas included in the group of characters, you must enclose the entire group of characters within quotation marks. And again, if you simply press the **ENTER** key, the phrase will be repeated for you.

The last option, option five, ends the program.

A few characters are not included in this program; these will have to be learned through other means. In all cases but two, this is because there are no ASCII characters on the keyboard to correspond with them (e.g., wait, double dash, error). The two exceptions are the quotation mark and the right parenthesis.

As mentioned above, quotation marks are used by BASIC to enclose a string of characters being entered by the operator. Since this would make it very awkward to include the quotation mark character in the program, and because the other characters are more important to learn, it has been omitted.

The right and left parenthesis are both supposed to use the same code. To avoid ambiguity in having you figure out whether the program was asking for the left or right parenthesis during the quiz options, we simply decided to treat the right one as an illegal character and thereby allow you to always respond with the left one.

Please be *very* careful when entering this program into your computer, especially for lines 3010 through 3130. If you make a mistake in typing the dots, dashes, commas, and X's, the program either will not work (Out of Data error, most likely), or you will teach yourself the wrong code! Be sure that you compare your results against the Sample Run photos to be sure that your codes look the same as ours.

**SAMPLE RUN**

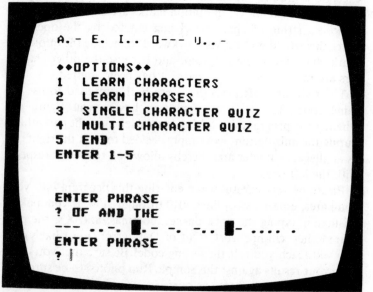

The program displays its title (both alphabetically and in code) and displays its options. The operator picks the first option and begins learning the vowels.

The operator proceeds to option 2, and begins by drilling on some common short words.

```
5   END
ENTER 1-5

WHAT CHARACTER IS THIS?
-...  B
RIGHT!
WHAT CHARACTER IS THIS?
..---  7
NO, IT WAS 2
TRY IT AGAIN.

WHAT CHARACTER IS THIS?
..---  2
RIGHT!
WHAT CHARACTER IS THIS?
....
```

Next the operator tries option 3, to be quizzed on individual characters. The first response is correct, but the next is not, the program repeats it to force the operator to respond correctly before going on to the next character.

```
3   SINGLE CHARACTER QUIZ
4   MULTI CHARACTER QUIZ
5   END
ENTER 1-5

WHAT'S THIS?
---..  --...  -.-.  ..-  ---
? 87CDO
NO, IT WAS 87CUO
LISTEN AGAIN.
---..  --...  -.-.  ..-  ---
? 87CUO
RIGHT!
WHAT'S THIS?
-  .---  -.-  ---...  .---
?
```

Finally, the operator asks for option 4, to test himself on random five character groups. After a mistake in his response for the first group, he replies correctly when it is repeated.

## PROGRAM LISTING

```
100 REM: HAM CODE
110 REM: (C) 1981, TOM RUGG AND PHIL
    FELDMAN
120 GOTO 2000
130 W=ASC(R$)-39:IF W<0 OR W>51 THEN 220
140 T$=C$(W):IF T$>"/" THEN 220
150 FOR J=1 TO LEN(T$):W$=MID$(T$,J,1)
160 D=3:IF W$="." THEN D=1
170 PRINT W$;
180 SOUND P,D
190 FOR D=1 TO 30:NEXT
200 NEXT:FOR J=1 TO 60*T:NEXT
210 PRINT" ";:RETURN
220 SOUND 8,8:RETURN
250 FOR K=1 TO LEN(P$):R$=MID$(P$,K,1)
260 IF ASC(R$)=32 THEN 280
270 GOSUB 130:NEXT:RETURN
280 PRINT CHR$(175);:FOR J=1 TO 90:NEXT
290 NEXT:PRINT:RETURN
300 PRINT"PRESS A KEY TO HEAR"
310 R$=INKEY$:IF R$="" THEN 310
320 W=ASC(R$):IF W=12 THEN 2100
330 IF W<39 OR W>90 THEN 350
340 IF C$(W-39)<>"X" THEN 360
350 SOUND 8,8:GOTO 310
360 PRINT R$;:GOSUB 130:GOTO 310
400 PRINT:PRINT"ENTER PHRASE"
410 INPUT P$
420 IF LEN(P$)=0 THEN P$=L$
430 IF P$="END" THEN 2100
440 GOSUB 250:L$=P$
450 GOTO 400
500 GOSUB 900
510 GOSUB 920
520 PRINT"WHAT CHARACTER IS THIS?"
540 GOSUB 130
550 T$=INKEY$:IF T$="" THEN 550
560 IF ASC(T$)=12 THEN 2100
570 IF ASC(T$)=13 THEN 540
580 PRINT T$:IF T$=R$ THEN 620
590 PRINT"NO, IT WAS ";R$
600 PRINT"TRY IT AGAIN.":PRINT
610 GOTO 510
```

```
620 PRINT"RIGHT!":GOTO 500
700 PRINT"WHAT'S THIS?"
710 P$="":FOR J=1 TO N
720 GOSUB 900
730 P$=P$+R$:NEXT
740 GOSUB 920:GOSUB 250:PRINT
750 INPUT T$:IF T$="" THEN 740
760 IF T$="END" THEN 2100
770 IF T$=P$ THEN PRINT"RIGHT!":GOTO 700
780 PRINT"NO, IT WAS ";P$
790 PRINT"LISTEN AGAIN."
800 GOTO 740
900 R=RND(52)-1:IF C$(R)="X" THEN 900
910 R$=CHR$(R+39):RETURN
920 FOR J=1 TO 800:NEXT:RETURN
950 END
2000 CLEAR 125
2010 DIM C$(51)
2020 FOR J=0 TO 51:READ C$(J):NEXT
2030 P=176:T=5
2050 CLS:P$="HAM CODE"
2060 PRINT TAB(12);P$:PRINT
2070 GOSUB 250
2080 N=5:L$=CHR$(32)
2100 PRINT
2110 PRINT:PRINT"**OPTIONS**"
2120 PRINT"1  LEARN CHARACTERS"
2130 PRINT"2  LEARN PHRASES"
2140 PRINT"3  SINGLE CHARACTER QUIZ"
2150 PRINT"4  MULTI CHARACTER QUIZ"
2160 PRINT"5  END"
2190 PRINT"ENTER 1-5"
2200 PRINT
2210 R$=INKEY$:R=RND(J)
2220 IF LEN(R$)=0 THEN 2210
2230 R=VAL(R$):IF R<1 OR R>5 THEN 2210
2240 ON R GOTO 300,400,500,700,950
3010 DATA .----,.,-.,-.-,X,X,X
3020 DATA --..,.--.,-....-,.-.-.-
3030 DATA -..-.,.,-----,.-----
3040 DATA ..---,...--,....-
3050 DATA .....,-....,--...
3060 DATA ---..,----.,-----
3070 DATA -.-.-..,X,X,X,..--..,X
3080 DATA .-,-....,-.-.,-..,.
```

```
3090 DATA . . ⁻ . , ⁻ ⁻ . , . . . . , . . , . ⁻ ⁻ ⁻
3100 DATA ⁻ . ⁻ . , . ⁻ . . , ⁻ ⁻ . , ⁻ . , ⁻ ⁻ ⁻
3110 DATA . ⁻ ⁻ . , ⁻ ⁻ . ⁻ . , . ⁻ . , . . . , ⁻
3120 DATA . . ⁻ . , . . . . ⁻ . , . ⁻ ⁻ . , ⁻ . . ⁻
3130 DATA ⁻ . ⁻ ⁻ . , ⁻ ⁻ . , ⁻ ⁻ . . .
```

## EASY CHANGES

1. To change the speed of the codes or the pitch at which they are sounded, change line 2030. T is the speed (time factor) and P is the pitch (see Appendix A of *Getting Started With Color BASIC*). Change T to 1 to make the speed about 19 or 20 words per minute, the top speed. Change T to 10 for about eight words per minute. Changing the speed only changes the length of time between letters and words, not the speed of dots and dashes or the short time interval between them. Currently the pitch is the C above middle C. Higher values of P give a higher pitch, and lower values give a lower pitch. For example, to get a higher pitched sound and the fastest speed, make this change:

    2030 P = 210:T = 1

2. If you have more than 4K of RAM (user memory) in your computer, you can set aside more string space for practicing longer phrases (option 2). Change line 2000 to:

    2000 CLEAR 1000

    By the way, if you have 4K, be sure that you are careful when entering the program not to include many extra spaces or text, or you may find that the program does not fit in 4K.

3. Change the number of characters in the multi-character quiz (option 4) by changing the value of N in line 2080.

4. Many experts stress that code is a language of *sound*, not sight, and should be learned that way. If you like, you can eliminate the displaying of dots and dashes on the screen by deleting line 170 and changing these lines:

    210 RETURN
    280 FOR J = 1 TO 90:NEXT

5. Eliminate the sounding of "HAM CODE" at the start of the program by deleting line 2070.

6. To drill on only alphabetic characters during options three and four, make this change:

    900 R = RND(26) + 25:IF C$(R) = "X" THEN 900

7 . A short delay is built into the program at several points. To lengthen it, replace the 800 in line 920 with 2000. To eliminate the delay, replace the 800 with 1.

## MAIN ROUTINES

| | |
|---|---|
| 130- 220 | Subroutine to sound and display character R$. |
| 250- 290 | Subroutine to sound and display phrase P$. |
| 300- 360 | Teaches characters by echoing keys until CLEAR is pressed. |
| 400- 450 | Teaches phrases by echoing entries until END is entered. |
| 500- 620 | Quizzes individual characters until CLEAR is pressed. |
| 700- 800 | Quizzes random N character phrases until END is entered. |
| 900- 910 | Subroutine to pick random character R$. |
| 920 | Delay subroutine. |
| 2000-2030 | Initializes variables. Stores codes in C$ array. |
| 2050-2080 | Displays and sounds title. Initializes more variables. |
| 2100-2240 | Displays options. Gets response. Initializes RND. Goes to option entered. |
| 3010-3130 | DATA statements with codes for ASCII 39 (apostrophe) through 90 (Z). X value is illegal code: A through Z are in 3080 through 3130. |

## MAIN VARIABLES

| | |
|---|---|
| W | Work variable and subscript. |
| R$ | Character to be sounded; work character. |
| T$ | Work string. |
| C$ | Array of code strings. |
| J,K | Loop and work variables. |
| W$ | Element (dot or dash) of code to be sounded. |
| D | Duration of sound to be made (dot = 1, dash = 3). Also loop variable. |
| P | Pitch of sound to be made. |
| T | Time factor to alter pauses between characters and words. |
| P$ | Phrase of characters to be sounded. |
| L$ | Last phrase entered. |
| N | Number of characters in multi-character quiz. |
| R | Random number for character selection; work variable. |

## SUGGESTED PROJECTS

1. Add another option to randomly quiz the operator on a series of common words and/or phrases that have been stored in DATA statements. You will need more than 4K of memory to have room for this.

2. Program some "intelligence" into the learning phase of the program. Have the program teach 3 or 4 common letters until the operator has mastered them, then begin teaching 3 or 4 more, etc.

3. Determine how to interface your Color Computer with amateur radio equipment so you can use the program to actually send code automatically under program control.

4. Now try the reverse of Project 3 — have the computer figure out how to decode a transmission that has been received over the radio, converting it into text. This will almost undoubtedly require some or all of the program to be in assembler language in order to run fast enough to handle this job in real time.

# METRIC

## PURPOSE

In case you don't realize it, we live in a metric world. The United States is one of the last holdouts, but that is changing rapidly. So if you're still inching along or watching those pounds, it's time to convert.

METRIC is an instructional program designed to familiarize you with the metric system. It operates in a quiz format; the program randomly forms questions from its data resources. You are then asked to compare two quantities — one in our old English units and one in the corresponding metric units. When you are wrong, the exact conversion and the rule governing it are given.

The two quantities to compare are usually within 50% of each other. Thus, you are constantly comparing an "English" quantity and a metric one which are in the same ball park. This has the effect of providing you some insight by sheer familiarity with the questions.

## HOW TO USE IT

The program first requests that you hit a key to begin. When this is done, it then asks how many questions you would like to do for the session. Any value of one or higher is acceptable.

The sample run shows how each question is formulated. A quantity in English units is compared with one in metric units. Either one may appear first in the question. Each quantity will have an integral value. The relating word ("longer," "hotter," "heavier," etc.) indicates what type of quantities are being compared.

There are three possible replies to each question. Pressing **Y** or **N** means that you think the answer is yes or no, respectively. Pressing any other key indicates that you have no idea as to the correct answer.

If you answer the question correctly, you will be duly congratulated and the program will proceed to the next question. A wrong answer or a response of "no idea," however, will generate some diagnostic information. The first value used in the question will be shown converted to its exact equivalent in the corresponding units. Also, the rule governing the situation will be displayed. At the end of any question, the program will request that you hit any key to proceed to the next question.

The program will continue generating the requested number of questions. Before ending, it will show you how many correct answers you gave and your percentage correct.

**SAMPLE RUN**

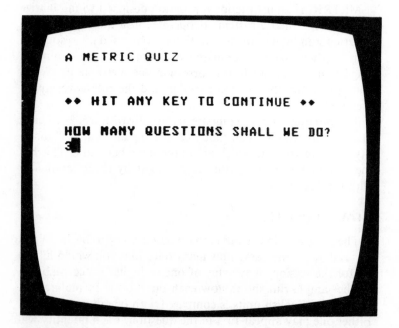

```
A METRIC QUIZ


** HIT ANY KEY TO CONTINUE **

HOW MANY QUESTIONS SHALL WE DO?
3
```

After hitting a key to begin the program, the operator requests a three question quiz.

```
A METRIC QUIZ

QUESTION 1 OF 3

IS 28 MILES PER HOUR
   FASTER THAN
      47 KILOMETERS PER HOUR ?

YOU SAY "NO" AND YOU'RE RIGHT
   -- VERY GOOD!

•• HIT ANY KEY TO CONTINUE ••
```

The first question is correctly answered "no." The program waits for a key to be pressed before continuing the quiz.

```
QUESTION 3 OF 3

IS 39 DEGREES CENTIGRADE
   HOTTER THAN
      149 DEGREES FAHRENHEIT ?

YOU SAY "YES" BUT YOU'RE WRONG

 39 DEGREES CENTIGRADE EQUALS
 102.2 DEGREES FAHRENHEIT

THE RULE IS:
DEG.F = (DEG.C • 1.8) + 32

•• HIT ANY KEY TO CONTINUE ••
```

Later, the third question is incorrectly answered with "yes." The correct conversion and governing rule are then displayed.

```
A METRIC QUIZ

YOU GOT 2 RIGHT OUT OF
  3 QUESTIONS

PERCENT CORRECT = 66.6666667
OK
```

The program shows the number and percentage of correctly answered questions.

## PROGRAM LISTING

```
100 REM: METRIC - 16K
110 REM: (C) 1981, PHIL FELDMAN AND TOM
    RUGG
140 CLEAR 50
150 B$=CHR$(32)
160 DIM ES$(10),MS$(10),R$(10)
170 DIM C(10),EF$(10),MF$(10)
200 GOSUB 400:GOSUB 500
210 GOSUB 1400
220 Q=RND(0):Q$=INKEY$
230 IF Q$="" THEN 220
240 PRINT:PRINT
250 PRINT"HOW MANY QUESTIONS ";
260 INPUT"SHALL WE DO";NQ
270 NQ=INT(NQ):IF NQ<1 THEN 250
300 FOR J=1 TO NQ:GOSUB 590
310 GOSUB 1400:GOSUB 1450:NEXT
320 GOSUB 500:PRINT"YOU GOT";
330 PRINT NR;"RIGHT OUT OF"
340 PRINT NQ;"QUESTIONS"
```

```
350 PRINT
360 P=100*NR/NQ
370 PRINT"PERCENT CORRECT =";P
380 END
400 RESTORE:ND=0
410 ND=ND+1
420 READ ES$(ND),MS$(ND),R$(ND)
430 READ C(ND),EP$(ND),MP$(ND)
440 IF ES$(ND)<>"XXX" THEN 410
450 ND=ND-1:RETURN
500 CLS:PRINT"A METRIC QUIZ"
510 PRINT:RETURN
590 N=RND(ND):F=RND(2)-1
600 V1=RND(98)+1:V3=V1*C(N)
610 IF F=1 THEN V3=V1/C(N)
620 IF N>1 THEN 650
630 V3=(V1-32)/1.8
640 IF F=1 THEN V3=(V1*1.8)+32
650 V2=INT(V3*(0.5+RND(0))+0.5)
660 T=0:IF V2<V3 THEN T=1
670 GOSUB 500
680 PRINT"QUESTION";J;"OF";NQ
690 PRINT:IF F=1 THEN 740
700 PRINT"IS";V1;EP$(N)
710 PRINT B$;B$;R$(N);" THAN"
720 PRINT B$;B$;V2;MP$(N);" ?"
730 GOTO 770
740 PRINT"IS";V1;MP$(N)
750 PRINT B$;B$;R$(N);" THAN"
760 PRINT B$;B$;V2;EP$(N);" ?"
770 GOSUB 1450
780 IF Q$<>"Y" THEN 820
790 PRINT:R=1
800 PRINT"YOU SAY 'YES' ";
810 GOTO 880
820 IF Q$<>"N" THEN 860
830 PRINT:R=0
840 PRINT"YOU SAY 'NO' ";
850 GOTO 880
860 PRINT
870 PRINT"YOU HAVE NO IDEA":R=2
880 X=T-R:IF R<>2 THEN 900
890 GOSUB 1000:GOTO 960
900 IF X=0 THEN 930
910 PRINT"BUT YOU'RE WRONG"
```

```
920 GOSUB 1000:GOTO 960
930 PRINT"AND YOU'RE RIGHT"
940 PRINT"   -- VERY GOOD!"
950 NR=NR+1
960 RETURN
1000 PRINT
1010 IF F=1 THEN 1050
1020 PRINT V1;EP$(N);" EQUALS"
1030 PRINT V3;MP$(N)
1040 GOTO 1070
1050 PRINT V1;MP$(N);" EQUALS"
1060 PRINT V3;EP$(N)
1070 PRINT:PRINT"THE RULE IS:"
1080 IF N>1 THEN 1140
1090 IF F=1 THEN 1120
1100 PRINT"DEG.C = (DEG.F - 32";
1110 PRINT")/1.8":RETURN
1120 PRINT"DEG.F = (DEG.C";
1130 PRINT" * 1.8) + 32":RETURN
1140 IF F=1 THEN 1170
1150 PRINT" 1 ";ES$(N);" EQUALS"
1160 PRINT C(N);MP$(N):RETURN
1170 Q=INT(1.E5/C(N))/1.E5
1180 PRINT" 1 ";MS$(N);" EQUALS"
1190 PRINT Q;EP$(N):RETURN
1400 PRINT:PRINT"** HIT ANY ";
1410 PRINT"KEY TO CONTINUE **";
1420 RETURN
1450 Q$="":Q$=INKEY$
1460 IF Q$="" THEN 1450
1470 RETURN
2000 DATA DEGREE FAHRENHEIT
2010 DATA DEGREE CENTIGRADE
2020 DATA HOTTER,0.5
2030 DATA DEGREES FAHRENHEIT
2040 DATA DEGREES CENTIGRADE
2100 DATA MILE PER HOUR
2110 DATA KILOMETER PER HOUR
2120 DATA FASTER,1.60935
2130 DATA MILES PER HOUR
2140 DATA KILOMETERS PER HOUR
2200 DATA FOOT,METER,LONGER
2210 DATA 0.3048,FEET,METERS
2300 DATA MILE,KILOMETER,LONGER
```

```
2310 DATA 1.60935,MILES
2320 DATA KILOMETERS
2400 DATA INCH,CENTIMETER
2410 DATA LONGER,2.54,INCHES
2420 DATA CENTIMETERS
2500 DATA GALLON,LITRE,MORE
2510 DATA 3.78533,GALLONS,LITRES
2600 DATA POUND,KILOGRAM,HEAVIER
2610 DATA 0.45359,POUNDS
2620 DATA KILOGRAMS
5999 DATA XXX,XXX,XXX,0,XXX,XXX
```

## EASY CHANGES

1. To have the program always ask a fixed number of questions, change line 250 to set NQ to the desired value and make line 260 a **REM** statement. For example:

   250 NQ = 10
   260 REM

   will cause the program to do 10 questions.

2. There are currently seven conversions built into the program:

   | N | Type | English Unit | Metric Unit |
   |---|------|--------------|-------------|
   | 1 | temperature | degrees F. | degrees C. |
   | 2 | speed | miles/hour | kilometers/hour |
   | 3 | length | feet | meters |
   | 4 | length | miles | kilometers |
   | 5 | length | inches | centimeters |
   | 6 | volume | gallons | litres |
   | 7 | weight | pounds | kilograms |

   If you wish to be quizzed on only one type of question, set N to this value by adding line 595. Thus,

   595 N = 4

   will cause the program to only produce questions comparing miles and kilometers. To add additional data to the program, see the first "Suggested Project."

3. You can easily have the questions posed in one "direction" only. To go only from English to metric units add

   597 F = 0

   while to go from metric to English units use

   597 F = 1

4.  You might want the converted value and governing rule to be displayed even when the correct answer is given. This is accomplished by adding line 955 as follows:

955 GOSUB 1000

## MAIN ROUTINES

140- 170 Dimensions and initializes variables.
200- 380 Mainline routine, drives other routines.
400- 450 Reads and initializes data.
500- 510 Displays header.
590- 960 Forms and asks questions. Processes user's reply.
1000-1190 Displays exact conversion and governing rule.
1400-1420 Requests the user to hit any key.
1450-1470 Waits for user to hit any key.
2000-5999 Data statements.

## MAIN VARIABLES

| | |
|---|---|
| ND | Number of conversions in the data. |
| ES$,EP$ | String arrays of English units' names (singular, plural). |
| MS$,MP$ | String arrays of metric units' names (singular, plural). |
| R$ | String array of the relation descriptors. |
| C | Array of the conversion factors. |
| Q | Work variable. |
| B$ | String constant of one blank character. |
| J | Current question number. |
| NR | Number of questions answered right. |
| P | Percentage answered right. |
| NQ | Number of questions in session. |
| N | Index number of current question in the data list. |
| F | Flag on question "direction" (0 = English to metric; 1 = metric to English). |
| V1,V2 | Numeric values on left, right sides of the question. |
| V3 | The correct value of the right hand side. |
| T | Flag on the question's correct answer (1 = true; 0 = false). |
| Q$ | User reply string. |
| R | User reply flag (0 = no; 1 = yes; 2 = no idea). |
| X | User's result (0 if correct answer was given). |

## SUGGESTED PROJECTS

1. Each built-in conversion requires six elements of data in this order:

   *Element   Data Description*
   1    English unit (singular)
   2    Metric unit (singular)
   3    Relation descriptor (e.g., "hotter," "faster," etc.)
   4    Conversion factor (from English to metric)
   5    English unit (plural)
   6    Metric unit (plural)

   Each of these elements, except the fourth, is a string. The data statements in the listing should make clear how the information is to be provided. You can add new data to the program with appropriate data statements in this format. New data should be added after the current data, i.e. just before line 5999. Line 5999 is a special data statement to trigger the end of all data to the program. The program is dimensioned up to ten entries while only seven are currently used. (Note: this format allows only conversions where one unit is a direct multiple of the other. Temperature, which does not fit this rule, is handled as a special case throughout the program.)

2. Convert the program to handle units conversion questions of any type.

3. Keep track of the questions asked and which ones were missed. Then do not ask the same questions too soon if they have been answered correctly. However, do re-ask those questions missed for additional practice.

# NUMBERS

## PURPOSE

This is an educational program for pre-school children. After a few weeks of watching Sesame Street on television, most three and four year old children will learn how to count from one to ten. The NUMBERS program allows these children to practice their numbers and have fun at the same time.

## HOW TO USE IT

We know a child who learned how to type CLOAD and RUN to get this program started before she turned three, but you'll probably have to help your child with this for a while. The program asks the question, "WHAT NUMBER COMES AFTER n?", where n is a number from one to eight. Even if the child can't read yet, he or she will soon learn to look for the number at the end of the line. The child should respond with the appropriate number, and then press the **ENTER** key.

If the answer is correct, the program displays the message "THAT'S RIGHT!", pauses for a couple of seconds, and then clears the screen and displays three geometric shapes. In the upper left of the screen a square is drawn. In the lower center, a triangle is drawn. Then an asterisk (or a snowflake, perhaps?) is drawn in the upper right portion of the screen. After a few seconds delay, the program clears the screen and asks another question. The same number is never asked twice in a row. The size of the three figures is chosen at random each time. If the child provides the wrong answer, a message indicates the error and the same question is asked again.

The program keeps on going until you hit the **BREAK** key. Remember that most children have a pretty short attention span, so please do not force your child to continue after his or her interest diminishes. Keep each session short and fun. This way, it will always be a treat to "play" with the computer.

**SAMPLE RUN**

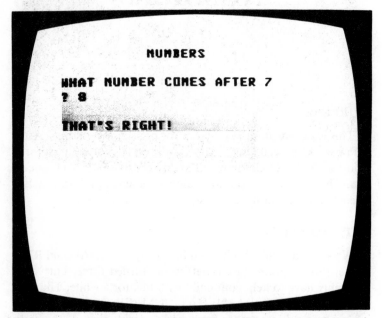

The program asks what number comes after 7, and waits for a response. The operator says "8", and the program acknowledges that the answer is correct.

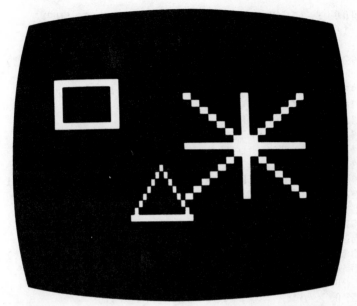

Because of the correct response, the program draws three geometric
figures.

## PROGRAM LISTING

```
100 REM: NUMBERS
110 REM: (C) 1981, TOM RUGG AND PHIL
    FELDMAN
120 CLEAR 200
130 M=8:TS=12
140 CLS
150 PRINT TAB(10);"NUMBERS"
170 R=RND(M):IF R=P THEN 170
180 PRINT
190 PRINT"WHAT NUMBER COMES AFTER";R
200 INPUT R$
210 PRINT
220 IF VAL(R$)=R+1 THEN 300
230 PRINT"NO, THAT'S NOT IT."
240 PRINT"TRY AGAIN.":GOTO 180
300 PRINT"THAT'S RIGHT!"
310 FOR J=1 TO 1000:NEXT
320 P=R:CLS(0)
330 E=RND(9)+2:C=RND(8)
```

```
400 Y=1:FOR X=1 TO 2*E:SET(X,Y,C):NEXT
410 X=2*E:FOR Y=1 TO E:SET(X,Y,C)
    :SET(X+1,Y,C):NEXT
420 Y=E:FOR X=2*E TO 1 STEP -1:SET(X,Y,C)
    :NEXT
430 X=1:FOR Y=E TO 1 STEP -1:SET(X,Y,C)
440 SET(X+1,Y,C):NEXT
450 C=RND(8):FOR J=1 TO E
460 Y=TS+J:X=TS+Y:SET(X,Y,C):NEXT
470 FOR J=1 TO E
480 Y=TS+J:X=TS+TS-J+2:SET(X,Y,C):NEXT
490 Y=TS+E+1:FOR X=TS+TS-E+1 TO TS+TS+E+1
500 SET(X,Y,C):NEXT
510 IF E>7 THEN E=7
520 C=RND(8):A=46:B=10
530 FOR J=1 TO E
540 X=A+J+J:Y=B+J:SET(X-1,Y,C):SET(X,Y,C)
550 Y=B-J:SET(X,Y,C):SET(X-1,Y,C)
560 Y=B:SET(X,Y,C):SET(X-1,Y,C)
570 X=A:SET(X,Y,C):SET(X-1,Y,C)
580 Y=B+J:SET(X,Y,C):SET(X-1,Y,C)
590 Y=B-J:SET(X-1,Y,C):SET(X,Y,C)
600 X=A-J-J:SET(X-1,Y,C):SET(X,Y,C)
610 Y=B:SET(X-1,Y,C):SET(X,Y,C)
620 Y=B+J:SET(X-1,Y,C):SET(X,Y,C)
630 NEXT
800 FOR J=1 TO 2000:NEXT
810 CLS
820 GOTO 170
```

## EASY CHANGES

1. Change the range of numbers that the program asks by altering the value of M in line 130. For a beginner, use a value of 3 for M instead of 8. Later, increase the value of M to 5, and then 8.

2. Alter the delay after "THAT'S RIGHT!" is displayed by altering the value of 1000 in statement 310. Double it to double the time delay, etc. The same can be done with the 2000 in line 800 to alter the delay after the figures are drawn.

3. To avoid randomness in the size of the figures that are drawn, replace line 330 with

$$330 \ E = 10:C = RND(8)$$

Instead of 10, you can use any integer from 2 to 11.

4. To slowly increase the size of the figures from small to large as correct answers are given (and the reverse for incorrect answers), do the following:
   a. Insert these lines:

       135 E = 1
       225 E = E − 1:IF E < 2 THEN E = 2

   b. Replace line 330 with:

       330 E = E + 1:C = RND (8):
       IF E > 11 THEN E = 11

## MAIN ROUTINES

| | |
|---|---|
| 120-150 | Initializes variables. Clears screen. |
| 170 | Picks random integer from 1 to M. |
| 180-240 | Asks question. Gets answer. Determines if right or wrong. |
| 310 | Delays about 2 seconds. |
| 320-440 | Draws a square. |
| 450-500 | Draws a triangle. |
| 520-630 | Draws an asterisk. |
| 800 | Delays about 4 seconds. |
| 810-820 | Clears screen. Goes back to ask next question. |

## MAIN VARIABLES

| | |
|---|---|
| M | Maximum number that will be asked. |
| E | Edge length of geometric figures. |
| R | Random integer in range from 1 to M. |
| P | Previous number that was asked. |
| R$ | Reply given by operator. |
| X,Y | Coordinates in CRT display. |
| TS | Triangle's starting location (top). |
| A,B | X,Y coordinate values. |
| J | Subscript variable. |
| C | Color of geometric shape. |

## SUGGESTED PROJECTS

1. Modify the program to ask the next letter of the alphabet. Use the ASC and CHR$ functions in picking a random letter from A to Y, and to check whether the response is correct or not.

2. Ask each number from 1 to M once (in a random sequence). At the end of the sequence, repeat those that were missed.

3. Add different shapes to the graphics display that is done after a correct answer. Try an octagon, a diamond, and a rectangle. Or, combine this program with one of the graphics display programs.

# TACHIST

## PURPOSE

This program turns your computer into a tachistoscope (tah-KISS-tah-scope). A tachistoscope is used in reading classes to improve reading habits and, as a result, improve reading speed. The program displays a word or phrase on the screen for a fraction of a second, then asks you what it was. With a little practice, you will find that you can read phrases that are displayed for shorter and shorter time periods.

## HOW TO USE IT

The program starts off by displaying a brief introduction and waiting for you to press any key (except the **BREAK** key or **SHIFT** keys, of course). After you press a key, the screen is blanked out except for two horizontal dash lines in the upper left-hand corner. After two and a half seconds, the phrase is flashed on the screen between the two lines. Then the screen is blanked again, and you are asked what the phrase was.

If you respond correctly, the next phrase is displayed for a shorter time period (half as long). If you respond incorrectly, the program shows you the correct phrase, and the next phrase is displayed for a longer period of time (twice as long).

The fastest the computer can display a phrase and erase it is about .02 seconds (one-fiftieth). See if you can reach the top speed and still continue to read the phrases correctly.

A great deal of research has been done to determine how people read and what they should do to read both faster and with better comprehension. We will not try to explain it all (see the bibliography), but a couple of things are worth mentioning.

To read fast, you should not read one word at a time. Instead, you should learn to quickly read an entire phrase at once. By looking at a point in the center of the phrase (and slightly above it), your eyes can see the whole phrase *without* the necessity of scanning it from left to right, word by word. Because the tachistoscope flashes an entire phrase on the screen at once, it forces you to look at a single point and absorb the whole phrase, rather than scanning left to right, word by word.

If you can incorporate this technique into your reading and increase the width of the phrases you absorb, your reading speed can increase dramatically.

**SAMPLE RUN**

The program displays an introduction, then waits.

The program clears the screen and displays two parallel lines in the upper left corner of the screen for a couple of seconds.

The program flashes a short phrase (chosen at random) between the two lines for a fraction of a second, then clears the screen.

The program asks what the phrase was. The operator responds correctly. The program acknowledges the correct response, and indicates that the next phrase will be shown for half as long.

## PROGRAM LISTING

```
100 REM: TACHIST
110 REM: (C) 1981, TOM RUGG AND PHIL
    FELDMAN
120 CLEAR 100
130 T=256
140 L=50
150 DIM T$(L)
160 C=0
170 READ R$
180 IF R$="XXX" THEN 260
190 C=C+1
200 IF C<=L THEN 230
210 PRINT"TOO MUCH DATA"
220 END
230 T$(C)=R$
240 GOTO 170
260 CLS
270 PRINT"TACHISTOSCOPE"
280 PRINT
```

```
290 PRINT"THIS PROGRAM IS DESIGNED TO"
300 PRINT"IMPROVE YOUR READING SPEED."
310 PRINT
320 PRINT"I'LL BRIEFLY DISPLAY A SHORT"
330 PRINT"PHRASE, AND YOU TRY TO READ IT."
340 PRINT
350 PRINT"TYPE WHAT YOU SEE, AND I'LL"
360 PRINT"TELL YOU IF YOU WERE RIGHT."
370 PRINT
410 PRINT"PRESS A KEY WHEN READY"
415 R=RND(2):R$=INKEY$
420 IF LEN(R$)=0 THEN 415
430 R=RND(C)
440 IF R=P1 OR R=P2 THEN 430
450 IF R=P3 OR R=P4 THEN 430
460 GOSUB 800
470 FOR K=1 TO 1500:NEXT
480 PRINT@32,T$(R);
490 FOR J=1 TO T:NEXT
500 CLS:FOR K=1 TO 500:NEXT
510 PRINT:PRINT:PRINT:PRINT
520 PRINT"WHAT WAS IT?"
530 INPUT R$
550 IF R$<>T$(R) THEN 700
560 PRINT"THAT'S RIGHT!"
570 T=T/2
590 R$="FOR HALF AS LONG."
600 P1=P2:P2=P3:P3=P4:P4=R
610 PRINT
620 IF T>8 THEN 640
630 T=8:R$="AT MAXIMUM SPEED."
640 PRINT"THE NEXT ONE WILL BE"
650 PRINT"DISPLAYED ";R$
660 PRINT:GOTO 410
700 PRINT"NO, THAT'S NOT IT."
710 PRINT"IT WAS--";T$(R)
720 T=T*2
730 IF T<=2048 THEN 760
740 T=2048:R$="AT THE SAME SPEED."
750 GOTO 600
760 R$="FOR TWICE AS LONG."
770 GOTO 600
800 CLS:PRINT"————————————————"
810 PRINT
820 PRINT"————————————————"
```

```
830 RETURN
910 DATA AT THE TIME
920 DATA THE BROWN COW
930 DATA LOOK AT THAT
940 DATA IN THE HOUSE
950 DATA THIS IS MINE
960 DATA SHE SAID SO
970 DATA THE BABY CRIED
980 DATA TO THE STORE
990 DATA READING IS FUN
1000 DATA HE GOES FAST
1010 DATA IN ALL THINGS
1020 DATA GREEN GRASS
1030 DATA TWO BIRDS FLY
1040 DATA LATE LAST NIGHT
1050 DATA THEY ARE HOME
1060 DATA ON THE PHONE
1070 DATA THROUGH A DOOR
1080 DATA WE CAN TRY
1090 DATA MY FOOT HURTS
1100 DATA HAPPY NEW YEAR
9999 DATA XXX
```

## EASY CHANGES

1. Change the phrases that are displayed by changing the DATA statements that start at line 910. Add more and/or replace those shown with your own phrases or words. Line 140 must specify a number that is at least as large as the number of DATA statements. So, to allow for up to 100 DATA statements, change line 140 to say

$$140 \ L = 100$$

Be sure to enter your DATA statements in the same form shown in the program listing. To begin with, you may want to start off with shorter phrases or single words. Later, try longer phrases. Do not alter line 9999, which has to be the last DATA statement. In a 4K Color Computer, you have room for about 40 or 50 phrases of the approximate size shown in the program listing. In a 16K Color Computer, you can have several hundred of them. Be sure to have at least 5.

2. To change the length of time the first phrase is displayed, change the value of T in line 130. Double it to double the length of time, etc. Don't make it less than eight.

3. To cause all phrases to be displayed for the same length of time, remove lines 570 and 720, and insert these lines:

```
595 R$ = "AT THE SAME SPEED"
725 R$ = "AT THE SAME SPEED":GOTO 600
```

4. If you want to change the waiting period before the phrase is flashed on the screen, change the 1500 in line 470. To make the delay five seconds, change it to 3000. To make it one second, change it to 600.

5. To put the program into a sort of flashcard mode, in which the phrases are flashed, but no replies are necessary, insert these three lines:

```
515 GOTO 710
595 R$ = "AT THE SAME SPEED"
715 GOTO 590
```

This will cause each phrase to be flashed (all for the same length of time), and then displayed again so you can verify what it was.

## MAIN ROUTINES

| | |
|---|---|
| 120- 150 | Initializes variables. |
| 160- 240 | Reads DATA statements into T$ array. |
| 260- 370 | Displays introduction. |
| 410- 420 | Waits for operator to press a key. |
| 430- 450 | Picks random phrase from T$ array. Ensures no duplication from previous four phrases. |
| 460 | Clears screen and displays horizontal lines. |
| 480- 500 | Displays phrase for appropriate length of time. |
| 510- 530 | Asks what the phrase was. |
| 550 | Determines if typed phrase matches the phrase displayed. |
| 560- 660 | Shortens time for next phrase if reply was correct. Saves subscript to avoid repetition. Goes back to wait for key to be pressed. |
| 700- 770 | Shows what phrase was. Lengthens time for next phrase. Ensures that time period does not exceed maximum. |

800- 830    Subroutine to display horizontal dash lines.
910-9999    DATA statements with phrases to be displayed.

## MAIN VARIABLES

| | |
|---|---|
| T | Time that phrase will be displayed. |
| J | Loop variable. |
| L | Limit of number of phrases. |
| T$ | Array of phrases (read into from DATA statements). |
| C | Count of number of phrases actually read. |
| R$ | Temporary string variable. Also, reply of operator. |
| R | Work variable. Also, subscript of phrase to be displayed. |
| P1,P2, P3,P4 | Subscripts of the four previous phrases. |
| K | Temporary work variable. |

## SUGGESTED PROJECTS

1. Instead of picking phrases at random, go through the list once sequentially.
2. Instead of only verifying that the current phrase does not duplicate any of the previous four phrases, modify the program to avoid duplication of the previous ten or more. Changes will be needed to lines 440, 450, and 600.
3. Keep score of the number of correct and incorrect replies, and display the percentage each time. Alternatively, come up with a rating based on the percentage correct and the speed attained, possibly in conjunction with a difficulty factor for the phrases used.
4. Add the capability to the program to also have a mode in which it can display a two to seven digit number, chosen at random. Have the operator try several of the numbers first (maybe five-digit ones) before trying the phrases. The phrases will seem easy after doing the numbers.

# VOCAB

## PURPOSE

Did you ever find yourself at a loss for words? Well, this vocabulary quiz can be used in a self-teaching environment or as reinforcement for classroom instruction to improve your ability to remember the jargon of any subject. It allows you to drill at your own pace, without the worry of ridicule from other students or judgment by an instructor. When you make mistakes, only the computer knows, and it's not telling anyone except you. Modifying the program to substitute a different vocabulary list is very simple, so you can accumulate many different versions of this program, each with a different set of words.

## HOW TO USE IT

This program is pretty much self-explanatory from the sample run. After you enter "RUN," it tells you to press a key to start, and indicates how many questions you will do (10).

Next, you get a series of multiple choice questions. Each question is formatted in one of two ways — either you are given a word and asked to select from a list of definitions, or you are given a definition and asked to select from a list of words. The format is chosen at random. You respond with the number of the choice you think is correct. If you are right, you are told so. If not, you are shown the correct answer. From the second answer on, you are shown a status report of the number correct out of the number attempted so far.

Finally, after the last question, you are shown the percentage you got correct, along with a comment on your performance. Then you have the option of going back for another round of questions or stopping.

**SAMPLE RUN**

```
THIS PROGRAM WILL TEST YOUR
KNOWLEDGE OF SOME USEFUL
VOCABULARY WORDS.

PRESS A KEY TO START.
WE'LL DO 10 QUESTIONS.


  1 WHAT WORD MEANS
    COMPANY LOVING?
    1 ANONYMOUS
    2 DISPARATE
    3 LACONIC
    4 VIVACIOUS
    5 GREGARIOUS
 ? 5
```

The program displays an introduction and asks the first question. The operator selects choice 5.

```
          COMPANY LOVING?
          1 ANONYMOUS
          2 DISPARATE
          3 LACONIC
          4 VIVACIOUS
          5 GREGARIOUS
        ? 5
        RIGHT!

          2 WHAT DOES ASTUTE MEAN?
            1 KEEN IN JUDGMENT
            2 WEAK OR EXHAUSTED
            3 FEARLESS OR COURAGEOUS
            4 TERSE
            5 LIVELY OR SPIRITED
          ?
```

The program responds that the first answer was correct, and asks the next question.

```
        THAT'S 7 RIGHT OUT OF 9

          10 WHAT WORD MEANS
             INDIFFERENT?
             1 OMINOUS
             2 ENERVATED
             3 LACONIC
             4 DISPARATE
             5 APATHETIC
        ? 5
        RIGHT!
        THAT'S 8 RIGHT OUT OF 10
        YOU HAD 80 PERCENT CORRECT.
        YOU CAN USE SOME MORE PRACTICE.

        WANT TO TRY AGAIN?
```

At the end of ten questions, the program gives a final score and asks about trying again.

## PROGRAM LISTING

```
100 REM: VOCABULARY QUIZ
110 REM: (C) 1981, TOM RUGG AND PHIL
    FELDMAN
120 CLEAR 50
300 GOSUB 1000:GOSUB 2000
500 GOSUB 3000:GOSUB 4000
700 GOSUB 5000:GOSUB 6000
900 IF E=0 THEN 500
910 GOTO 300
1000 IF E<>0 THEN 1060
1010 CLS:PRINT"VOCABULARY QUIZ"
1030 PRINT:PRINT"THIS PROGRAM WILL TEST
     YOUR"
1040 PRINT"KNOWLEDGE OF SOME USEFUL"
1050 PRINT"VOCABULARY WORDS."
1060 PRINT:PRINT"PRESS A KEY TO START."
1070 R$=INKEY$:A=RND(2)
1080 IF R$="" THEN 1070
1110 L=10
1120 PRINT"WE'LL DO";L;"QUESTIONS."
1200 PRINT:RETURN
2000 IF E<>0 THEN 2200
2010 C=5
2020 D=16
2030 DIM D$(D),E$(D),P(C):J=1
2060 READ D$(J)
2070 IF D$(J)="XXX" THEN 2140
2090 READ E$(J):J=J+1
2110 IF J<=D THEN 2060
2120 PRINT"OVER";D;"DATA STATEMENTS."
2140 D=J-1
2200 Q=1:E=0:Q1=0
2300 RETURN
3000 FOR J=1 TO C:P(J)=0:NEXT
3030 FOR J=1 TO C
3040 P=RND(D)
3050 IF P=P1 OR P=P2 OR P=P3 THEN 3040
3060 FOR K=1 TO J:IF P(K)=P THEN 3040
3070 NEXT K:P(J)=P:NEXT J
3200 A=RND(C):RETURN
4000 PRINT:M=RND(2)
4020 IF M=2 THEN 4100
```

```
4030 PRINT Q;"WHAT WORD MEANS"
4040 PRINT TAB(3);E$(P(A));"?"
4050 FOR J=1 TO C
4060 PRINT TAB(2);J;D$(P(J))
4070 NEXT:GOTO 4210
4100 PRINT Q;"WHAT DOES ";D$(P(A));" MEAN?"
4110 FOR J=1 TO C
4120 PRINT TAB(2);J;E$(P(J))
4130 NEXT
4210 RETURN
5000 INPUT R
5010 IF R>=1 AND R<=C THEN 5050
5020 PRINT"MUST BE FROM 1 TO";C
5030 GOTO 5000
5050 IF R=A THEN 5100
5060 PRINT"NO, THE ANSWER IS NUMBER";A
5070 GOTO 5210
5100 PRINT"RIGHT!":Q1=Q1+1
5210 IF Q=1 THEN 5300
5220 PRINT"THAT'S";Q1;"RIGHT OUT OF";Q
5300 P3=P2:P2=P1:P1=P(A)
5330 RETURN
6000 Q=Q+1:IF Q<=L THEN RETURN
6020 E=1:Q=Q1*100/(Q-1)
6070 PRINT"YOU HAD";Q;"PERCENT CORRECT."
6080 IF Q>80 THEN 6110
6090 PRINT"YOU CAN USE SOME MORE PRACTICE."
6100 GOTO 6200
6110 PRINT"VERY GOOD!"
6200 PRINT
6210 INPUT"WANT TO TRY AGAIN";R$
6220 R$=LEFT$(R$,1):IF R$<>"N" THEN 6240
6230 PRINT:PRINT"BYE.":PRINT:END
6240 IF R$<>"Y" THEN 6210
6250 RETURN
7010 DATA ANONYMOUS,OF UNKNOWN ORIGIN
7020 DATA OMINOUS,THREATENING OR MENACING
7030 DATA AFFLUENT,WEALTHY
7040 DATA APATHETIC,INDIFFERENT
7050 DATA LACONIC,TERSE
7060 DATA INTREPID,FEARLESS OR COURAGEOUS
7070 DATA GREGARIOUS,COMPANY LOVING
7080 DATA ENERVATED,WEAK OR EXHAUSTED
```

```
7090 DATA VENERABLE,WORTHY OF RESPECT
7100 DATA DISPARATE,DIFFERENT AND DISTINCT
7110 DATA VIVACIOUS,LIVELY OR SPIRITED
7120 DATA ASTUTE,KEEN IN JUDGMENT
7999 DATA XXX
```

## EASY CHANGES

1. Add more DATA statements between lines 7010 and 7999, or replace them all with your own. Be careful not to use two or more words with very similar definitions; the program might select more than one of them as possible answers to the same question. Note that each DATA statement first has the vocabulary word, then a comma, and then the definition or synonym. Be sure there are no commas or colons in the definition (unless you enclose the definition in quotes). If you add more DATA statements, you have to increase the value of D in line 2020 to be at least one greater than the number of words. The number of DATA statements you can have depends on how long each one is and how much user memory your computer has. Using DATA statements that average the same length as these, you can probably have about 12 to 15 of them in a 4K Color Computer, or as many as 400 in a 16K model. Be sure to leave statement 7999 as it is — it signals that there are no more DATA statements.

2. To get something other than five choices for each question, change the value of C in line 2010. You might want only three or four choices per question.

3. If you want to ask some number of questions other than 10, change the value of L in line 1110.

4. To make the program pause longer after a wrong answer, insert:

$$5065 \text{ FOR } J = 1 \text{ TO } 5000\text{:NEXT}$$

## MAIN ROUTINES

120- 910 Mainline routine. Calls major subroutines.
1000-1200 Displays introduction. Initializes RND function. Displays number of questions to be asked.
2000-2300 Reads vocabulary words and definitions into arrays. Performs housekeeping.

3000-3200 Selects choices for answers and determines which will be the correct one.

4000-4210 Determines in which format the question will be asked. Asks it.

5000-5330 Accepts answer from operator. Determines if right or wrong. Keeps score. Saves subscripts of last three correct answers.

6000-6250 Gives final score. Asks about doing it again.

7010-7999 DATA statements with vocabulary words and definitions.

## MAIN VARIABLES

E           Set to 1 to avoid repeating introduction after the first round.

L           Limit of number of questions to ask.

R           Work variable. Also used for operator's reply to each question.

C           Number of choices of answers given for each question.

D           At least one greater than number of DATA statements. Used to DIM arrays.

D$          Array of vocabulary words.

E$          Array of definitions.

P           Array for numbers of possible answers to each question.

J           Work variable (subscript for FOR-NEXT loops).

Q           Number of questions asked so far (later used to calculate percent correct).

Q1          Number of questions correct so far.

P           Work variable.

P1,P2,P3    Last three correct answers.

A           Subscript of correct answer in P array.

M           Work variable to decide which way to ask question.

R$          Yes or no reply about doing another round.

## SUGGESTED PROJECTS

1. Modify lines 6070 through 6200 to display the final evaluation messages based on a finer breakdown of the percent correct. For example, show one message if 100 percent, another if 95 to 99, another if 90 to 94, etc.

2. Ask the operator's name in the introduction routine, and personalize some of the messages with his/her name.
3. Instead of just checking about the last three questions, be sure that the next question has not been asked in the last eight or ten questions. (Check lines 3050 and 5300.)
4. Keep track of which questions the operator misses. Then, after going through the number of questions he/she requested, repeat those that were missed.

# Section 3

# Game Programs

## INTRODUCTION TO GAME PROGRAMS

Almost everyone likes to play games. Computer games are a fun and entertaining use of your TRS-80 Color Computer. Besides providing relaxation and recreation, they have some built-in practical bonuses. They often force you to think strategically, plan ahead, or at least be orderly in your thought processes. They are also a good way to help some friends over their possible "computer phobia." We present a collection of games to fit any game playing mood.

Maybe you desire a challenging all-skill game? Like chess or checkers, WARI involves no luck and considerable thinking. The computer will be your opponent, and a formidable one indeed.

Perhaps you're in the mood for a game with quick action and mounting excitement. GROAN is a fast-paced dice game involving mostly luck with a dash of skill (or intuition) thrown in. The Color Computer is ready to take you on anytime.

Two word games are included. In JOT, you and the computer each pick secret words and then try to home in on each other's selection. In ARGO, you are challenged to make words by unscrambling letters in a race against time.

Do you like solving puzzles? If so, try DECODE. The computer will choose a secret code and then challenge you to find it.

Graphic electronic arcade games are a prevalent landmark of our times. We include two such games. ROADRACE puts you behind the wheel of a high speed race car. You must steer accurately to stay on course. OBSTACLE lets you and a friend compete in a game of cut and thrust. Each of you must avoid crossing the path laid by the other, and by yourself!

# ARGO

## PURPOSE

Argo is a word game that is both challenging and a lot of fun. The program displays 13 random letters, and your object is to try to score as many points as possible by creating words from them.

## HOW TO USE IT

The program begins by displaying its name and asking you to press a key to start the game. After you press a key (other than **SHIFT** or **BREAK**, of course), the program displays 13 letters in alphabetical order and starts its "timer." When the timer in the upper left corner reaches 5000, the game is over.

Your object is to create words that are at least three, but no more than seven letters long. You can enter as many as six words of each length, but only the first five will score points. This is to give you a chance to enter an extra word of some length in case you mis-typed a word or entered a word that is later disallowed.

Each word is entered by simply typing the letters of the word and pressing the **ENTER** key. As each letter of the word is typed, it is displayed at the top of the screen. When **ENTER** is pressed, the word is moved to the lower part of the screen, where a column of words is displayed for each length. The three letter words are at the left of the screen, and the seven letter words are at the right.

If a typing error is made before pressing **ENTER**, you can simply correct it as usual by using the "back arrow" key. If you do not see the error until after you pressed **ENTER**, there is no way to erase the erroneous word.

The program displays an error message to the right of your word if you enter a duplicate word or if you try to enter a word that is not made up of the letters shown. Of course, you can only use a letter the number of times it is shown—to use a letter twice, there need to be two of them.

The program has no way of knowing whether or not you are entering legitimate words. It only checks that you are using the proper letters. It's up to you to determine if you want to allow slang, proper names, foreign words, etc. If you are going to compete with a friend, be sure you establish the ground rules first.

At the end of your time limit, the program displays the score and ends. Scoring is based on how many words you entered of each length. Each word counts the square of its word length in points. So, each three letter word counts nine points. Each four letter word is 16 points, a five letter word is 25 points, a six letter word is 36 points, and a seven letter word is 49 points. This means that the maximum possible score is

$$5 \times (9 + 16 + 25 + 36 + 49) = 675.$$

In our experience, however, any score over 200 is very good, and anything over 300 is excellent. Needless to say, the scores vary widely based on what letters you happen to get.

The program gives you a fair chance by making sure that you have at least two vowels among your 13 letters. Other than that, the letters are simply chosen at random.

## SAMPLE RUN

The program waits for the operator to press a key to start the game.

The program selects 13 random letters and starts the timer.

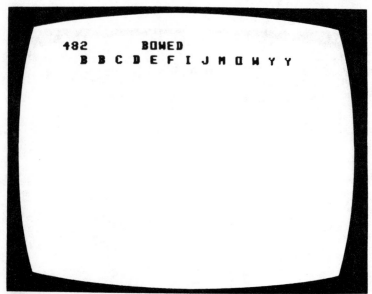

```
482        BOWED
    B B C D E F I J M O W Y Y
```

The operator enters the first word, which will go in the column of five letter words when ENTER is pressed.

```
5000
      B B C D E F I J M O W Y Y

BOW DICE BOWED
CIW MICE MOWED
COW DIME
MOW DOME
BID
FED

TIME'S UP.    SCORE = 159

OK
```

The timer reaches 5000 to end the game, causing the score to be displayed. Note that a typing error was made (CIW), so the operator entered an extra three letter word. This caused the scoring of five words of three letters to be correct.

## PROGRAM LISTING

```
100 REM: ARGO
110 REM: (C) 1981, TOM RUGG AND PHIL
    FELDMAN
140 CLEAR 200:CLS:N=13
150 DIM W$(7,6),A(N),E(N),V(5)
160 V(1)=65:V(2)=69:V(3)=73
165 V(4)=79:V(5)=85
170 D(3)=96:D(4)=100:D(5)=105
175 D(6)=111:D(7)=118
180 GOSUB 6000
190 GOSUB 900:CLS:C=0:M=5000
195 D=10:GOTO 5010
200 W$=""
210 A$=INKEY$:C=C+1
215 IF C>M THEN 810
220 PRINT@0,C;:IF A$="" THEN 210
230 IF ASC(A$)=13 THEN 300
260 IF ASC(A$)=8 THEN 1500
270 IF A$<"A" OR A$>"Z" THEN 210
280 W$=W$+A$:PRINT@D,W$;
285 IF LEN(W$)>8 THEN 300
290 GOTO 210
300 L=LEN(W$)
310 IF L<3 OR L>7 THEN 400
320 GOSUB 3010
330 IF F=1 THEN M$="DUPLICATE":GOTO 700
340 GOSUB 4010:IF F=1 THEN 400
350 T(L)=T(L)+1
360 IF T(L)>6 THEN 500
370 W$(L,T(L))=W$
380 PRINT@D(L),W$;
390 PRINT@D," "
395 D(L)=D(L)+32:GOTO 200
400 M$="ILLEGAL":GOTO 700
500 T(L)=T(L)-1:M$="TOO MANY"
510 GOTO 700
700 PRINT@D+10,M$;
710 FOR J=1 TO 30:C=C+1
720 PRINT@0,C;:NEXT
730 PRINT@D," "
740 GOTO 200
810 PRINT@320,"TIME'S UP.   ";
820 SC=0:FOR J=3 TO 7
830 K=T(J):IF K>5 THEN K=5
```

```
840 SC=SC+J*J*K:NEXT
850 PRINT" SCORE =";SC
855 PRINT
860 END
900 FOR J=1 TO N:R=RND(26)+64
910 A(J)=R:NEXT
920 FOR J=1 TO 2
930 A(J)=V(RND(5)):NEXT
940 RETURN
1500 IF LEN(W$)<2 THEN 730
1510 W$=LEFT$(W$,LEN(W$)-1)
1520 PRINT@D," "
1530 PRINT@D,W$;:GOTO 210
3010 F=0:IF T(L)=0 THEN RETURN
3020 FOR J=1 TO T(L)
3030 IF W$(L,J)=W$ THEN F=1
3040 NEXT:RETURN
4010 F=0:FOR J=1 TO N:E(J)=A(J)
4020 NEXT:FOR J=1 TO L
4030 K=ASC(MID$(W$,J,1))
4040 FOR X=1 TO N
4050 IF E(X)=K THEN E(X)=0:GOTO 4070
4060 NEXT:F=1
4070 NEXT J:RETURN
5010 FOR J=N TO 2 STEP -1:X=A(1):F=1
5020 FOR L=2 TO J:IF A(L)>X THEN X=A(L):F=L
5030 NEXT:A(F)=A(J):A(J)=X:NEXT
5050 FOR J=1 TO N
5060 PRINT@33+J+J,CHR$(A(J));
5070 NEXT:GOTO 730
6000 PRINT TAB(12);"A R G O"
6010 PRINT:PRINT"PRESS A KEY"
6020 J=RND(2):A$=INKEY$
6030 IF LEN(A$)=0 THEN 6020
6040 RETURN
```

## EASY CHANGES

1. You can easily change the program to give you more or less
   than 13 letters to choose from. In a 4K computer, you can
   use any number from three to 17, but more than 15 causes
   the last ones to extend to a second line. Values from nine to
   15 are best. As an example, make this change to use 15
   letters:

   140 CLEAR 200:CLS:N=15

2. The program currently guarantees at least two vowels among the list of letters. Change the "2" at the end of line 920 to alter this. For example, to guarantee at least three vowels, it should be:

   920 FOR J = 1 TO 3

3. Give the player more or less time to create words by changing the value of M in line 190. For example, to make each game last about twice as long, make this change:

   190 GOSUB 900:CLS:C = 0:M = 10000

## MAIN ROUTINES

| | |
|---|---|
| 140- 195 | Initializes variables, displays title, chooses letters. |
| 200- 290 | Gets word from player. Increments timer while waiting. |
| 300- 510 | Examines word for legality. Saves it. |
| 700- 740 | Displays and erases error message. |
| 810- 860 | Computes score and ends program. |
| 900- 940 | Subroutine to select N letters. |
| 1500-1530 | Backspaces during word entry. |
| 3010-3040 | Subroutine to check for duplicate word. |
| 4010-4070 | Subroutine to check that legal letters were used. |
| 5010-5070 | Alphabetizes and displays letters. |
| 6000-6040 | Subroutine to display title and initialize RND. |

## MAIN VARIABLES

| | |
|---|---|
| N | Number of letters to choose from. |
| W$ | Array that words are saved in. |
| A | Array holding ASCII values of letters. |
| E | Array for evaluating whether legal letters were used. |
| V | Array with ASCII values of the vowels. |
| D | Array of screen locations of each word length. |
| C | Counter for timer. |
| M | Maximum value for timer. |
| D | Screen location for word being entered. |
| W$ | Word being entered. |
| A$ | Key pressed during word entry. |
| L | Length of word entered. Also work variable. |
| F | Flag set to 1 if word is illegal. Also work variable. |
| M$ | Error message. |

| | |
|---|---|
| T | Array to count the number of words entered of each length. |
| J,X | Loop and work variables. |
| R | Random number used in selecting letters. |

## SUGGESTED PROJECTS

1. Display the score as each word is entered, so the player can see the score while the game is in progress.
2. Allow the player to erase the last word entered, in case of typographical error.

# Color Section

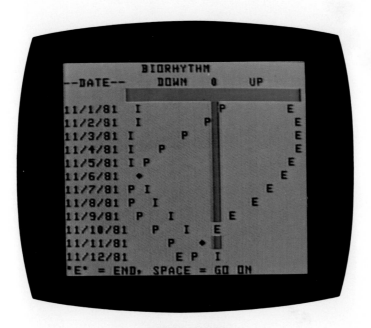

**BIORHYTHM**

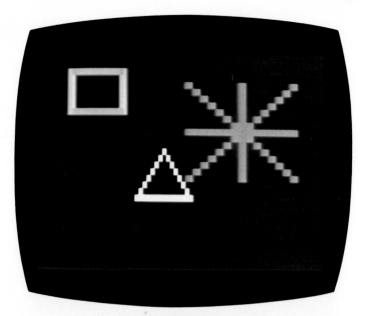

**NUMBERS**

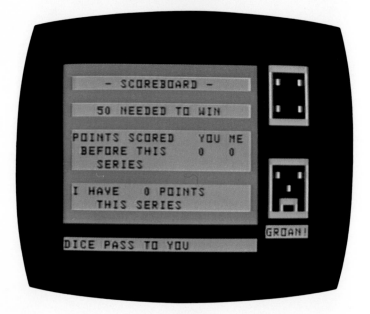

**GROAN**

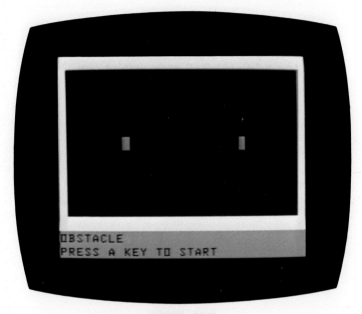

**OBSTACLE**

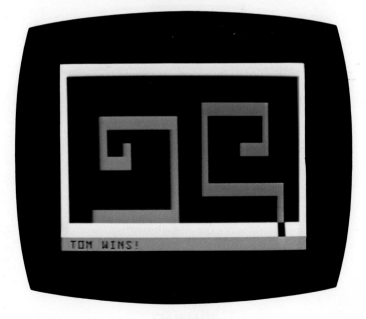

**OBSTACLE**

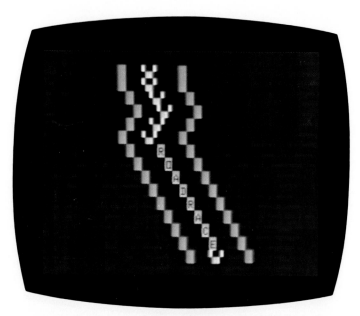

**ROADRACE**

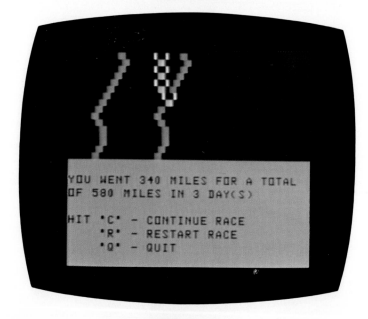

**ROADRACE**

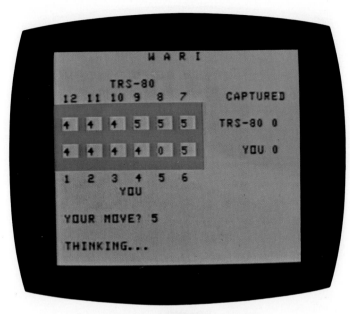

**WARI**

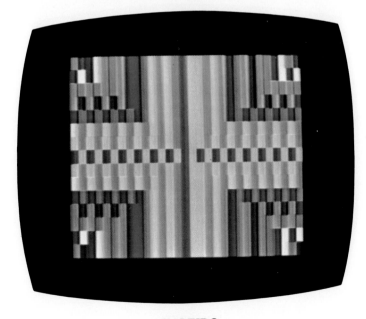

**KALEIDO**

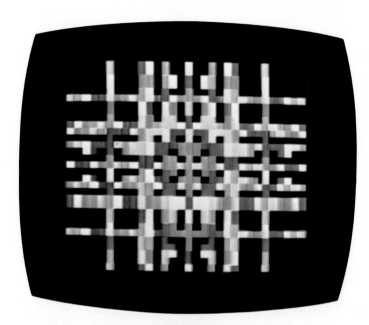

**SPARKLE**

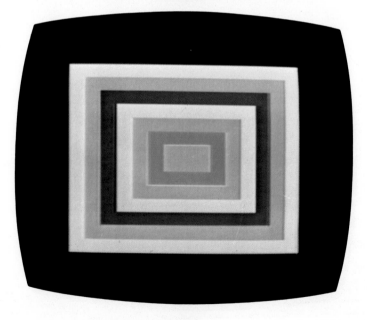

**SQUARES**

**WALLOONS**

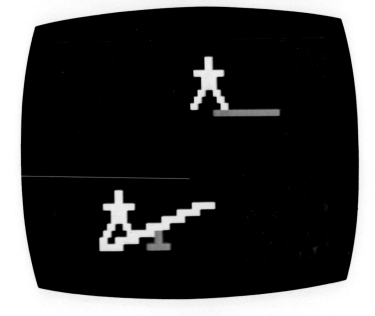

**WALLOONS**

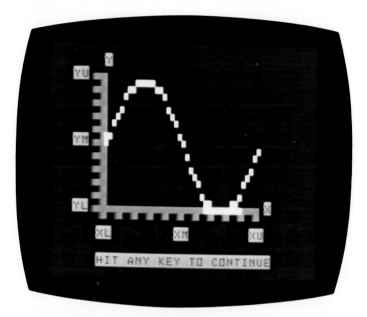

**GRAPH**

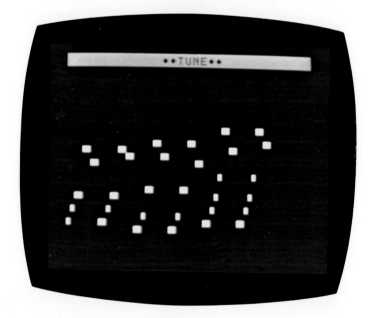

**TUNE**

# DECODE

## PURPOSE

Decode is really more of a puzzle than a game, although you can still compete with your friends to see who can solve the puzzles the fastest. Each time you play, you are presented with a new puzzle to solve.

The object is to figure out the computer's secret code in as few guesses as possible. The program gives you information about the accuracy of each of your guesses. By carefully selecting your guesses to make use of the information you have, you can determine what the secret code must be in a surprisingly small number of guesses. Five or six is usually enough.

The first few times you try, you will probably require quite a few more guesses than that, but with practice, you'll discover that you can learn a lot more from each guess than you originally thought.

## HOW TO USE IT

The program starts off by displaying a brief introduction. Here are some more details.

The program selects a secret code for you to figure out. The code is a four digit number that uses only the digits 1 through 6. For example, your TRS-80 Color Computer might pick 6153 or 2242 as a secret code.

Your object is to guess the code in the fewest possible guesses. After each of your guesses, the program tells you a "black" and a "white" number. The black number indicates the number of digits in your guess that were correct — the digit was correct *and* in the correct position. So, if the secret code is 6153 and your guess is 4143, you will told that black is 2 (because the 1 and the 3 will have been correct). Of course, you aren't told *which* digits are correct. That is for you to figure out by making use of the information you get from other guesses.

Each of the white numbers indicates a digit in your guess that was correct, but which is in the wrong position. For example, if the secret code is 6153 and your guess is 1434, you will be told that white is 2. The 1 and 3 are correct, but in wrong positions.

The white number is determined by ignoring any digits that accounted for a black number. Also, a single position in the secret code or guess can only account for one black or white number. These facts become significant when the secret code and/or your guess have duplicate digits. For example, if the code is 1234 and your guess is 4444, there is only one black, and no whites. If the code is 2244 and your guess is 4122, there are no blacks and three whites.

This may sound a little tricky, but you will quickly get the hang of it.

At any time during the game, you can ask for a "SUMMARY" by entering an S instead of a guess. This causes the program to clear the screen and display each guess (with the corresponding result) that has occurred so far.

Also, if you get tired of trying and want to give up, you can enter a Q (for "quit") to end your misery and find out the answer. Otherwise, you continue guessing until you get the code right (four black, zero white), or until you have used up the maximum of twelve guesses.

**SAMPLE RUN**

```
FIGURE OUT A 4 POSITION CODE
USING THE DIGITS 1 THROUGH 6

"BLACK" MEANS A CORRECT DIGIT
IN THE CORRECT POSITION.
"WHITE" MEANS ANOTHER CORRECT
DIGIT IN THE WRONG POSITION.

PRESS A KEY TO START
I'VE CHOSEN MY SECRET CODE.

GUESS NUMBER 1 ? 6413
GUESS 1 -- BLACK = 2   WHITE = 0

GUESS NUMBER 2 ?
```

The program displays an introduction, chooses its secret code, and asks for the operator's first guess. After the operator makes a guess, the program responds with a "black" and a "white" number, and asks for the second guess.

```
                    SUMMARY
       NO.      GUESS    BLACK     WHITE
        1       6413       2         0
        2       6414       1         1
        3       6452       1         0
        4       6611       0         0
        5       4433       3         0

GUESS NUMBER 6 ? 4443
GUESS 6 -- BLACK = 4   WHITE = 0


YOU GOT IT IN 6 GUESSES.
....THAT'S NOT BAD
WANT TO TRY AGAIN?
```

Later in the same game, the operator asks for a summary, then makes the guess that turns out to be correct. The program acknowledges that the guess is correct and asks about trying another game.

## PROGRAM LISTING

```
100 REM: DECODE
110 REM: (C) 1981, TOM RUGG AND PHIL
    FELDMAN
120 CLEAR 200:D=6:P=4:L=12
130 DIM G$(L),G(P),C(P)
140 DIM B(L),W(L)
150 GOSUB 1200
160 GOSUB 300
180 PRINT"GUESS NUMBER";G;
190 INPUT A$
200 IF LEFT$(A$,1)="S" THEN 500
210 IF LEFT$(A$,1)="Q" THEN 600
220 GOSUB 700
230 GOSUB 800
240 GOSUB 1000
250 IF B(G)=P THEN 2000
260 G$(G)=A$
270 G=G+1:IF G>L THEN 2200
280 GOTO 180
300 G=1:C$=""
310 FOR J=1 TO P
320 R=RND(D)
330 C$=C$+MID$(STR$(R),2,1)
340 NEXT
350 PRINT"I'VE CHOSEN MY SECRET CODE."
360 PRINT:RETURN
500 IF G=1 THEN PRINT"NO GUESSES YET"
    :GOTO 180
510 CLS:PRINT TAB(12);"SUMMARY"
520 PRINT"NO.    GUESS    BLACK    WHITE"
530 FOR J=1 TO G-1
540 PRINT J;TAB(7);G$(J);TAB(16);B(J);
    TAB(24);W(J)
560 NEXT:PRINT
570 GOTO 180
600 PRINT
610 PRINT"MY CODE WAS...";
620 FOR J=1 TO 1000:NEXT
630 PRINT C$:PRINT
640 FOR J=1 TO 500:NEXT
650 GOTO 2090
700 IF LEN(A$)<>P THEN 780
710 FOR J=1 TO P
```

```
720  R=VAL(MID$(A$,J,1))
730  IF R<1 OR R>D THEN 780
740  NEXT
750  RETURN
780  PRINT"ILLEGAL,  TRY AGAIN,"
790  GOTO 180
800  B=0:W=0
810  FOR J=1 TO P
820  G(J)=VAL(MID$(A$,J,1))
830  C(J)=VAL(MID$(C$,J,1))
840  IF G(J)=C(J) THEN B=B+1:G(J)=0:C(J)=0
850  NEXT
860  FOR J=1 TO P:IF C(J)=0 THEN 920
870  H=0:FOR K=1 TO P
880  IF C(J)=0 THEN 910
890  IF C(J)<>G(K) THEN 910
900  H=1:G(K)=0:C(J)=0
910  NEXT K:W=W+H
920  NEXT J
930  RETURN
1000 B(G)=B:W(G)=W
1010 PRINT"GUESS";G;"-- BLACK =";B;
     " WHITE =";W
1020 RETURN
1200 CLS
1210 PRINT"**** DECODE ****"
1220 PRINT
1230 PRINT"FIGURE OUT A";P;"POSITION CODE"
1240 PRINT"USING THE DIGITS 1 THROUGH";D
1260 PRINT
1270 PRINT"'BLACK' MEANS A CORRECT DIGIT"
1280 PRINT"IN THE CORRECT POSITION,"
1290 PRINT"'WHITE' MEANS ANOTHER CORRECT"
1300 PRINT"DIGIT IN THE WRONG POSITION,"
1310 PRINT:PRINT"PRESS A KEY TO START"
1320 IF LEN(INKEY$)<>0 THEN RETURN
1340 J=RND(2):GOTO 1320
2000 PRINT
2010 PRINT"YOU GOT IT IN";G;"GUESSES,"
2020 IF G<6 THEN B$="VERY GOOD"
2040 IF G=6 THEN B$="NOT BAD"
2050 IF G>6 THEN B$="A BIT WEAK"
2070 PRINT"....THAT'S ";B$
2090 INPUT"WANT TO TRY AGAIN";A$
2100 IF LEFT$(A$,1)="Y" THEN 150
```

```
2110 IF LEFT$(A$,1)<>"N" THEN 2090
2120 PRINT:PRINT"COWARD,":PRINT
2130 END
2200 PRINT
2210 PRINT"THAT'S YOUR LIMIT OF"
2220 PRINT L;"GUESSES,"
2230 PRINT"MY CODE WAS ";C$
2240 GOTO 2090
```

## EASY CHANGES

1. Modify line 120 to change the complexity of the code and/or the number of guesses you are allowed. For example, the following line would allow fifteen guesses at a five position code using the digits 1 through 8:

   120 CLEAR 200: D = 8:P = 5:L = 15

   The introduction will automatically reflect the new values for D and P. Be sure that neither D nor P is set greater than 9. You will need a 16K computer to make this change, unless you delete some text in the program (such as lines 1260-1300 or line 350).

2. To change the program so it will always display the "Summary" information after each guess automatically, replace line 280 with this:

   280 GOTO 500

## MAIN ROUTINES

120- 160 Initializes variables. Displays introduction. Chooses secret code.
180- 240 Gets a guess from operator. Analyzes reply. Displays result.
250      Determines if operator guessed correctly.
260- 280 Saves guess. Adds one to guess counter. Determines if limit on number of guesses was exceeded.
300- 360 Subroutine to initialize variables, choose secret code and inform operator.
500- 570 Subroutine to display summary of guesses so far.
600- 650 Subroutine to slowly display secret code when operator quits.
700- 790 Subroutine to determine if operator's guess was legal.

800- 930 Subroutine to determine number of black and white responses for the guess.
1000-1020 Subroutine to display number of black and white responses for guess.
1200-1340 Subroutine to display title and introduction.
2000-2130 Subroutine to analyze operator's performance after correct answer is guessed and ask about playing again.
2200-2240 Subroutine to display secret code after operator exceeds limit of number of guesses.

## MAIN VARIABLES

D        Number of possible digits in each position of the code (i.e., a digit from 1 to D).
P        Number of positions in the code.
L        Limit of number of guesses that can be made.
G$       Array in which guesses are saved.
G,C      Work arrays in which each guess is analyzed.
B,W      Arrays in which the number of black and white responses is saved for each guess.
R,H      Work variables.
G        Counter of the number of guesses made.
A$       Reply by the operator.
C$       Secret code chosen by the program.
J,K      Loop variables.
B,W      Number of black and white responses for this guess.
B$       String with message about operator's performance.

## SUGGESTED PROJECTS

1. Change the analysis at the end of the game to take into account the difficulty of the code as well as the number of guesses it took to figure the code out. A four position code using the digits 1 through 6 has 1296 possibilities, but a five position code using 1 through 8 has 32768 possibilities. Change lines 2020 through 2050 to determine the message to be displayed based on the number of possibilities in the code as well as G.

2. At the beginning of the game, give the operator the option of deciding the complexity of the code. Ask for the number of positions and the number of digits. Make sure only "rea-

sonable" numbers are used — do not try to create a code with zero positions, for example. Another approach is to ask the operator if he/she wants to play the easy, intermediate, or advanced version. Then set the values of D and P accordingly. Suggestions are:

|  |  |
|---|---|
| Easy: | D = 3 and P = 3 |
| Intermediate: | D = 6 and P = 4 |
| Advanced: | D = 8 and P = 5 |

3. In addition to using the number of guesses to determine how well the operator did, keep track of the amount of time. This will require use of the INKEY\$ function instead of the INPUT function in line 190, and a bit of logic to "build" the A\$ reply one character at a time. By counting the number of null strings encountered while waiting for keys to be pressed, you can "time" the operator.

# GROAN

## PURPOSE

Do you like the thrills of fast-paced dice games? If so, GROAN is right up your alley. It is a two-person game with the computer playing directly against you. There is a considerable amount of luck involved. However, the skill of deciding when to pass the dice to your opponent also figures prominently.

The Color Computer will roll the dice for both players, but don't worry—it will not cheat. (We wouldn't think of stooping to such depths.)

Why is the game called GROAN? You will know soon after playing it.

## HOW TO USE IT

The game uses two dice. They are just like regular six-sided dice except for one thing. The die face where the "1" would normally be has a picture of a frowning face instead. The other five faces of each die have the usual numbers two through six on them.

The object is to be the first player to achieve a score agreed upon before the start of the game. Players alternate taking turns. A turn consists of a series of dice rolls (at least one roll, possibly several) subject to the following rules.

As long as no frown appears on either die, the roller builds a running score for this current series of rolls. After each roll with no frown, he has the choice of rolling again or passing the dice to his opponent. If he passes the dice, his score achieved on the current series is added to any previous total he may have had.

But if he rolls and a frown appears, he will be groaning. A frown on only one die cancels any score achieved for the current series of rolls. Any previous score is retained in this case. However, if he rolls a double frown, his entire previous total is wiped out as well as his current total. Thus, he reverts back to a total score of zero — true despair.

The program begins by asking what the winning score should be. Values between 50 and 100 tend to produce the best games, but any positive value less than 1000 is acceptable. Next, you are asked to hit any key to begin the simulated coin toss which randomly decides who will get the first roll.

Each dice roll is portrayed with a short graphics display. The dice are shown rolling and then the outcome is displayed pictorially. Before each roll, the Color Computer indicates whose roll is coming up.

Each roll is followed by a display of the scoreboard. This scoreboard gives all relevant information: score needed to win, both players' scores before the current series of rolls, and the total score for the current series.

If a frown should appear on a die, the scoreboard will indicate the current running total as zero. In addition, the previous total will become zero in the case of the dreaded double frown. In either case, the dice will be passed automatically to the other player.

If a scoring roll results, the roller must decide whether to roll again or to pass the dice. The program has a built-in strategy to decide this for the computer. For you, the question will be asked after the scoreboard is displayed. The two legal replies are **P** and **R**. The **R** means that you wish to roll again. The **P** means that you choose to pass the dice to the computer. If you should score enough to win, you must still pass the dice to add the current series to your previous total.

The first player to pass the dice with a score greater than or equal to the winning score is the victor. This will surely cause his opponent to GROAN. The computer will acknowledge the winner before signing off.

**SAMPLE RUN**

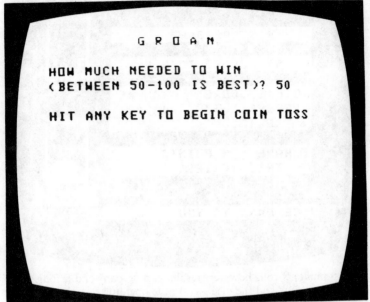

The operator has decided to challenge the computer to a fifty point game of GROAN. He must now hit any key to begin the simulated coin toss.

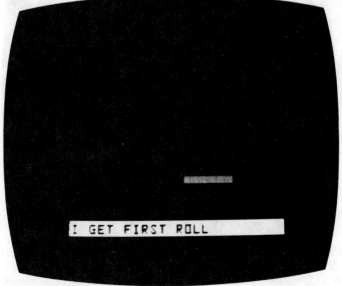

The computer wins the coin toss and gets the first dice roll.

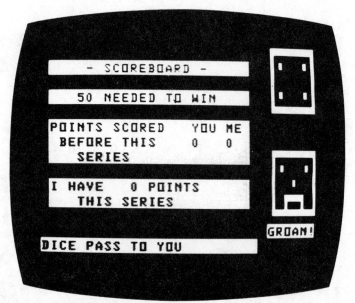

The computer's roll, however, results in a "groan" and a four. This scores no points and the dice pass to the operator.

Much later in the same game, the operator rolls an 8 to start a series of rolls. The score was operator—23, Color Computer—36 before the roll. The operator must now decide whether to pass the dice or risk rolling again.

## PROGRAM LISTING

```
100 REM: GROAN - 16K
110 REM: (C) 1981, PHIL FELDMAN AND TOM
    RUGG
150 CLEAR 400
160 C=3
170 A=8
210 B$=CHR$(143):C$=""
220 FOR J=1 TO 25:C$=C$+B$:NEXT
230 B$=CHR$(127+C*16):D$=""
240 FOR J=1 TO 25:D$=D$+B$:NEXT
250 GOSUB 5000
300 CLS
310 PRINT TAB(10);"G R O A N"
320 PRINT:PRINT"HOW MUCH NEEDED TO WIN"
330 INPUT"(BETWEEN 50-100 IS BEST)";W
340 W=INT(W):IF W<=0 THEN 300
350 IF W>999 THEN 300
360 PRINT:PRINT"HIT ANY KEY TO BEGIN COIN
    TOSS"
370 Q=RND(6):Q$=INKEY$
380 IF Q$="" THEN 370
390 GOSUB 1600
400 T=0:IF Q=2 THEN 700
500 P$="YOU":CLS
510 PRINT@201,"YOU'RE ROLLING";
520 GOSUB 2700:GOSUB 2800
530 T=T+R1+R2:IF F>0 THEN T=0
540 IF F=2 THEN H=0
550 GOSUB 2000
560 IF F=0 THEN 590
570 PRINT@416,"DICE PASS TO ME";
580 GOSUB 2750:GOTO 700
590 GOSUB 2200
600 Q$=INKEY$:IF Q$="" THEN 600
610 IF Q$="R" THEN 500
620 IF Q$<>"P" THEN 600
630 H=H+T:IF H>=W THEN 4000
640 T=0:F=1:PRINT@416,C$;
650 PRINT@448,C$;:GOTO 560
700 T=0:P$="I"
710 CLS:PRINT@203,"I'M ROLLING";
720 GOSUB 2700:GOSUB 2800
730 T=T+R1+R2:IF F>0 THEN T=0
```

```
740  IF F=2 THEN P=0
750  GOSUB 2000:IF F=0 THEN 790
760  PRINT@416,C$;
770  PRINT@416,"DICE PASS TO YOU";
780  GOSUB 2750:T=0:GOTO 500
790  GOSUB 7000:PRINT@416,C$;
800  IF X=0 THEN 830
810  PRINT@416,"I'LL ROLL AGAIN";
820  GOSUB 2750:GOTO 710
830  PRINT@416,"I'LL STOP WITH THIS";
840  GOSUB 2700:P=P+T
850  IF P>=W THEN 4000
860  PRINT@448,C$;
870  PRINT@448,"DICE PASS TO YOU";
880  T=0:GOSUB 2750:GOTO 500
1600 CLS(0):Q=365:FOR J=1 TO 5
1610 PRINT@Q,CH$;:Q=Q-62
1620 GOSUB 2770:CLS(0)
1630 PRINT@Q,CV$;:Q=Q-2
1640 GOSUB 2770:CLS(0):NEXT
1650 FOR J=1 TO 5:PRINT@Q,CH$;
1660 Q=Q+2:GOSUB 2770:CLS(0)
1670 PRINT@Q,CV$;:Q=Q+62
1680 GOSUB 2770:CLS(0):NEXT
1690 PRINT@365,CH$;:Q$="YOU"
1700 Q=RND(2):IF Q=2 THEN Q$="I"
1710 PRINT@448,C$;
1720 PRINT@448,Q$;" GET FIRST ROLL";
1730 GOSUB 2750:RETURN
2000 FOR J=32 TO 320 STEP 32
2010 PRINT@J,C$;:NEXT
2020 FOR J=0 TO 128 STEP 64
2030 PRINT@J,D$;:NEXT
2040 PRINT@256,D$;:PRINT@352,D$;
2050 FOR J=0 TO 352 STEP 32
2060 PRINT@J,E$;:PRINT@J+24,E$;
2070 NEXT
2080 PRINT@37,"- SCOREBOARD -";
2090 PRINT@99,W;"NEEDED TO WIN";
2100 PRINT@161,"POINTS SCORED";
2110 PRINT@194,"BEFORE THIS";
2120 PRINT@228,"SERIES";
2130 PRINT@177,"YOU ME";
2140 PRINT@208,H;:PRINT@212,F;
2150 PRINT@289,P$;" HAVE";
```

```
2160 PRINT@297,T;"POINTS";
2170 PRINT@324,"THIS SERIES";
2180 RETURN
2200 PRINT@416,C$;:PRINT@448,C$;
2210 PRINT@416,"(P=PASS DICE - R=REROLL)";
2220 PRINT@448,"YOUR DECISION (P OR R) ?";
2230 RETURN
2700 FOR K=1 TO 1000:NEXT:RETURN
2750 FOR K=1 TO 2000:NEXT:RETURN
2770 FOR K=1 TO 50:NEXT:RETURN
2800 CLS(0):R1=RND(6):R2=RND(6)
2810 GOSUB 6000:XC=58:YC=4:R=R1
2820 GOSUB 3000:YC=18:R=R2
2830 GOSUB 3000:F=0
2840 IF R1=1 THEN F=1:GOSUB 3400
2850 IF R2=1 THEN F=F+1
2860 IF R2=1 THEN GOSUB 3500
2870 IF F=2 THEN GOSUB 3600
2880 RETURN
3000 XL=XC-3:XR=XC+3:YU=YC-2
3010 YD=YC+2
3020 IF R=1 THEN 3100
3030 IF R=2 THEN 3160
3040 IF R=3 THEN 3180
3050 IF R=4 THEN 3200
3060 IF R=5 THEN 3220
3070 IF R=6 THEN 3240
3100 SET(XL,YU,A):SET(XR,YU,A)
3110 SET(XC,YC,A)
3120 FOR J=XL+1 TO XR-1
3130 SET(J,YD,A):NEXT
3140 SET(XL+1,YD+1,A)
3150 SET(XR-1,YD+1,A):RETURN
3160 SET(XL,YU,A):SET(XR,YD,A)
3170 RETURN
3180 GOSUB 3160:SET(XC,YC,A)
3190 RETURN
3200 GOSUB 3160:SET(XR,YU,A)
3210 SET(XL,YD,A):RETURN
3220 GOSUB 3180:GOSUB 3200
3230 RETURN
3240 GOSUB 3200:SET(XL,YC,A)
3250 SET(XR,YC,A):RETURN
3400 PRINT@186,"GROAN!";
3410 SOUND 10,10:RETURN
```

```
3500 PRINT@410,"GROAN!";
3510 SOUND 10,10:RETURN
3600 PRINT@502,"-DESPAIR-";
3610 SOUND 2,50:RETURN
4000 T=0:CLS(0):GOSUB 2000
4010 PRINT@416,C$;
4020 PRINT@448,C$;
4030 IF P>=W THEN 4070
4040 PRINT@416,"YOU WIN";
4050 PRINT@448,"IT WAS SHEER LUCK";
4060 SOUND 2,20:GOTO 4110
4070 PRINT@416,"I WIN";
4080 PRINT@448,"SKILL TRIUMPHS AGAIN";
4090 FOR J=1 TO 15
4100 SOUND 200,1:NEXT
4110 GOSUB 2750:END
5000 RESTORE:T$="":FOR J=1 TO 6
5010 READ Q:Q=Q+A*16
5020 T$=T$+CHR$(Q):NEXT
5030 Q=117+A*16:FOR J=1 TO 3
5040 GOSUB 5500:T$=T$+CHR$(Q)
5050 T$=T$+CHR$(128)+CHR$(128)
5060 T$=T$+CHR$(128)+CHR$(128)
5070 T$=T$+CHR$(Q):NEXT
5080 GOSUB 5500:FOR J=1 TO 6
5090 READ Q:Q=Q+A*16
5100 T$=T$+CHR$(Q):NEXT
5200 Q=RND(7)+1:CH$="":CV$=""
5210 FOR J=1 TO 6
5220 CH$=CH$+CHR$(124+Q*16)
5230 NEXT:FOR J=1 TO 3
5240 CV$=CV$+CHR$(127+Q*16)
5250 FOR K=1 TO 31
5260 CV$=CV$+CHR$(128):NEXT
5270 NEXT:RETURN
5500 FOR K=1 TO 26
5510 T$=T$+CHR$(128):NEXT:RETURN
5700 DATA 117,124,124,124,124
5710 DATA 125,116,124,124,124
5720 DATA 124,124
6000 Q=0
6010 Q=Q+33:PRINT@Q,T$;
6020 PRINT@Q+224,T$;
6030 Q=Q-31:CLS(0):PRINT@Q,T$;
6040 PRINT@Q+224,T$;
```

```
6050  IF  Q=26  THEN  RETURN
6060  CLS(0):GOTO  6010
7000  V=P+T:IF  V>=W  THEN  7200
7010  IF  (W-H)<10  THEN  7250
7020  IF  P>=H  THEN  L=T/25
7030  IF  P>=H  THEN  7100
7040  IF  V<H  THEN  L=T/35
7050  IF  V<H  THEN  7100
7060  L=T/30
7100  IF  RND(0)>L  THEN  7250
7200  X=0:RETURN
7250  X=1:RETURN
```

**EASY CHANGES**

1.  If you wish to set the program for a fixed value of the winning score, it can be done by changing line 320 and deleting lines 330-350. Simply set W to the winning score desired. For example:

    320 W = 100

    would make the winning score 100. Don't forget to delete lines 330, 340, and 350.

2.  The rolling dice graphics display before each roll can be eliminated by changing line 6000 as follows:

    6000 Q = 57:GOTO 6030

    This has the effect of speeding up the game by showing each dice roll immediately.

3.  After you play the game a few times, you may wish to change the delay constants in lines 2700 and 2750. They control the "pacing" of the game; i.e., the time delays between various messages, etc. To speed up the game try

    2700 FOR K = 1 TO  500:NEXT:RETURN
    2750 FOR K = 1 TO 1000:NEXT:RETURN

    Of course, if desired, the constants can be set to larger values to slow down the pacing.

4.  The color of the scoreboard and the color of the dice are set in lines 160 and 170 with the variables C and A respectively. You can make them any of the 8 available colors as explained in your manual. For example to get a red scoreboard and yellow dice, change lines 160 and 170 to

    160 C = 4
    170 A = 2

5. If your computer has only 4K of memory, you can get a playable version of the game by making the following changes:

```
150   CLEAR 75
330   INPUT W
360   PRINT:PRINT "HIT ANY KEY"
570   PRINT@416, "MY DICE";
770   PRINT@416, "YOUR DICE";
870   PRINT @448, "YOUR DICE";
1600  CLS (0):Q$ = "YOU"
2700  REM
2810  R = R1:Q = 124:GOSUB 3000
2820  R = R2:Q = 348
2830  GOSUB 3000:F = 0:Q = 186
2850  IF R2 = 1 THEN F = F + 1:Q = 410
2860  IF R2 = 1 THEN GOSUB 3400
3000  IF R = 1 THEN 3020
3010  PRINT@Q,R; :RETURN
3020  PRINT@Q," G "; :RETURN
3400  PRINT@Q,"GROAN!";
```

In addition, the following lines must be deleted: 100-110, 170, 250, 310, 340-350, 1610-1690, 2770, 3030-3250, 3500-3510, 4020, 4050, 4080, and 5000-6060.

These changes will remove many of the program's fancy effects but will not materially affect the performance of the game. In order to save the program on cassette or load it later from cassette, you may need to execute a CLEAR 0 statement before the cassette input/output.

## MAIN ROUTINES

160- 250  Initializes constants.
300- 400  Initial display. Gets winning score.
500- 650  Human rolls.
700- 880  Color Computer rolls.
1600-1730  Coin toss for first roll.
2000-2230  Displays scoreboard.
2700-2770  Delay loops.
2800-2880  Determines dice roll, drives its display.
3000-3250  Draws die face.
3400-3610  Displays groan messages.

4000-4110   Ending messages.
5000-5720   Initializes string variables.
6000-6060   Graphics dice rolling.
7000-7250   Computer's strategy. Sets $X = 0$ to stop rolling or $X = 1$ to continue rolling.

## MAIN VARIABLES

| | |
|---|---|
| W | Amount needed to win. |
| H | Previous score of human. |
| P | Previous score of computer. |
| C | Scoreboard color. |
| A | Dice color. |
| T | Score of current series of rolls. |
| X | Computer strategy flag ($0 =$ stop rolling; $1 =$ roll again). |
| L | Cutoff threshold used in computer's built-in strategy. |
| V | Score computer would have if it passed the dice. |
| Q,Q$ | Work variable, work string variable. |
| J,K | Loop indices. |
| P$ | String of name of current roller. |
| R1,R2 | Outcome of roll for die 1, die 2. |
| R | Outcome of a die roll. |
| F | Result of roll ($0 =$ no frown; $1 =$ one frown; $2 =$ double frown). |
| XC,YC | Horizontal, vertical die printing positions. |
| XL,XR | Screen printing positions. |
| YU,YD | |
| B$,C$,D$ | Strings for graphics displays. |
| CV$, | |
| CH$,T$ | |

## SUGGESTED PROJECTS

1.  The computer's built-in strategy is contained from line 7000 on. Remember, after a no frown roll, the Color Computer must decide whether or not to continue rolling. See if you can improve on the current strategy. You may use, but not modify, the variables P, T, H, W. The variable X must be set before returning. Set $X = 0$ to mean the computer passes the dice or $X = 1$ to mean the computer will roll again.

2. Ask the operator for his/her name. Then personalize the messages and scoreboard more.

3. Dig into the workings of the graphics routines connected with the dice rolling. Then modify them to produce new, perhaps more realistic, effects.

# JOT

## PURPOSE

JOT is a two player word game involving considerable mental deduction. The TRS-80 Color Computer will play against you. But be careful! You will find your computer quite a formidable opponent.

The rules of JOT are fairly simple. The game is played entirely with three-letter words. All letters of each word must be distinct — no repeats. (See the section on Easy Changes for further criteria used in defining legal words.)

To begin the game, each player chooses a secret word. The remainder of the game involves trying to be the first player to deduce the other's secret word.

The players take turns making guesses at their opponent's word. After each guess, the asker is told how many letters (or hits) his guess had in common with his opponent's secret word. The position of the letters in the word does not matter. For example, if the secret word was "own," a guess of "who" would have 2 hits. The winner is the first person to correctly guess his opponent's secret word.

## HOW TO USE IT

The program starts by requesting that you hit any key to begin. It then displays some introductory messages while asking you to think of your secret word. It then asks whether or not you wish to make the first guess. This is followed by you and the Color Computer alternating guesses at each other's secret word.

After the computer guesses, it will immediately ask you how it did. Possible replies are **0, 1, 2, 3,** or **R**. The response of **R** (for right) means the Color Computer has just guessed your word correctly—a truly humbling experience. The numerical replies indicate that the word guessed by the computer had that number of hits in your secret word. A response of **3** means that all the letters were correct, but they need to be rearranged to form the actual secret word (e.g. a guess of "EAT" with the secret word being "TEA").

After learning how it did, the computer will take some time to process its new information. If this time is not trivial, the Color Computer will display the message: "I'M THINKING" so you do not suspect it of idle daydreaming. If it finds an inconsistency in its information, it will ask you for your secret word and then analyze what went wrong.

When it is your turn to guess, there are two special replies you can make. These are the single letters **S** or **Q**. The **S**, for summary, will display a table of all previous guesses and corresponding hits. This is useful as a concise look at all available information. It will then prompt you again for your next guess. The **Q**, for quit, will simply terminate the game.

When not making one of these special replies, you will input a guess at the computer's secret word. This will be, of course, a three letter word. If the word used is not legal, the computer will so inform you. After a legal guess, you will be told how many hits your guess had. If you correctly guess the computer's word, you will be duly congratulated. The computer will then ask you for your secret word and verify that all is on the "up and up."

**SAMPLE RUN**

```
              J O T

HIT ANY KEY TO BEGIN

JUST A MOMENT ....

THANKS, NOW LET'S EACH THINK
OF OUR SECRET WORD

(THIS TAKES ME A WHILE ...)

I'VE ALMOST GOT IT ..

OK, DO YOU WANT TO GO FIRST? N
```

The player hits a key to begin. Then he and the computer each select their secret words. The computer is given the first guess.

```
OK, DO YOU WANT TO GO FIRST? N

MY GUESS IS -- HAM
HOW DID I DO (0-3 OR R)? 0

I'M THINKING ...

YOUR GUESS (OR S OR Q)? FAT
# OF HITS IS 0

MY GUESS IS -- RIB
HOW DID I DO (0-3 OR R)? 0

I'M THINKING ...

YOUR GUESS (OR S OR Q)?
```

The computer and player exchange the first few guesses and their results with each other.

```
MY GUESS IS -- KEY
HOW DID I DO (0-3 OR R)? 1

YOUR GUESS (OR S OR Q)? S

----------------------------------
YOUR GUESSES      #      MY GUESSES
WORD    HITS             WORD   HITS
 FAT     0          1     HAM     0
 RED     1          2     RIB     0
 OAR     0          3     DUG     0
 GEM     1          4     COW     0
                    5     KEY     1

YOUR GUESS (OR S OR Q)?
```

Later in the same game, the player requests a summary before making his guess.

```
 GEM     1          4      COW     0
                    5      KEY     1

YOUR GUESS (OR S OR Q)? MEM
# OF HITS IS 2

MY GUESS IS -- PET
HOW DID I DO (0-3 OR R)? R

IT SURE FEELS GOOD

MY WORD WAS - PEN

HOW ABOUT ANOTHER GAME? N
OK
```

The computer, however, guesses correctly to win the game. After revealing its secret word, the computer offers another game but the player has had enough.

## PROGRAM LISTING

```
100 REM: JOT - 16K
110 REM: (C) 1981, PHIL FELDMAN AND TOM
    RUGG
150 CLEAR 200
160 M=25
170 N=405
180 DIM A$(N),G1$(M),G2$(M)
190 DIM H1(M),H2(M)
200 G1=0:G2=0
210 L=N
220 CLS:PRINT TAB(12);"J O T"
230 PRINT
240 PRINT"HIT ANY KEY TO BEGIN"
250 Q=Q+1:P$=INKEY$
260 IF P$="" THEN 250
270 Q=RND(-Q):PRINT
280 PRINT"JUST A MOMENT ...."
290 RESTORE:FOR P=1 TO N
300 READ A$(P):NEXT:PRINT
310 PRINT"THANKS, NOW LET'S EACH THINK"
320 PRINT"OF OUR SECRET WORD"
325 PRINT
330 PRINT"(THIS TAKES ME A WHILE ...)"
340 FOR A=N TO 100 STEP -1
350 B=RND(A):GOSUB 4000:NEXT
360 PRINT:Q=RND(N)
370 PRINT"I'VE ALMOST GOT IT .."
380 FOR A=99 TO 2 STEP -1
390 B=RND(A):GOSUB 4000:NEXT
400 M$=A$(Q):PRINT
410 PRINT"OK, DO YOU WANT TO ";
420 INPUT"GO FIRST";Q$
430 Q$=LEFT$(Q$,1)
440 IF Q$="N" THEN 700
450 IF Q$="Y" THEN 500
460 PRINT
470 PRINT"YES OR NO PLEASE"
480 PRINT:GOTO 410
500 PRINT
510 INPUT"YOUR GUESS (OR S OR Q)";P$
520 IF P$="S" THEN GOSUB 1200
530 IF P$="S" THEN 500
540 IF P$="Q" THEN 2000
```

```
550 IF P$<>M$ THEN 580
560 G1=G1+1:G1$(G1)=P$
570 H1(G1)=9:GOTO 5000
580 GOSUB 3000
590 IF F=1 THEN 630
600 PRINT"THAT'S NOT A LEGAL WORD !"
610 PRINT"   -- TRY AGAIN"
620 GOTO 500
630 Q$=M$:GOSUB 4200:Q$=P$
640 GOSUB 2600
650 PRINT"# OF HITS IS";Q
660 G1=G1+1:G1$(G1)=Q$:H1(G1)=Q
670 IF G1=M THEN 5400
700 Q$=A$(L):G2=G2+1:G2$(G2)=Q$
710 PRINT
720 PRINT"MY GUESS IS -- ";Q$
730 INPUT"HOW DID I DO (0-3 OR R)";P$
740 P$=LEFT$(P$,1)
750 IF P$="R" THEN H2(G2)=9
760 IF P$="R" THEN 4400
770 P=VAL(P$):IF P>3 THEN 800
780 IF P>0 THEN 810
790 IF P$="0" THEN 810
800 PRINT"BAD ANSWER":GOTO 710
810 IF L<100 THEN 840
820 PRINT
830 PRINT"I'M THINKING ..."
840 H2(G2)=P:GOSUB 900:GOTO 500
900 Q$=G2$(G2):H=H2(G2):J=0
910 GOSUB 4200:L=L-1
920 IF L<1 THEN 1000
930 J=J+1:IF J>L THEN 990
940 Q$=A$(J):GOSUB 2600
950 IF Q=H THEN 930
960 A=J:B=L:GOSUB 4000:L=L-1
970 IF L<1 THEN 1000
980 IF L>=J THEN 940
990 RETURN
1000 PRINT
1010 PRINT"SOMETHING'S WRONG !"
1020 PRINT
1030 INPUT"WHAT'S YOUR SECRET WORD";P$
1040 GOSUB 3000
1050 IF F<>0 THEN 1090
1060 PRINT"ILLEGAL WORD"
```

```
1070 PRINT"I NEVER HAD A CHANCE"
1080 GOTO 2000
1090 PRINT
1100 PRINT"   YOU GAVE A BAD"
1110 PRINT"ANSWER SOMEWHERE"
1120 PRINT
1130 PRINT"HIT ANY KEY TO SEE THE SUMMARY"
1140 Q$=INKEY$
1150 IF Q$="" THEN 1140
1160 GOSUB 1200:GOTO 2000
1200 PRINT:Q=G1:Q$="  "
1210 IF G2>G1 THEN Q=G2
1220 IF Q>0 THEN 1250
1230 PRINT"NO GUESSES YET"
1240 RETURN
1250 FOR J=1 TO 30:PRINT"-";
1260 NEXT:PRINT"-"
1270 PRINT"YOUR GUESSES";
1280 PRINT TAB(16);"#";
1290 PRINT TAB(21);"MY GUESSES"
1300 PRINT"WORD   HITS";
1310 PRINT TAB(21);"WORD   HITS"
1320 FOR J=1 TO Q:K=1
1330 IF J>9 THEN K=0
1340 IF J>G1 THEN 1400
1350 IF J>G2 THEN 1440
1360 PRINT"  ";G1$(J);Q$;H1(J);
1370 PRINT TAB(14+K);J;
1380 PRINT TAB(22);G2$(J);
1390 PRINT"  ";H2(J):GOTO 1470
1400 PRINT TAB(14+K);J;
1410 PRINT TAB(22);G2$(J);
1420 PRINT"  ";H2(J):GOTO 1470
1440 PRINT"  ";G1$(J);Q$;H1(J);
1450 PRINT TAB(14+K);J
1470 NEXT:RETURN
2000 PRINT
2010 INPUT"HOW ABOUT ANOTHER GAME";Q$
2020 Q$=LEFT$(Q$,1)
2030 IF Q$="Y" THEN 200
2040 IF Q$="N" THEN END
2050 PRINT
2060 PRINT"YES OR NO PLEASE"
2070 GOTO 2000
2600 P$=LEFT$(Q$,1):Q=0
```

```
2610 GOSUB 2700
2620 P$=MID$(Q$,2,1)
2630 GOSUB 2700
2640 P$=RIGHT$(Q$,1)
2650 GOSUB 2700
2660 RETURN
2700 IF P$=M1$ THEN Q=Q+1
2710 IF P$=M2$ THEN Q=Q+1
2720 IF P$=M3$ THEN Q=Q+1
2730 RETURN
3000 F=0
3010 FOR J=1 TO N
3020 IF A$(J)=P$ THEN F=1:RETURN
3030 NEXT:RETURN
4000 Q$=A$(B):A$(B)=A$(A)
4010 A$(A)=Q$:RETURN
4200 M1$=LEFT$(Q$,1)
4210 M2$=MID$(Q$,2,1)
4220 M3$=RIGHT$(Q$,1):RETURN
4400 PRINT
4410 PRINT"IT SURE FEELS GOOD"
4420 PRINT
4430 PRINT"MY WORD WAS - ";M$
4440 GOTO 2000
5000 PRINT
5010 PRINT"CONGRATULATIONS - THAT'S IT"
5020 PRINT
5030 INPUT"WHAT'S YOUR WORD";P$
5040 GOSUB 3000:J=1
5050 IF F<>0 THEN 5090
5060 PRINT:PRINT"ILLEGAL WORD"
5070 PRINT"I HAD NO CHANCE !"
5080 GOTO 2000
5090 IF A$(J)<>P$ THEN 5120
5100 PRINT:PRINT"NICE WORD"
5110 GOTO 2000
5120 J=J+1:IF J<=L THEN 5090
5130 PRINT
5140 PRINT"YOU MADE AN ERROR SOMEWHERE !"
5150 PRINT"HIT ANY KEY TO SEE THE SUMMARY"
5160 Q$=INKEY$
5170 IF Q$="" THEN 5160
5180 GOSUB 1200:GOTO 2000
5400 PRINT"SORRY, I'M OUT OF MEMORY"
5410 PRINT
```

```
5420 PRINT"MY WORD WAS - ";M$
5430 GOTO 2000
6000 DATA ACE,ACT,ADE,ADO,ADS
6010 DATA AFT,AGE,AGO,AID,AIL
6020 DATA AIM,AIR,ALE,ALP,AND
6030 DATA ANT,ANY,APE,APT,ARC
6040 DATA ARE,ARK,ARM,ART,ASH
6050 DATA ASK,ASP,ATE,AWE,AWL
6060 DATA AXE,AYE,BAD,BAG,BAN
6070 DATA BAR,BAT,BAY,BED,BEG
6080 DATA BET,BID,BIG,BIN,BIT
6090 DATA BOA,BOG,BOW,BOX,BOY
6100 DATA BUD,BUG,BUM,BUN,BUS
6110 DATA BUT,BUY,BYE,CAB,CAD
6120 DATA CAM,CAN,CAP,CAR,CAT
6130 DATA COB,COD,COG,CON,COP
6140 DATA COT,COW,COY,CRY,CUB
6150 DATA CUD,CUE,CUP,CUR,CUT
6160 DATA DAB,DAM,DAY,DEN,DEW
6170 DATA DIE,DIG,DIM,DIN,DIP
6180 DATA DOE,DOG,DON,DOT,DRY
6190 DATA DUB,DUE,DUG,DYE,DUO
6200 DATA EAR,EAT,EGO,ELK,ELM
6210 DATA END,ELF,ERA,FAD,FAG
6220 DATA FAN,FAR,FAT,FED,FEW
6230 DATA FIG,FIN,FIR,FIT,FIX
6240 DATA FLY,FOE,FOG,FOR,FOX
6250 DATA FRY,FUN,FUR,GAP,GAS
6260 DATA GAY,GEM,GET,GIN,GNU
6270 DATA GOB,GOD,GOT,GUM,GUN
6280 DATA GUT,GUY,GYP,HAD,HAG
6290 DATA HAM,HAS,HAT,HAY,HEN
6300 DATA HEX,HID,HIM,HIP,HIS
6310 DATA HIT,HER,HEM,HOE,HOG
6320 DATA HOP,HOT,HOW,HUB,HUE
6330 DATA HUG,HUM,HUT,ICE,ICY
6340 DATA ILK,INK,IMP,ION,IRE
6350 DATA IRK,ITS,IVY,JAB,JAR
6360 DATA JAW,JAY,JOB,JOG,JOT
6370 DATA JOY,JUG,JAG,JAM,JET
6380 DATA JIG,JUT,KEG,KEY,KID
6390 DATA KIN,KIT,LAB,LAD,LAG
6400 DATA LAP,LAW,LAY,LAX,LED
6410 DATA LEG,LET,LID,LIE,LIP
6420 DATA LIT,LOB,LOG,LOP,LOT
```

```
6430 DATA LOW,LYE,MAD,MAN,MAP
6440 DATA MAR,MAT,MAY,MEN,MET
6450 DATA MID,MOB,MOP,MOW,MUD
6460 DATA MIX,MUG,NAB,NAG,NAP
6470 DATA NAY,NET,NEW,NIL,NIP
6480 DATA NOD,NOT,NOR,NOW,NUT
6490 DATA OAF,OAK,OAR,OAT,ODE
6500 DATA OIL,OLD,ONE,OPT,ORE
6510 DATA OUR,OUT,OVA,OWE,OWL
6520 DATA OWN,PAD,PAL,PAN,PAR
6530 DATA PAT,PAW,PAY,PEA,PEG
6540 DATA PEN,PET,PEW,PIE,PIG
6550 DATA PIT,PLY,POD,POT,POX
6560 DATA PER,PIN,PRO,PRY,PUB
6570 DATA PUN,PUS,PUT,RAG,RAM
6580 DATA RAN,RAP,RAT,RAW,RAY
6590 DATA RED,RIB,RID,REV,RIG
6600 DATA RIM,RIP,ROB,ROD,ROE
6610 DATA ROT,ROW,RUB,RUE,RUG
6620 DATA RUM,RUN,RUT,RYE,SAD
6630 DATA SAG,SAP,SAT,SAW,SAY
6640 DATA SET,SEW,SEX,SHY,SEA
6650 DATA SIN,SHE,SIP,SIR,SIT
6660 DATA SIX,SKI,SKY,SLY,SOB
6670 DATA SOD,SON,SOW,SOY,SPA
6680 DATA SPY,STY,SUE,SUM,SUN
6690 DATA TAB,TAD,TAG,TAN,TAP
6700 DATA TAX,TAR,TEA,TEN,THE
6710 DATA THY,TIC,TIE,TIN,TIP
6720 DATA TOE,TON,TOP,TOW,TOY
6730 DATA TRY,TUB,TUG,TWO,URN
6740 DATA USE,UPS,VAN,VAT,VEX
6750 DATA VIA,VIE,VIM,VOW,YAK
6760 DATA YAM,YEN,YES,YET,YOU
6770 DATA WAD,WAG,WAN,WAR,WAS
6780 DATA WAX,WAY,WEB,WED,WET
6790 DATA WHO,WHY,WIG,WIN,WIT
6800 DATA WOE,WON,WRY,ZIP,FIB
```

## EASY CHANGES

1. It is fairly common for players to request a summary before most guesses that they make. If you want the program to automatically provide a summary before each guess, change lines 500 through 530 to read

```
500  Q = G1 + G2
510  IF Q > 0 THEN GOSUB 1200
520  PRINT
530  INPUT "YOUR GUESS (OR Q)";P$
```

2. The maximum number of guesses allowed, M, can be changed in line 160. You may wish to increase it in conjunction with Suggested Project 2. You might decrease it to free some memory needed for other program additions. The current value of twenty-five is really somewhat larger than necessary. An actual game almost never goes beyond fifteen guesses. To set M to 15 change line 160 to read

$$160 \ M = 15$$

3. Modifying the data list of legal words is fairly easy. Our criteria for legal words were as follows: they must have three distinct letters and *not* be

   — capitalized
   — abbreviations
   — interjections (like "ugh," "hey" etc.)
   — specialized words (like "ohm," "sac," "yaw" etc.)

In line 170, N is set to be the total number of words in the data list. The data list itself is from line 6000 on.

To add word(s), do the following. Enter them in data statements after the current data (use line numbers larger than 6800). Then redefine the value of N to be 405 plus the number of new words added. For example, to add the words "ohm" and "yaw" onto the list, change line 170 to read

$$170 \ N = 407$$

and add a new line

### 6810 DATA OHM,YAW

To delete word(s), the opposite must be done. Remove the words from the appropriate data statement(s) and decrease the value of N accordingly.

## MAIN ROUTINES

| | |
|---|---|
| 150- 190 | Dimensions arrays. |
| 200- 480 | Initializes new game. |
| 340- 390 | Shuffles A$ array randomly. |
| 500- 670 | Human guesses at the computer's word. |
| 700- 840 | Computer guesses. |
| 900- 990 | Evaluates human's possible secret words. Moves them to the front of A$ array. |
| 1000-1160 | Processes inconsistency in given information. |
| 1200-1470 | Displays the current summary table. |
| 2000-2070 | Inquires about another game. |
| 2600-2730 | Compares a guess with key word. |
| 3000-3030 | Checks if input word is legal. |
| 4000 | Swaps elements A and B in the A$ array. |
| 4200-4220 | Breaks word Q$ into separate letters. |
| 4400-4440 | Post-mortem after computer wins. |
| 5000-5180 | Post-mortem after human wins. |
| 5400-5430 | Error routine — too many guesses. |
| 6000-6800 | Data. |

## MAIN VARIABLES

| | |
|---|---|
| N | Total number of data words. |
| M | Maximum number of guesses allowed. |
| A$ | String array holding data words. |
| G1$,G2$ | String arrays of human's, computer's guesses. |
| H1,H2 | Arrays of human's, computer's hits corresponding to G1$,G2$. |
| G1,G2 | Current number of human's, computer's guesses. |
| M$ | Computer's secret word. |
| M1$,M2$, M3$ | First, second, and third letters of a word. |
| P$,Q$ | String temporaries and work variables. |
| L | Current number of human's possible secret words. |
| F | Flag for input word legality. |
| H | Number of hits in last guess. |
| A,B | A$ array locations to be swapped. |
| J,P,Q | Temporaries; array and loop indices. |
| K | TAB argument. |

## SUGGESTED PROJECTS

1. Additional messages during the course of the game can personify the program even more. After the Color Computer finds out how its last guess did, you might try an occasional message like one of these:

   JUST AS I THOUGHT...
   HMM, I DIDN'T EXPECT THAT...
   JUST WHAT I WAS HOPING TO HEAR...

   The value of L is the number of words to which the computer has narrowed down the human's secret word. You might check its value regularly and when it gets low, come out with something like

   BE CAREFUL, I'M CLOSING IN ON YOU.

2. Incorporate a feature to allow the loser to continue guessing at the other's word. The summary display routine will already work fine even if G1 and G2 are very different from each other. It will display a value of "9" for the number of hits corresponding to the correct guess of a secret word.

# OBSTACLE

## PURPOSE

This program allows you and a friend (or enemy) to play the game of OBSTACLE, an arcade-like game that's one of our favorites. A combination of physical skills (reflex speed, hand to eye coordination, etc.) and strategic skills are needed to beat your opponent. Each game generally takes only a minute or two, so you'll want to play a match of several games to determine the better player.

## HOW TO USE IT

The object of the game is to keep moving longer than your opponent without bumping into an obstacle. When the program starts, it asks in turn for the name of the player on the left and on the right. Then it displays the playing field, shows the starting point for each player, and tells you to press any key to start.

After a key is pressed, each player begins moving independently in one of four random directions — up, down, left, or right. As each player moves, he or she builds a "wall" inside the playing field. The computer determines the speed of the move; the player can only control his own direction. The player on the left can change direction to up, down, left, or right by pressing the key **W**, **Z**, **A**, or **D**, respectively. The player on the right does the same by using the keys for **O** (not zero), **,** (comma), **K**, and **;** (semi-colon). Find these keys on the TRS-80 Color Computer keyboard and you will see the logic behind these choices.

The first time either player bumps into the wall surrounding the playing field or the obstacle wall built by either player, he or she loses. When this happens, the program indicates the point of impact for a few seconds and displays the name of the winner. Then the game starts over.

The strategic considerations for this game are interesting. Should you attack your opponent, trying to build a wall around him that he must crash into? Or should you stay away from him and try to make efficient moves in an open area until your opponent runs out of room on his own? Try both approaches and see which yields the most success.

When pressing a key to change direction, be sure to press it quickly and release it. *Do not* hold a key down—you might inhibit the computer from recognizing a move your opponent is trying to make. Once in a while, only one key will be recognized when two are hit at once.

**SAMPLE RUN**

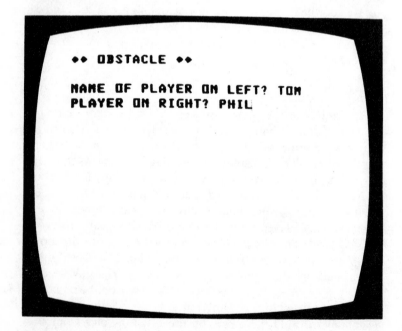

```
●● OBSTACLE ●●

NAME OF PLAYER ON LEFT? TOM
PLAYER ON RIGHT? PHIL
```

The program starts off by asking for the names of the two players.

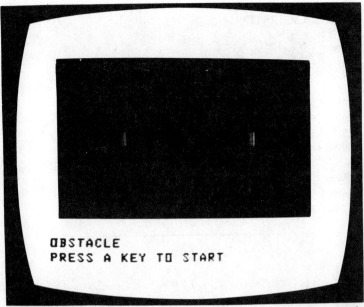

The program draws the playing field and waits for a key to be pressed.

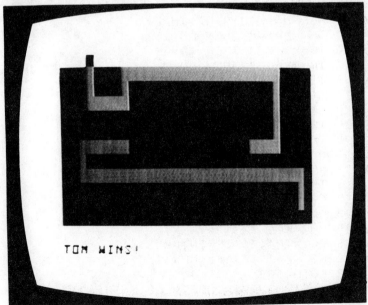

The program redraws the playing field and starts both players moving in a random direction (in this case, both start moving to the left). Phil (on the right) doesn't change directions soon enough and crashes into the wall, making Tom the winner.

## PROGRAM LISTING

```
100 REM: OBSTACLE
110 REM: (C) 1981, TOM RUGG AND PHIL
    FELDMAN
120 CLEAR 200:GOSUB 600
130 CLS(0):PRINT@416,"OBSTACLE"
150 PRINT"PRESS A KEY TO START"
155 A$=CHR$(175):B$=CHR$(191)
160 A=200:B=215
165 E$=CHR$(207):S=1024:AD=RND(4):BD=RND(4)
170 GOSUB 950:GOSUB 900
175 FOR J=1 TO 5:R$=INKEY$:NEXT
180 R$=INKEY$:J=RND(2)
190 IF LEN(R$)=0 THEN 180
200 CLS(0):GOSUB 950:GOSUB 900
210 X=A:D=AD:GOSUB 1000
220 AR=R:A=X
230 X=B:D=BD:GOSUB 1000
240 BR=R:B=X
245 IF AR=1 OR BR=1 THEN 400
250 GOSUB 900
260 FOR J=1 TO 8:R$=INKEY$
270 IF R$="W" THEN AD=1
280 IF R$="Z" THEN AD=2
290 IF R$="A" THEN AD=3
300 IF R$="D" THEN AD=4
310 IF R$="O" THEN BD=1
320 IF R$="," THEN BD=2
330 IF R$="K" THEN BD=3
340 IF R$=";" THEN BD=4
350 NEXT:GOTO 210
400 GOSUB 700:IF AR=1 THEN R$=CHR$(128)
410 IF BR=1 THEN Z$=CHR$(128)
420 FOR J=1 TO 15:PRINT@A,A$;
430 PRINT@B,B$;
440 FOR K=1 TO 100:NEXT
450 PRINT@A,R$;:PRINT@B,Z$;
460 FOR K=1 TO 100:NEXT:NEXT J
490 GOTO 130
600 CLS:PRINT"** OBSTACLE **":PRINT
610 INPUT"NAME OF PLAYER ON LEFT";AN$
620 INPUT"PLAYER ON RIGHT";BN$
650 RETURN
```

```
700 SOUND 4,4:PRINT@416," ";
710 IF AR=0 OR BR=0 THEN 730
720 PRINT"YOU BOTH LOSE!":RETURN
730 R$=AN$:IF AR=1 THEN R$=BN$
740 PRINT R$;" WINS!"
750 R$=A$:Z$=B$:RETURN
900 PRINT@A,A$;:PRINT@B,B$;
920 RETURN
950 FOR X=0 TO 31:PRINT@X,E$;
960 PRINT@X+384,E$;:NEXT
970 FOR X=0 TO 384 STEP 32
980 PRINT@X,E$;:PRINT@X+31,E$;
990 NEXT:RETURN
1000 IF D=1 THEN X=X-32
1010 IF D=2 THEN X=X+32
1020 IF D=3 THEN X=X-1
1030 IF D=4 THEN X=X+1
1040 R=0:IF PEEK(S+X)<>128 THEN R=1
1050 RETURN
```

## EASY CHANGES

1.  To speed the game up, change the 8 in line 260 to a 5 or so. To slow it down, make it 12 or 15.
2.  To make both players always start moving upward at the beginning of each game (instead of in a random direction), insert the following statement:

    168 AD = 1:BD = 1

    To make the players always start off moving toward each other, use this statement instead:

    168 AD = 4:BD = 3

3.  To change the length of time that the final messages are displayed after each game, modify line 420. Change the 15 to 8 (or so) to shorten it, or to 25 to lengthen it.
4.  Change the colors of the players and/or the boundary of the playing field by changing lines 155 and 165. For example, to make the player on the left magenta and the player on the right orange, make this change:

    155 A$ = CHR$(239):B$ = CHR$(255)

    The color of the playing field boundary can be changed by changing the value of E$ in line 165. Refer to the appendix on color graphics characters in your "Getting Started With Color BASIC" manual for other color possibilities.

5. Change the keys that are used to determine each player's direction by altering the appropriate values in lines 270 through 340. For example, to make the X key cause the player on the left to go down, make this change:

280 IF R$ = "X" THEN AD = 2

## MAIN ROUTINES

120- 170   Initializes variables. Gets players' names. Displays titles, playing field.
180- 200   Waits for key to be pressed to start game. Redisplays playing field.
210- 250   Makes move for player A (on left side) and B (on right). Saves results.
260- 350   Accepts moves from keyboard and translates direction.
400- 490   Displays winner's name at bottom of screen. Flashes a square where collision occurred. Goes back to start next game.
600- 650   Subroutine that gets each player's name.
700- 750   Subroutine that displays winner's name.
900- 920   Subroutine that displays each graphics color of each player's obstacle on the screen.
950- 990   Subroutine that displays playing field.
1000-1050  Subroutine that moves marker and determines if space moved to is empty.

## MAIN VARIABLES

A          Player A's current position.
B          Player B's current position.
A$         A's marker.
B$         B's marker.
S          Starting address of CRT memory area.
AD,BD      Current direction that A and B are going (1 = up, 2 = down, 3 = left, 4 = right).
E$         Graphics character for edge of playing field.
R$         Character being read from keyboard; also work variable.

X           Temporary position on screen.
D           Temporary direction.
AR,BR       Result of A's and B's moves (0 = okay, 1 = loser).
AN$,BN$     Names of players A and B.
Z$          Work variable.
J,K         Loop variables.

## SUGGESTED PROJECTS

1. Keep score over a seven game (or so) match. Display the current score after each game. Don't forget to allow for ties.
2. Modify the program to let each player press only two keys — one to turn left from the current direction of travel, and one to turn right.
3. Instead of a game between two people, make it a game of a person against the computer. Develop a computer strategy to keep finding open areas to move to and/or to cut off open areas from the human opponent.

# ROADRACE

## PURPOSE

Imagine yourself at the wheel of a high-speed race car winding your way along a treacherous course. The road curves unpredictably. To stay on course, you must steer accurately or risk collision. How far can you go in one day? How many days will it take you to race cross-country? Thrills galore without leaving your living room.

The difficulty of the game is completely under your control. By adjusting the road width and visibility conditions, ROAD-RACE can be made as easy or as challenging as you wish.

## HOW TO USE IT

The program begins with a short graphics display. It then asks you to hit any key to begin. Next you are requested to provide two inputs: road width and visibility. The road width (in characters) can be set anywhere between 4 and 15. The degree of difficulty changes appreciably with different widths. A very narrow setting will be quite difficult and a wide one relatively easy. Visibility can be set to any of four settings, ranging from "terrible" to "good." When visibility is good, the car appears high on the screen. This allows a good view of the twisting road ahead. When visibility is poor, the car appears low on the screen allowing only a brief look at the upcoming road.

Having set road width and visibility, the race is ready to start. The car appears on the road at the starting line. A five-step starting light counts down the start. When the bottom light goes on, the race begins. The road moves continually up the screen. Its twists and turns are controlled randomly. You must steer the car accurately to keep it on track.

The car is controlled with the use of two keys near the upper right corner of the keyboard. Pressing the left arrow (←) will cause the car to move to the left while pressing the right arrow (→) will cause a move to the right. Doing neither will cause the car to continue straight down.

The race proceeds until the car goes "off the road." Each such collision is considered to terminate one day of the race. After each day, you are shown the number of miles achieved that day along with the cumulative miles achieved for consecutive days of the race.

After each collision, you can proceed by pressing either **C**, **R**, or **Q**. Selecting **C** will continue the race for another day with the same road conditions. Cumulative totals will be retained. **R** will restart the race. This allows changing the road conditions and initializing back to day one. **Q** simply quits the race and returns the computer back to direct Basic. Either of the last two options will produce a display of the average miles travelled per day for the race.

There are several different ways to challenge yourself with the program. You can try to see how far you get in a given number of days. You might see how many days it takes you to go a given number of miles — say 3000 miles for a cross-country trip. As you become proficient at one set of road conditions, make the road narrower and/or the visibility poorer. This will increase the challenge. Different road conditions can also be used as a handicapping aid for two unequally matched opponents.

**SAMPLE RUN**

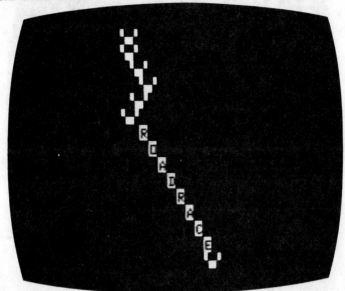

The program displays its logo.

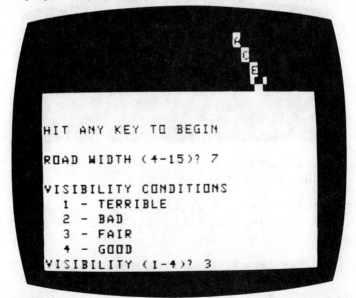

After requesting a key be hit to begin, the short input phase begins. The operator selects a course with a 7 character road width and fair visibility.

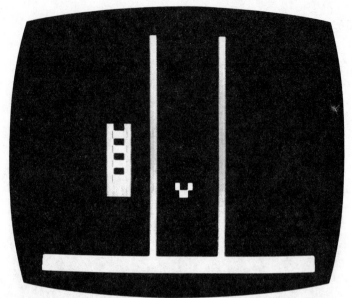

The car is on the starting line. The starting light counts down the beginning of the race. When the last light goes on, the race will be off and running.

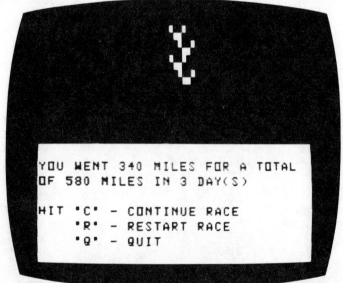

The operator, steering the car from the keyboard, finally crashes. A distance of 340 miles is obtained on this leg for a total of 580 miles in 3 days (legs). The options for continuing are displayed while the program waits for the operator's choice.

## PROGRAM LISTING

```
100 REM: ROADRACE - 16K
110 REM: (C) 1981, PHIL FELDMAN AND TOM
    RUGG
140 CLEAR 200
150 LC=0.45
160 CR=3:CC=8
170 L$=CHR$(8):R$=CHR$(9)
200 RC=1-LC
210 G=1024
250 GOSUB 3000
300 GOSUB 3600
310 PRINT:T=0:N=0
320 INPUT"ROAD WIDTH (4-15)";W
330 W=INT(W):PRINT
340 IF W<4 OR W>15 THEN 310
350 PRINT"VISIBILITY CONDITIONS"
360 PRINT"  1 - TERRIBLE"
370 PRINT"  2 - BAD"
380 PRINT"  3 - FAIR"
390 PRINT"  4 - GOOD"
400 INPUT"VISIBILITY (1-4)";V
410 V=INT(V):GOSUB 2000
420 IF V<1 OR V>4 THEN 400
500 N=N+1:EL=449:ER=478-W:H=0
510 Z=527-64*V:L=463-INT(W/2)
520 FOR J=1 TO 16:PRINT@480,B$;
530 GOSUB 1400:Q$=INKEY$:NEXT
540 PRINT@Z,C$;:GOSUB 4000
600 H=H+1:Q=RND(0):PRINT@480,B$;
610 IF Q>RC AND L<ER THEN 640
620 IF Q<LC AND L>EL THEN 650
630 GOSUB 1400:GOTO 700
640 GOSUB 1600:GOTO 700
650 GOSUB 1500
700 Q$=INKEY$
710 IF Q$=L$ THEN Z=Z-1
720 IF Q$=R$ THEN Z=Z+1
730 IF PEEK(Z+G)<>128 THEN 800
740 IF PEEK(Z+G+1)<>128 THEN 800
750 PRINT@Z,C$;:GOTO 600
800 FOR J=1 TO 8:Q$=INKEY$
810 PRINT@Z,D$;:SOUND 150,3
820 FOR K=1 TO 10:NEXT
```

```
830 PRINT@Z,C$;
840 FOR K=1 TO 10:NEXT:NEXT
900 M=H*5:T=T+M
910 PRINT@480,CHR$(143)
920 PRINT"YOU WENT";M;"MILES FOR A TOTAL"
930 PRINT"OF";T;"MILES IN";N;"DAY(S)":PRINT
940 PRINT"HIT 'C' - CONTINUE RACE"
950 PRINT"     'R' - RESTART RACE"
960 PRINT"     'Q' - QUIT"
970 Q$=INKEY$
980 IF Q$="C" THEN 500
990 IF Q$="R" THEN 1010
1000 IF Q$<>"Q" THEN 970
1010 PRINT
1020 PRINT"AVERAGE MILES PER DAY WAS"
1030 PRINT T/N
1040 IF Q$="R" THEN 310
1050 END
1400 PRINT@L,RS$;:RETURN
1500 L=L-1:PRINT@L,RL$;:RETURN
1600 PRINT@L,RR$;:L=L+1:RETURN
2000 Q=121+CC*16:K=118+CC*16
2010 C$=CHR$(Q)+CHR$(K)
2020 Q=127+CR*16:RS$=CHR$(Q)
2030 FOR J=1 TO W
2040 RS$=RS$+CHR$(128):NEXT
2050 RS$=RS$+CHR$(Q)
2060 Q=119+CR*16:K=120+CR*16
2070 RL$=CHR$(Q)+CHR$(K)
2080 FOR J=1 TO (W-1)
2090 RL$=RL$+CHR$(128):NEXT
2100 RL$=RL$+CHR$(Q)+CHR$(K)
2110 Q=116+CR*16:K=123+CR*16
2120 RR$=CHR$(Q)+CHR$(K)
2130 FOR J=1 TO (W-1)
2140 RR$=RR$+CHR$(128):NEXT
2150 RR$=RR$+CHR$(Q)+CHR$(K)
2160 B$="":FOR J=1 TO 32
2170 B$=B$+CHR$(128):NEXT
2180 D$=CHR$(128)+CHR$(128)
2200 RETURN
3000 W=7:GOSUB 2000:CLS(0)
3010 FOR J=1 TO 15:READ Q
3020 PRINT@Q,RS$;:NEXT
```

```
3030  FOR J=1 TO 600:NEXT
3040  RESTORE:FOR J=1 TO 6
3050  READ Q:PRINT@Q+3,C$;
3060  FOR K=1 TO 100:NEXT:NEXT'
3070  T$="ROADRACE":FOR J=1 TO 8
3080  READ Q:PRINT@Q+3,C$;
3090  Q$=CHR$(128)+MID$(T$,J,1)
3100  FOR K=1 TO 100:NEXT
3110  PRINT@Q+3,Q$;:NEXT
3120  READ Q:PRINT@Q+3,C$;
3130  SOUND 150,20
3140  FOR J=1 TO 500:NEXT
3150  PRINT@480,""
3160  RETURN
3200  DATA 12,44,77,110,141,172
3210  DATA 205,238,271,304,337
3220  DATA 370,403,436,469
3600  PRINT
3610  PRINT"HIT ANY KEY TO BEGIN"
3620  Q=RND(0):Q$=INKEY$
3630  IF Q$="" THEN 3620
3640  RETURN
4000  Q=175:K=195
4010  N$=CHR$(Q)+CHR$(Q)+CHR$(Q)
4020  M$=CHR$(Q)+CHR$(K)+CHR$(Q)
4030  Q=Z-INT(W/2)-5:K=Q-128
4040  FOR J=K TO Q STEP 32
4050  PRINT@J,N$;:NEXT
4060  FOR J=K TO Q STEP 32
4070  FOR R=1 TO 300:NEXT
4080  PRINT@J,M$;:SOUND 100,4
4090  NEXT:RETURN
```

## EASY CHANGES

1. The keys which cause the car to move left and right can be
   easily changed. You may wish to do this if you are left-
   handed or find that two widely separated keys would be
   more convenient. The changes are to be made in line 170.
   Left and right movements are controlled by the two string
   variables L$ and R$. If, for example, you wanted 1 to cause
   a left move and 9 to cause a right move, change line 170 to
   read

   170 L$ = "1":R$ = "9"

2. The amount of windiness in the road can be adjusted by changing the value of LC in line 150. Maximum windiness is achieved with a value of 0.5 for LC. To get a straighter road, make LC smaller. A value of 0. will produce a completely straight road. LC should lie between 0. and 0.5 or else the road will drift to one side and linger there. To get a somewhat less winding road, you might change line 150 to read

150 LC = 0.4

3. The colors used for the road and for the car are assigned to the variables CR and CC respectively. These are set in line 160. Currently blue is used for the road and orange for the car. You may wish to use different colors for variety. (Don't use black, however, for that is the color of the background.) Consult your reference manual for the numerical values corresponding to the eight possible colors. For example, to get a yellow road and red car, change line 160 to read

160 CR = 2:CC = 4

4. Instead of the keyboard, the car's movement can be controlled by one of the optional joysticks. Connect the right joystick and make these program changes

700 Q = JOYSTK (0)<br>710 IF Q < 21 THEN Z = Z - 1<br>720 IF Q > 42 THEN Z = Z + 1

The left to right movement of the joystick will now control the car. When the paddle lies in the central third of its range, the car will continue straight down the road. If the paddle is in the leftmost third of its range, the car will *continue* to move left. Similarly, if the paddle is turned to right side, the car will *continue* to move right.

5. If you have a 4K machine, the program can be made to fit by deleting lines 3010-3220 and changing line 3000 to

3000 RETURN

This has the effect of removing the initial graphics display but otherwise unaffecting the program.

## MAIN ROUTINES

140- 250 Variable initialization and graphics display.
300- 420 Gets road conditions from user.

500- 540 Initializes the road.
600- 650 Determines the next road condition.
700- 750 Updates the car position.
800-1050 Processes end of race day.
1400-1600 Draws next road segment.
2000-2200 Initializes string variables.
3000-3220 Initial graphics display.
3600-3640 Waits for user to hit any key.
4000-4090 Graphics to begin race.

## MAIN VARIABLES

| | |
|---|---|
| W | Road width. |
| V | Visibility. |
| M | Miles driven on current day. |
| N | Number of days of the race. |
| T | Total miles driven for whole race. |
| H | Elapsed time during race. |
| L$,R$ | String characters to move car left, right. |
| L | Position of left side of road. |
| LC,RC | Random value cutoff to move road left, right. |
| EL,ER | Leftmost, rightmost allowable road position. |
| Q$ | User replies. |
| Z | Screen location of car. |
| RS$,RL$, RR$ | Strings to display road segments. |
| CR | Color of road. |
| CC | Color of car. |
| G | First address of screen memory. |
| C$ | Character string for car. |
| J,K,Q,R | Loop indices and work variables. |
| B$,D$,T$, N$,M$ | Miscellaneous strings. |

## SUGGESTED PROJECTS

1. Write a routine to evaluate a player's performance after each collision. Display a message rating him anywhere from "expert" to "back seat driver." This should involve comparing his actual miles achieved against an expected (or average) number of miles for the given road width and visibility. For starters, you might use

$$\text{Expected miles} = W^3 + (10*V) - 35$$

This formula is crude, at best. The coding can be done between lines 930 and 940.

2. Incorporate provisions for two players racing one at a time. Keep cumulative totals separately. After each collision, display the current leader and how far he is ahead.

3. Add physical obstacles or other hazards onto the road in order to increase the challenge. This can be done with appropriate PRINT statements before the various RETURNs in lines 1400-1600. The program will recognize a collision if the car moves into any non-blank square.

# WARI

## PURPOSE

Wari is an old game with roots that are much older. Its origins go back thousands of years to a variety of other similar games, all classified as being members of the Mancala family. Other variations are Awari, Oware, Pallanguli, Kalah, and countless other offshots.

The program matches you against the computer. You are probably going to lose a few games before you win one—the computer plays a pretty good game. This may hurt your ego a little bit, since Wari is purely a skill game (like chess or checkers). There is no element of luck involved, as would be the case with backgammon, for example. When you lose, it's because you were outplayed.

## HOW TO USE IT

When you start the program, the first thing it does is display the Wari board and ask you if you want to go first. The board is made up of twelve squares in two rows of six. Your side is the bottom side, numbered one through six from left to right. The computer's side is on the top, numbered seven through twelve from right to left.

At the start of the game, each square has four "stones" in it. There is no way to differentiate between your stones and the computer's. They all look alike and will move from one side to the other during the course of play.

The first player "picks up" all the stones in one of the squares on his side of the board and drops them, one to a square, starting with the next highest numbered square. The stones continue to be dropped consecutively in each square, continuing over onto the opponent's side if necessary (after square number 12 comes square number 1 again).

If the last stone is dropped onto the opponent's side *and* leaves a total of either two or three stones in that square, these stones are captured by the player who moved, and removed from the board. Also, if the next-to-last square in which a stone was dropped meets the same conditions (on the opponent's side and now with two or three stones), its stones are also captured. This continues backwards until the string of consecutive squares of two or three on the opponent's side is broken.

Regardless of whether any captures are made, play alternates back and forth between the two players.

The object of the game is to be the first player to capture twenty-four or more stones. That's half of the forty-eight stones that are on the board at the beginning of the game.

There are a few special rules to cover some situations that can come up in the game. It is not legal to capture all the stones on the opponent's side of the board, since this would leave the opponent with no moves on his next turn. By the same token, when your opponent has no stones on his side (because he had to move his last one to your side on his turn), you have to make a move that gives him at least one stone to move on his next turn, if possible. If you cannot make such a move, the game is over and counted as a draw.

During the course of the game, it's possible for a square to accumulate twelve or more stones in it. Moving from such a square causes stones to be distributed all the way around the board. When this happens, the square from which the move was made is skipped over. So, the square moved from is always left empty.

It takes the computer anywhere from five seconds to about forty seconds to make a move, depending on the complexity of the board position. The word THINKING is displayed during this time, and a period is added to it as each possible move is evaluated in sequence (seven through twelve).

This program is a little too large to fit into a 4K Color Computer. You will need 16K or more.

## SAMPLE RUN

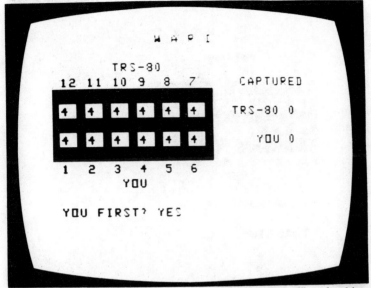

The program starts off by drawing the playing "board" and asking who should move first. The operator decides to go first.

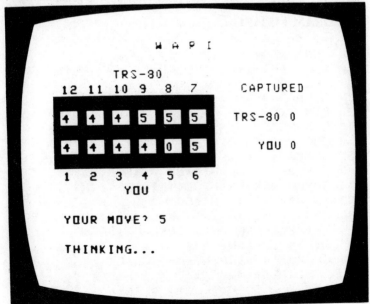

The program asks for the operator's move. He or she decides to move square number 5. The program alters the board accordingly, and begins "thinking" about what move to make.

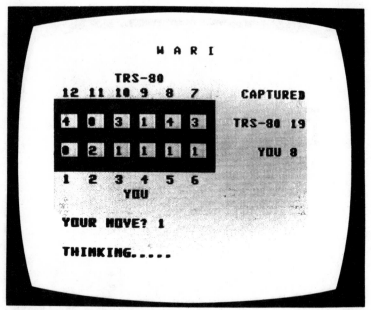

Later in the same game, the computer is about to move square number
12, which will capture seven more stones and win the game.

## PROGRAM LISTING

```
100 REM: WARI - 16K
110 REM: (C) 1981, TOM RUGG AND PHIL
    FELDMAN
120 CLEAR 200:Q=14:P=13:F=50:D=12
130 DIM T(Q),Y(Q),W(Q),V(6),E(6),B(Q)
140 GOSUB 750
150 FOR J=1 TO D:B(J)=4:NEXT:B(P)=0:B(Q)=0
155 GOSUB 1200:GOSUB 900
160 GOSUB 990:INPUT"YOU FIRST";R$
170 GOSUB 990:PRINT D$:R$=LEFT$(R$,1)
180 IF R$="Y" THEN 250
190 GOSUB 1050:PRINT D$;D$;D$;:GOSUB 1050
195 PRINT"THINKING";:GOSUB 510
    :IF M<1 THEN 2000
200 GOSUB 1050:PRINT D$;:GOSUB 1050
    :PRINT"MY MOVE IS";M
210 FOR J=1 TO Q:T(J)=B(J):NEXT:GOSUB 350
220 FOR J=1 TO Q:B(J)=T(J):NEXT:GOSUB 900
230 IF B(Q)<24 THEN 250
240 GOSUB 1050:PRINT"I WIN!";D$:GOTO 810
```

```
250 GOSUB 990:PRINT D$;D$:GOSUB 990:INPUT
    "YOUR MOVE";R$
260 M=INT(VAL(R$)):IF M>6 OR M<1 THEN 330
270 FOR J=1 TO Q:T(J)=B(J):NEXT
280 GOSUB 350:IF M<0 THEN 330
290 FOR J=1 TO Q:B(J)=T(J):NEXT
310 GOSUB 900:IF B(P)<24 THEN 190
320 GOSUB 1050:PRINT"YOU WIN!";D$:GOTO 810
330 PRINT@398,"ILLEGAL";:SOUND 8,8
340 FOR J=1 TO 2000:NEXT:GOTO 250
350 IF T(M)=0 THEN M=-1:RETURN
360 R$="H":IF M>6 THEN R$="C":GOTO 380
370 FOR J=1 TO Q:Y(J)=T(J):NEXT:GOTO 400
380 FOR J=1 TO 6:Y(J)=T(J+6):Y(J+6)=T(J)
    :NEXT
390 Y(P)=T(Q):Y(Q)=T(P):M=M-6
400 C=M:N=Y(C):FOR J=1 TO N:C=C+1
410 IF C=P THEN C=1
420 IF C=M THEN C=C+1:GOTO 410
430 Y(C)=Y(C)+1:NEXT:Y(M)=0:L=C
440 IF L<7 OR Y(L)>3 OR Y(L)<2 THEN 460
450 Y(P)=Y(P)+Y(L):Y(L)=0:L=L-1:GOTO 440
460 S=0:FOR J=7 TO D:S=S+Y(J):NEXT
470 IF S=0 THEN M=-2:RETURN
480 IF R$="H" THEN FOR J=1 TO Q:T(J)=Y(J)
    :NEXT:RETURN
490 FOR J=1 TO 6:T(J)=Y(J+6):T(J+6)=Y(J)
    :NEXT
500 T(Q)=Y(P):T(P)=Y(Q):RETURN
510 FOR A=1 TO 6:M=A+6
520 IF B(M)=0 THEN E(A)=-F:GOTO 690
530 FOR J=1 TO Q:T(J)=B(J):NEXT:GOSUB 350
540 IF M<0 THEN E(A)=-F:GOTO 690
550 IF T(Q)>23 THEN M=A+6:RETURN
560 FOR J=1 TO Q:W(J)=T(J):NEXT
    :FOR K=1 TO 6
570 IF T(K)=0 THEN V(K)=F:GOTO 670
580 FOR J=1 TO Q:T(J)=W(J):NEXT:M=K
    :GOSUB 350
590 IF M<0 THEN V(K)=F:GOTO 670
600 FA=0:FB=.05:FC=0:FD=0:FOR J=7 TO D
610 FB=FB+T(J):IF T(J)>0 THEN FA=FA+1
620 IF T(J)<3 THEN FC=FC+1
630 IF T(J)>FD THEN FD=T(J)
640 NEXT:FE=FB:FOR J=1 TO 6:FE=FE+T(J):NEXT
```

```
650  FA=FA/6:FD=1-FD/FB:FC=1-FC/6:FB=FB/FE
660  V(K)=.3*(FA+FB)+.2*(FC+FD)+T(Q)+B(P)
     -B(Q)-T(P)
670  NEXT:E(A)=F:FOR J=1 TO 6
675  IF V(J)<E(A) THEN E(A)=V(J)
680  NEXT
690  PRINT",";:NEXT:M=0:FA=-F:FOR J=1 TO 6
700  IF E(J)>FA THEN FA=E(J):M=J+6
710  NEXT:RETURN
750  D$=CHR$(32):FOR J=1 TO 4
760  D$=D$+D$:NEXT:A$=CHR$(175):RETURN
810  PRINT"GOOD GAME!"
840  INPUT"WANT TO PLAY AGAIN";R$
850  R$=LEFT$(R$,1):IF R$="Y" THEN 120
860  IF R$<>"N" THEN 840
880  PRINT:END
900  FOR J=0 TO 5
910  PRINT@160+3*J,B(12-J);
920  PRINT@224+3*J,B(J+1);
930  NEXT
940  PRINT@181,"TRS-80";B(Q);
950  FOR J=0 TO 18 STEP 3
960  PRINT@160+J,A$;
970  PRINT@224+J,A$;:NEXT
980  PRINT@248,"YOU";B(P);:RETURN
990  PRINT@384," ";:RETURN
1050 PRINT@448," ";:RETURN
1200 CLS:PRINT@12,"W A R I"
1220 PRINT@71,"TRS-80";
1230 FOR J=0 TO 5
1235 PRINT@288+3*J,J+1;
1240 PRINT@96+3*J,12-J;:NEXT
1250 PRINT@118,"CAPTURED";
1260 PRINT@328,"YOU";
1270 FOR J=1 TO 19
1280 PRINT@127+J,A$;
1290 PRINT@191+J,A$;
1300 PRINT@255+J,A$;
1310 NEXT:RETURN
2000 PRINT"NO LEGAL MOVES":GOTO 840
```

**EASY CHANGES**

1. Want a faster moving game against an opponent who isn't
   quite such a good player? Insert the following two lines:

555 GOTO 600
665 E(A) = V(K):GOTO 690

In the standard version of the game, the computer looks at each of its possible moves and each of your possible replies when evaluating which move to make. This change causes the computer to look only at each of its moves, without bothering to look at any of your possible replies. As a result, the computer does not play as well, but it takes only a few seconds to make each move.

2.  If you are curious about what the computer thinks are the relative merits of each of its possible moves, you can make this change to find out. Change line 690 so it looks like this:

    690 PRINT E(A);:NEXT:M = 0:FA = − F:FOR J = 1 TO 6

    and replace the 448 in line 1050 with 416. This will cause the program to display its evaluation number for each of its moves in turn (starting with square seven). It will select the largest number of the six. A negative value means that it will lose stones if that move is made, assuming that you make the best reply you can. A value of negative 50 indicates an illegal move. A positive value greater than one means that a capture can be made by the computer, which will come out ahead after your best reply.

## MAIN ROUTINES

120- 155  Initializes variables. Displays board.
160- 180  Asks who goes first. Evaluates answer.
190- 220  Determines computer's move. Displays new board position.
230- 240  Determines if computer's move resulted in a win. Displays a message if so.
250- 290  Gets operator's move. Checks for legality. Displays new board position.
310- 320  Determines if operator's move resulted in a win.
330       Displays message if illegal move attempted.
350- 500  Subroutine to make move M in T array.
360- 390  Copies T array into Y array (inverts if computer is making the move).
400- 430  Makes move in Y array.
440- 450  Checks for captures. Removes stones. Checks previous square.

460- 470 Sees if opponent is left with a legal move.
480- 500 Copies Y array back into T array.
510- 710 Subroutine to determine computer's move.
750- 760 Subroutine to create graphics strings for board display.
810- 880 Displays ending message. Asks about playing again.
900- 980 Subroutine to display stones on board and captured, and "cross-bars" of board squares.
990 Subroutine to move cursor to "YOUR MOVE" position on screen.
1050 Subroutine to move cursor to "MY MOVE" position on screen.
1200-1310 Subroutine to display Wari board (without stones), titles, and square numbers.
2000 Displays message when computer has no legal move.

## MAIN VARIABLES

J,K  Subscript variables.
Q,P,F,D  Constant values of 14, 13, 50 and 12, respectively.
T,Y,W  Arrays with temporary copies of the Wari board.
V  Array with evaluation values of operator's six possible replies to computer's move being considered.
E  Array with evaluation values of computer's six possible moves.
B  Array containing Wari board. Thirteenth element has stones captured by operator. Fourteenth has computer's.
R$  Operator's reply. Also used as switch to indicate whose move it is (C for computer, H for human).
M  Move being made (1-6 for operator, 7-12 for computer). Set negative if illegal.
C  Subscript used in dropping stones around board.
L  Last square in which a stone was dropped.
S  Stones on opponent's side of the board after a move.
A  Subscript used to indicate which of the six possible computer moves is currently being evaluated.
FA  First evaluation factor used in determining favorability of board position after a move (indicates computer's number of occupied squares).
FB  Second evaluation factor (total stones on computer's side of the board).

| FC | Third evaluation factor (number of squares with two or less stones). |
| FD | Fourth evaluation factor (number of stones in most populous square on computer's side). |
| FE | Total stones on board. |
| A$ | String of graphics color used to display the Wari board. |
| D$ | String of 16 blanks. |

## SUGGESTED PROJECTS

1. Modify the program to declare the game a draw if neither player has made a capture in the past thirty moves. Insert a line 300 to add one to a counter of the number of moves made. To make the change, keep track of the move number of the last capture, and compare the difference between it and the current move number with 30.
2. Modify the evaluation function used by the computer strategy to see if you can improve the quality of its play. Lines 600 through 660 examine the position of the board after the move that is being considered. Experiment with the factors and/or the weighting values, or add a new factor of your own.
3. Change the program so it can allow two people to play against each other, instead of just a person against the computer.

# Section 4

# Graphics Display Programs

**INTRODUCTION TO GRAPHICS DISPLAY PROGRAMS**

The TRS-80 Color Computer is an amazing machine. It has very useful color graphics capabilities in addition to its other capacities. Programs in the other sections of this book take advantage of these graphics to facilitate and "spice up" their various output. Here we explore their use for sheer fun, amusement, and diversion.

Ever look through a kaleidoscope and enjoy the symmetric changing patterns produced? KALEIDO will create such effects to keep you hypnotized.

Two other programs produce ever changing patterns but with much different effects. SPARKLE will fascinate you with a changing shimmering collage. SQUARES uses geometric shapes to obtain its pleasing displays.

WALLOONS demonstrates a totally different aspect of the computer. This program will keep you entertained with an example of computer animation.

# KALEIDO

**PURPOSE**

If you have ever played with a kaleidoscope, you were probably fascinated by the endless symmetrical patterns you saw displayed. This program creates a series of kaleidoscope-like designs, with each one overlaying the previous one.

**HOW TO USE IT**

There is not much to say about how to use this one. Just type RUN, then sit back and watch. Turning down the lights and playing a little music is a good way to add to the effect.

Have a few friends bring their Color Computers over (all your friends *do* have Color Computers, don't they?), and get them all going with KALEIDO at once. Let us know if you think you have set a new world's record. Please note that we will not be responsible for any hypnotic trances induced this way.

**SAMPLE RUN**

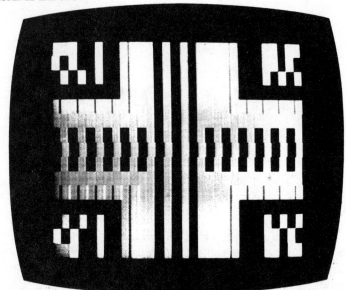

One of the patterns generated by the KALEIDO program.

**PROGRAM LISTING**

```
100 REM: KALEIDO
110 REM: (C) 1981, TOM RUGG AND PHIL
    FELDMAN
120 CLEAR 200:GOSUB 400:CLS(0)
130 A=239:D=-1
140 W=2:S=7:L=32:M=8
150 DIM R$(S)
160 FOR J=0 TO S:A$="":FOR K=1 TO W
170 A$=A$+CHR$(RND(M)*16+127):NEXT
180 R$(J)=A$:NEXT
190 D=-D
200 P=0:Q=S:IF D<0 THEN Q=0:P=S
210 FOR K=P TO Q STEP D
220 FOR J=K TO Q STEP D
230 PRINT@A+J*W+K*L,R$(K);
240 PRINT@A+K*W+J*L,R$(K);
250 PRINT@A+J*W-K*L,R$(K);
260 PRINT@A+K*W-J*L,R$(K);
270 PRINT@A-J*W+K*L,R$(K);
280 PRINT@A-K*W+J*L,R$(K);
290 PRINT@A-J*W-K*L,R$(K);
```

```
300 PRINT@A-K*W-J*L,R$(K);
310 NEXT:NEXT
320 GOTO 160
400 CLS
410 PRINT"** KALEIDO **"
420 PRINT
430 PRINT"PRESS A KEY TO START"
440 A$=INKEY$:J=RND(2)
450 IF A$="" THEN 440
460 RETURN
```

## EASY CHANGES

1. To clear the screen before the next pattern about 20% of the time (chosen at random), insert this:

   185 IF RND (100) < = 20 THEN CLS(0)

   For 50%, use 50 instead of 20, etc.

2. To randomly select either a wide or narrow pattern, insert:

   315 W = RND(2)

   To always get a narrow pattern, use this instead:

   145 W = 1

3. To randomly change the size of the patterns, insert:

   187 S = RND (5) + 2

4. To cause only the outward patterns to be displayed, change line 190 to say

   190 D = 1

   To cause only inward patterns, change it to say

   190 D = − 1

5. To alter the number of graphics colors used in the pattern, insert:

   316 M = RND(7) + 1

6. To lengthen the delay after each pattern is drawn, insert this line:

   317 FOR J = 1 TO 3000:NEXT

   Use a number larger than 3000 to increase the length of the delay even more.

*Note:* These changes add a lot to the appeal of the designs. Experiment! Each change can be done by itself or in combination with other changes.

## MAIN ROUTINES

| | |
|---|---|
| 120-150 | Housekeeping. Initializes variables, RND. |
| 160-180 | Picks S + 1 random graphics colors, each W characters wide. |
| 190 | Reverses direction of display (inward-outward). |
| 200-310 | Displays a full screen of the pattern. |
| 320 | Goes back to create next pattern. |
| 400-460 | Subroutine to display title and initialize RND. |

## MAIN VARIABLES

| | |
|---|---|
| A | Pointer to center of design. |
| D | Direction in which design is drawn (1 = outward, − 1 = inward). |
| W | Width of each graphics string. |
| S | Size of one-quarter of the pattern. |
| L | Length of one line on the screen (32). |
| M | Multiplier used to determine the range of random graphics colors. |
| R$ | Array for the S random graphics strings. |
| J,K | Subscript variables. |
| P,Q | Inner and outer bounds of design (distance from center). |
| A$ | Temporary string variable used to build graphics strings. |

# SPARKLE

## PURPOSE

This graphics display program provides a continuous series of hypnotic patterns, some of which seem to sparkle at you while they are created. Two types of patterns are used. The first is a set of colored concentric diamond shapes in the center of the screen. Although the pattern is somewhat regular, the sequence in which it is created is random, which results in the "sparkle" effect.

The second type of pattern starts about two seconds after the first has finished. It is a series of "sweeps" across the screen— left to right and top to bottom. Each sweep uses a random graphics color that is spaced equally across the screen. The spacing distance is chosen at random for each sweep. Also, the number of sweeps to be made is chosen at random each time in the range from 11 to 30.

After the second type of pattern is complete, the program goes back to the first type, which begins to overlay the second type.

## HOW TO USE IT

Confused by what you just read? Never mind. You have to see it to appreciate it. Just enter the program into your Color Computer, then sit back and watch the results of your labor.

## SAMPLE RUN

One of the patterns generated by the SPARKLE program.

## PROGRAM LISTING

```
100 REM: SPARKLE
110 REM: (C) 1981, TOM RUGG AND PHIL
    FELDMAN
120 CLEAR 200:GOSUB 950:S=15
130 DIM A(S),B(S):X=S+S:Y=S
140 T=RND(8)
150 FOR J=0 TO S:A(J)=J:B(J)=J:NEXT
160 FOR J=0 TO S:R=RND(S+1)-1
170 W=A(J):A(J)=A(R):A(R)=W:NEXT
180 FOR J=0 TO S:R=RND(S+1)-1
190 W=B(J):B(J)=B(R):B(R)=W:NEXT
200 FOR J=0 TO S:FOR K=0 TO S
210 R=A(J):W=B(K):C=R+W+T
220 IF C>8 THEN C=C-8:GOTO 220
240 SET(X+R+R,Y+W,C)
245 SET(X+R+R+1,Y+W,C)
250 SET(X+R+R,Y-W,C)
255 SET(X+R+R+1,Y-W,C)
260 SET(X-R-R,Y-W,C)
265 SET(X-R-R+1,Y-W,C)
270 SET(X-R-R,Y+W,C)
```

```
275  SET(X-R-R+1,Y+W,C)
280  SET(X+W+W,Y+R,C)
285  SET(X+W+W+1,Y+R,C)
290  SET(X+W+W,Y-R,C)
295  SET(X+W+W+1,Y-R,C)
300  SET(X-W-W,Y-R,C)
305  SET(X-W-W+1,Y-R,C)
310  SET(X-W-W,Y+R,C)
315  SET(X-W-W+1,Y+R,C)
320  NEXT K:NEXT J
350  FOR J=1 TO 2000:NEXT
400  M=8:N=RND(20)+10
410  FOR J=1 TO N
420  R=RND(18):W=RND(M)
450  FOR L=Y-S TO Y+S STEP INT(R/4)+2
460  FOR K=X-S-S TO X+S+S STEP R
470  SET(K,L,W)
480  NEXT K:NEXT L:NEXT J
490  GOTO 140
950  CLS
960  PRINT"** SPARKLE **"
970  PRINT
980  PRINT"PRESS A KEY TO START"
990  A$=INKEY$:J=RND(2)
1000 IF A$="" THEN 990
1010 CLS(0):RETURN
```

## EASY CHANGES

1. Make the second type of pattern appear first by inserting this line:

   135 GOTO 400

   Or, eliminate the first type of pattern by inserting:

   145 GOTO 400

   Or, eliminate the second type of pattern by inserting:

   360 GOTO 140

2. Increase the delay after the first type of pattern by increasing the 2000 in line 350 to, say, 5000. Remove line 350 to eliminate the delay.

3. Increase the number of sweeps across the screen of the second type of pattern by changing the 10 at the right end of line 400 into a 30 or a 50, for example. Decrease the number of sweeps by changing the 10 to a 1, and also changing the 20 in line 400 to 5 or 10.

4.  Watch the effect on the second type of pattern if you change
    the 18 in line 420 into various integer values between 2
    and 60.
5.  Change the value of M in line 400 to alter the graphics colors
    used in the second type of pattern. For example, try

$$M = 4$$

    Be sure M is an integer from 2 to 8.

## MAIN ROUTINES

| | |
|---|---|
| 120- 130 | Initializes variables. |
| 140- 320 | Displays first type of pattern. |
| 150- 190 | Shuffles the numbers 0 through 15 in the A and B arrays. |
| 200- 320 | Displays graphics colors on the screen. |
| 350 | Delays for about 2 seconds. |
| 400- 480 | Overlays the entire screen with a random graphics color spaced at a fixed interval chosen at random. |
| 950-1010 | Displays title, initializes RND, clears screen. |

## MAIN VARIABLES

| | |
|---|---|
| S | Size of the first type of pattern. |
| R | Random integer. Also, work variable. |
| A,B | Arrays in which shuffled integers from 0 to 15 are stored for use in making first type of pattern. |
| X,Y | Coordinates of center of screen (30 across, 15 down). |
| T | Integer from 1 to 8, used in creating random graphics colors. |
| J,K,L | Work and loop variables. |
| W | Work variable. |
| C | Graphics color to be displayed on screen at X,Y. |
| N | Number of repetitions of second type of pattern. |
| M | Multiplier used in getting a random color for the second type of pattern. |
| A$ | Input key to start the display. |

## SUGGESTED PROJECTS

Make the second type of pattern alternate between "falling
from the top" (as it does now) and rising from the bottom of the
screen.

# SQUARES

## PURPOSE

This is another graphics-display program. It draws a series of concentric squares with the graphics color used for each one chosen at random. After a full set of concentric squares is drawn, the next set starts again at the center and overlays the previous one. They are actually rectangles, not squares, but let's not be nit-pickers.

## HOW TO USE IT

As with most of the other graphics display programs, you just sit back and enjoy watching this one once you get it started.

**SAMPLE RUN**

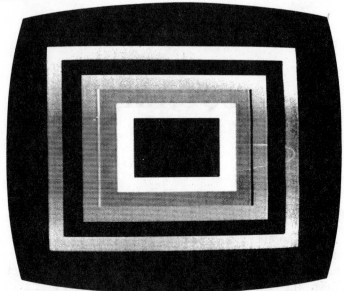

One of the patterns generated by the SQUARES program.

## PROGRAM LISTING

```
100 REM: SQUARES
110 REM: (C) 1981, TOM RUGG AND PHIL
    FELDMAN
120 CLEAR 200
130 GOSUB 300
140 N=1:L=272
150 C=127+16*RND(8):C$=CHR$(C)
170 FOR J=1 TO N:PRINT@L,C$;
175 PRINT@L+1,C$;:L=L+1
180 L=L+1:NEXT:N=N+1
190 FOR J=1 TO N:PRINT@L,C$;
195 PRINT@L+1,C$;
200 L=L-32:NEXT:L=L+31
210 FOR J=1 TO N:PRINT@L,C$;
215 PRINT@L-1,C$;:L=L-1
220 L=L-1:NEXT:L=L+33
230 N=N-1
240 FOR J=1 TO N:PRINT@L,C$;
245 PRINT@L+1,C$;
250 L=L+32:NEXT:N=N+2
```

```
260 IF N<14 THEN 150
270 FOR J=1 TO 1000:NEXT
280 GOTO 140
300 CLS
310 PRINT"** SQUARES **"
320 PRINT:PRINT
330 PRINT"PRESS A KEY TO START"
340 IF LEN(INKEY$)<>0 THEN 360
350 J=RND(2):GOTO 340
360 CLS(0):RETURN
```

## EASY CHANGES

1. Change the delay after each set of patterns by changing the 1000 in line 270. A bigger number causes a longer delay.
2. To occasionally blank out the screen (about 20% of the time), insert this:

   275 IF RND(100) < = 20 THEN CLS(0)

## MAIN ROUTINES

| | |
|---|---|
| 130 | Displays title and initializes RND function. |
| 140 | Initializes counters for the pattern. Points to the center of the screen. |
| 150 | Picks a graphics color and creates a string of it. |
| 170-180 | Draws the bottom side of the square. |
| 190-200 | Draws the right side. |
| 210-230 | Draws the top side. |
| 240-250 | Draws the left side. |
| 260 | Tests if the outermost square has been drawn. |
| 270 | Delays about one second. |
| 280 | Goes back to start at the center again. |
| 300-360 | Subroutine to display title and set RND. |

## MAIN VARIABLES

| | |
|---|---|
| N | Length of the side currently being drawn. |
| L | Location on the screen where colors are currently being displayed. |
| C | Numeric equivalent of the random graphics color chosen. |
| C$ | String representation of the random graphics color. |
| J | Loop variable. |

# WALLOONS

## PURPOSE

The TRS-80 Color Computer is quite a versatile machine. This program takes advantage of its powerful graphics capability to produce computer animation. That's right, animation! WALLOONS will entertain you with a presentation from the Color Circus.

The Color Circus searches the world over to bring you the best in circus acts and other performing artists. Today, direct from their performance before the uncrowned heads of Europe, the Circus brings you the Flying Walloons.

## HOW TO USE IT

Just sit back, relax, and get ready to enjoy the show. (Don't forget to turn on the sound on your TV set.) Type RUN and the Flying Walloons will be ready to perform. You have a front row center seat and the show is about to begin.

Applause might be appropriate if you enjoy their performance. Please note that the Walloons have been working on a big new finish to their act which they haven't yet quite perfected.

**SAMPLE RUN**

The billboard announces a new presentation of the (in)famous Color
Circus.

"The Flying Walloons" are to perform!

The Walloons attempt a dangerous trick from their repertoire.

## PROGRAM LISTING

```
100 REM: WALLOONS - 16K
110 REM: (C) 1981, PHIL FELDMAN AND TOM
    RUGG
150 CLEAR 200
200 CLS(0):FOR J=1 TO 5
210 SOUND 200,2:NEXT
220 CLS(0):GOSUB 2100:GOSUB 2000
230 CLS:GOSUB 2400
300 C=2
310 CF=3
320 GOSUB 7000:F=461:LU=390
330 LD=486:WL=360:WR=370
340 FOR K=1 TO 1000:NEXT
350 GOSUB 4000:CLS
360 PRINT@234,"F I N I S"
370 FOR K=1 TO 2000:NEXT
380 PRINT:PRINT
390 END
2000 FOR J=1 TO 7
2010 CLS(J):SOUND J*30,4:NEXT
2020 FOR J=6 TO 0 STEP -1:CLS(J)
2030 SOUND J*30+1,4:NEXT
```

```
2040 FOR J=1 TO 300:NEXT:RETURN
2100 T$=CHR$(143):G$=""
2110 FOR J=1 TO 22:G$=G$+T$:NEXT
2120 FOR J=69 TO 389 STEP 32
2130 PRINT@J,G$;:NEXT
2140 PRINT@138,"COLOR CIRCUS";
2150 PRINT@236,"PROUDLY";
2160 PRINT@332,"PRESENTS";
2200 FOR K=1 TO 3:FOR J=36 TO 59
2210 GOSUB 2900:NEXT
2220 FOR J=91 TO 443 STEP 32
2230 GOSUB 2900:NEXT
2240 FOR J=442 TO 420 STEP -1
2250 GOSUB 2900:NEXT
2260 FOR J=388 TO 68 STEP -32
2270 GOSUB 2900:NEXT:NEXT
2280 FOR J=1 TO 2000:NEXT
2300 FOR J=0 TO 7
2310 PRINT@J+236,"-";
2320 FOR K=1 TO 400:NEXT:NEXT
2330 FOR J=1 TO 1000:NEXT:RETURN
2400 T$="T H E"
2410 G$="F L Y I N G"
2420 B$="W A L L      N S"
2450 FOR J=122 TO 97 STEP -1
2460 PRINT@J,T$:GOSUB 2800:NEXT
2470 FOR J=244 TO 229 STEP -1
2480 PRINT@J,G$:GOSUB 2800:NEXT
2490 FOR J=368 TO 361 STEP -1
2500 PRINT@J,B$:GOSUB 2800:NEXT
2510 FOR J=1 TO 700:NEXT
2520 T$=CHR$(32)
2530 FOR J=17 TO 337 STEP 32
2540 PRINT@J,"O";:GOSUB 2790
2550 PRINT@J,T$;:NEXT
2560 PRINT@369,"O";
2570 FOR J=19 TO 339 STEP 32
2580 PRINT@J,"O";:GOSUB 2790
2590 PRINT@J,T$;:NEXT
2600 PRINT@371,"O";
2610 RETURN
2790 SOUND 5,1:RETURN
2800 FOR K=1 TO 20:NEXT:RETURN
2900 C=C+1:IF C=8 THEN C=0
2910 PRINT@J,CHR$(143+16*C);
```

```
2920 RETURN
3000 READ J,K:IF J=0 THEN RETURN
3010 SOUND J,K:GOTO 3000
3100 DATA 108,4
3110 DATA 108,4,147,4,159,4
3120 DATA 170,8,170,2,170,2
3130 DATA 176,4,125,4,125,4
3140 DATA 159,8,108,4
3150 DATA 108,4,140,4,147,4
3160 DATA 159,4,170,4,159,4
3170 DATA 159,4,147,4,125,4
3180 DATA 108,8,108,4
3190 DATA 108,4,147,4,159,4
3200 DATA 170,4,170,4,170,4
3210 DATA 176,4,125,4,125,4
3220 DATA 159,8,108,2,108,2
3230 DATA 108,4,140,4,147,4
3240 DATA 159,4,170,4,159,4
3250 DATA 147,12,0,0
4000 W=354:CLS(0):GOSUB 7600
4010 GOSUB 7900:W=59:GOSUB 7600
4020 PRINT@181,U$;:FOR J=1 TO 90
4030 NEXT:GOSUB 3000
4040 FOR W=354 TO 98 STEP -32
4050 GOSUB 6500:NEXT
4060 FOR W=99 TO 104:GOSUB 6500
4070 NEXT
4080 FOR W=136 TO 264 STEP 32
4090 GOSUB 6500:NEXT
4100 W=59:CLS(0):GOSUB 7600
4110 PRINT@181,U$;:W=WL
4120 GOSUB 7600:GOSUB 7800
4130 SET(19,28,C):FOR J=1 TO 3
4140 SOUND 200,2:NEXT
4150 FOR K=1 TO 700:NEXT
4200 FOR W=59 TO 58 STEP -1
4210 GOSUB 6500:NEXT
4220 K=25:FOR W=57 TO 51 STEP -1
4230 GOSUB 7600:FOR J=1 TO K
4240 NEXT:K=K*2:GOSUB 7700:NEXT
4250 FOR W=52 TO 54:GOSUB 6500
4260 NEXT:W=55:GOSUB 7600
4270 FOR J=1 TO 1000:NEXT
4300 FOR J=1 TO 2
4310 SET(13,23,C):SET(20,23,C)
```

```
4320 FOR K=1 TO 150:NEXT
4330 RESET(13,23):RESET(20,23)
4340 FOR K=1 TO 150:NEXT:NEXT
4350 PRINT@55,CHR$(191);
4360 SOUND 2,15
4370 FOR K=1 TO 1500:NEXT
4400 FOR W=55 TO 51 STEP -1
4410 GOSUB 7600:FOR K=1 TO 200
4420 NEXT:GOSUB 7700:NEXT
4500 FOR J=1 TO 4
4510 FOR W=50 TO 274 STEP 32
4520 GOSUB 6500:NEXT
4530 W=WR:CLS(0):GOSUB 7600
4540 GOSUB 7900:SET(34,28,C)
4550 SOUND 200,1
4560 FOR W=264 TO 40 STEP -32
4570 GOSUB 6500:NEXT
4580 FOR W=72 TO 264 STEP 32
4590 GOSUB 6500:NEXT
4600 W=WL:CLS(0):GOSUB 7600
4610 GOSUB 7800:SET(19,28,C)
4620 SOUND 200,1
4630 FOR W=274 TO 82 STEP -32
4640 GOSUB 6500:NEXT:NEXT
4700 FOR W=50 TO 54
4710 GOSUB 6500:NEXT
4720 FOR W=86 TO 278 STEP 32
4730 GOSUB 6500:NEXT
4800 W=502:PRINT@W,W1$;
4810 PRINT@W-34,D3$;
4820 PRINT@W-65,D2$;
4830 PRINT@W-98,D1$;
4840 FOR K=1 TO 100:NEXT
4850 PRINT@W,CHR$(191);
4860 SOUND 2,15
4870 FOR K=1 TO 2000:NEXT
4880 RETURN
6500 GOSUB 7600:FOR K=1 TO 25
6510 NEXT:GOSUB 7700:RETURN
7000 J=16*(C-1):W1$=CHR$(143+J)
7010 W2$=CHR$(132+J)+CHR$(141+J)
7020 T$=CHR$(143+J):U$=CHR$(142+J)
7030 F$=CHR$(136+J)
7040 W2$=W2$+T$+U$+F$
7050 T$=CHR$(135+J)
```

```
7060 U$=CHR$(140+J)
7070 F$=CHR$(139+J):W3$=T$+U$+F$
7080 L$=CHR$(136+J)
7090 B$=CHR$(128):N$=CHR$(132+J)
7100 W4$=T$+L$+B$+N$+F$
7110 E$=B$+B$+B$+B$+B$
7120 L$=CHR$(131+J)
7130 U$=CHR$(140+J)
7140 F$=CHR$(143+J)
7150 M$=U$+U$+U$
7160 N$=L$+L$+F$+U$+U$
7170 R$=U$+U$+F$+L$+L$
7200 K=141+J:L=130+J
7210 D1$=CHR$(K)+CHR$(L)+B$
7220 D1$=D1$+CHR$(L-1)+CHR$(K+1)
7230 D2$=CHR$(K)+CHR$(L+1)
7240 D2$=D2$+CHR$(K+1)
7250 D3$=CHR$(L-1)+CHR$(L+5)
7260 D3$=D3$+CHR$(K+2)
7270 D3$=D3$+CHR$(K-2)+CHR$(L)
7300 J=16*(CF-1):T$=CHR$(143+J)
7310 F$=CHR$(140+J)
7320 L$=F$+F$+F$:U$=L$+L$+L$
7400 RETURN
7500 PRINT@F,T$;:PRINT@F+31,L$;
7510 RETURN
7600 PRINT@W,W1$;
7610 PRINT@W+30,W2$;
7620 PRINT@W+63,W3$;
7630 PRINT@W+94,W4$;:RETURN
7700 PRINT@W,B$;
7710 PRINT@W+30,E$;
7720 PRINT@W+62,E$;
7730 PRINT@W+94,E$;:RETURN
7800 PRINT@LD,M$;
7810 PRINT@LD-30,N$;
7820 PRINT@LD-58,N$;
7830 PRINT@LD-86,N$;
7840 GOSUB 7500:RETURN
7900 PRINT@LU,R$;
7910 PRINT@LU+36,R$;
7920 PRINT@LU+72,R$;
7930 PRINT@LU+108,M$;
7940 GOSUB 7500:RETURN
```

## EASY CHANGES

1. If you wish to have the Walloons perform more (or less) jumps during their performance, change the loop bound value of 4 in line 4500 accordingly. To get six jumps, use

    4500 FOR J = 1 TO 6

2. The color of the Walloons and their performing lever is controlled by the variable C set in line 300. Try the effect of making C any of the integers from 1 through 8. (However, C = 4 should be avoided as this conflicts with one of the special effects.) Your Basic manual indicates which colors correspond to which integers. To get orange Walloons, for example, change line 300 to

    300 C = 8

3. In a similar manner to that above, the color of the fulcrum and entrance platform is controlled by the variable CF set in line 310. To get a green fulcrum, change line 310 to

    310 CF = 1

4. The speed of the Walloon's movement is controlled by the delay constant in line 6500. This constant is currently set to 25. To make the Walloons move faster, try changing line 6500 to

    6500 GOSUB 7600:FOR K = 1 TO 5

    To have them move slower, try

    6500 GOSUB 7600:FOR K = 1 TO 50

5. You might want to personalize the title placard and make yourself the presenter of the Walloons. This can be done by altering the string literal, "COLOR CIRCUS" in line 2140 to something else. However, you cannot use a string with a length of much more than 16 characters or it will print beyond the end of the placard. To say, for example, that Simon Fenster presents the Walloons, change line 2140 to:

    2140 PRINT@138, "SIMON FENSTER";

## MAIN ROUTINES

200- 390 Main routine—drives Walloon's performance.
2000-2040 Subroutine to flash screen.
2100-2330 Subroutine to display placard.

**MAIN VARIABLES**

| | |
|---|---|
| A$-Z$ | Various graphics strings. |
| C | Color of Walloons and lever. |
| CF | Color of fulcrum and platform. |
| F | Location of fulcrum. |
| LU,LD | Lever locations. |
| WL,WR | Walloon locations on lever. |
| W | Location of Walloon's head. |
| J,K,L | Loop indices and work variables. |

**SUGGESTED PROJECTS**

1. There are many possibilities for "spicing up" the Walloons' act with extra tricks or improved ones. Perhaps you would like to change their finish to something less crude. To get you started, here are the changes to produce one alternate ending:

```
4625 IF J = 4 THEN 4650
4650 FOR W = 273 TO 9 STEP  − 33
4655 GOSUB 6500:NEXT
4660 FOR W = 40 TO 232 STEP 32
4665 GOSUB 6500:NEXT
4670 W = 264:GOSUB 7600
4675 PRINT@WL,CHR$(127 + C*16);
4680 GOTO 4870
```

2. If you add some alternate tricks or endings as suggested in the previous project, try randomizing if and when they will be done. Thus, the Walloon's performance will be different each time the program is run. At least their ending may be variable.

3. Scour the world yourself for other acts to include in the Color Circus. Maybe someday we will have a complete software library of performing artists.

# Section 5

# Mathematics Programs

## INTRODUCTION TO MATHEMATICS PROGRAMS

Since their invention, computers have been used to solve mathematical problems. Their great speed and reliability render solvable many otherwise difficult (or impossible) calculations. Several different numerical techniques lend themselves naturally to computer solution. The following programs explore some of them. They will be of interest mainly to engineers, students, mathematicians, statisticians, and others who encounter such problems in their work.

GRAPH takes advantage of the Color Computer's graphic powers to draw the graph of a function $Y = f(X)$. The function is supplied by you. INTEGRATE calculates the integral, or "area under the curve," for any such function.

Experimental scientific work frequently results in data at discrete values of X and Y. CURVE finds a polynomial algebraic expression to express this data with a formula.

Theoretical scientists (and algebra students) often must find the solution to a set of simultaneous linear algebraic equations. SIMEQN does the trick.

Much modern engineering work requires the solution of differential equations. DIFFEQN will solve any first-order ordinary differential equation that you provide.

STATS will take a list of data and derive standard statistical information describing it. In addition, it will sort the data list into ranking numerical order.

# CURVE

## PURPOSE AND DISCUSSION

CURVE fits a polynomial function to a set of data. The data must be in the form of pairs of X-Y points. This type of data occurs frequently as the result of some experiment, or perhaps from sampling tabular data in a reference book.

There are many reasons why you might want an analytic formula to express the functional relationship inherent in the data. Often you will have experimental errors in the Y values. A good formula expression tends to smooth out these fluctuations. Perhaps you want to know the value of Y at some X not obtained exactly in the experiment. This may be a point between known X values (interpolation) or one outside the experimental range (extrapolation). If you wish to use the data in a computer program, a good formula is a convenient and efficient way to do it.

This program fits a curve of the form

$$Y = C_0 + C_1 X^1 + C_2 X^2 + \ldots + C_D X^D$$

to your data. You may select D, the degree (or power) of the highest term, to be as large as 5. The constant coefficients, $C_0$-$C_D$, are the main output of the program. Also calculated is the goodness of fit, a guide to the accuracy of the fit. You may fit different degree polynomials to the same data and also ask to have Y calculated for specific values of X.

The numerical technique involved in the computation is known as least squares curve fitting. It minimizes the sum of the squares of the errors. The least squares method reduces the problem to a set of simultaneous algebraic equations. Thus these equations could be solved by the algorithm used in SIMEQN. In fact, once the proper equations are set up, CURVE uses the identical subroutine found in SIMEQN to solve the equations. For more information, the bibliography contains references to descriptions of the numerical technique.

## HOW TO USE IT

The first thing you must do, of course, is enter the data into the program. This consists of typing in the pairs of numbers. Each pair represents an X value and its corresponding Y value. The two numbers (of each pair) are separated by a comma. A question mark will prompt you for each data pair. After you have entered them all, type

$$999,999$$

to signal the end of the data. When you do this, the program will respond by indicating how many data pairs have been entered. A maximum of 500 data pairs is allowed.

Next, you must input the degree of the polynomial to be fitted. This can be any non-negative integer subject to certain constraints. The maximum allowed is 5. Also, D must be less than the number of data pairs.

A few notes regarding the selection of D may be of interest. If $D = 0$, the program will output the mean value of Y as the coefficient $C_0$. If $D = 1$, the program will be calculating the best straight line through the data. This special case is known as "linear regression." If D is one less than the number of data pairs, the program will find an exact fit to the data (barring round-off and other numerical errors). This is a solution which passes exactly through each data point.

Once you have entered the desired degree, the program will begin calculating the results. There may be a slight pause while this calculation is performed. The time involved depends on the number of data pairs and the degree selected.

The results are displayed in a table. It gives the values of the coefficients for each power of X from 0 to D. That is, the values of $C_0$-$C_D$ are output. Also shown is the goodness of fit, a number between 0 and 1. This is a measure of how accurately the program was able to fit the given case. A value of 1 means perfect fit, lesser values indicate correspondingly poorer fits. It is hard to say what value denotes *satisfactory* fit since much depends on the accuracy of data and the purpose at hand. But as a rule of thumb, anything above 0.95 is quite good. For those interested, the formula to calculate the goodness of fit is

$$G.F. = \sqrt{1 - \frac{\sum_i (Y_i - \hat{Y}_i)^2}{\sum_i (Y_i - \bar{Y})^2}}$$

where $Y_i$ are the actual Y data values, $\hat{Y}_i$ are the calculated Y values (through the polynomial expression), and $\bar{Y}$ is the mean value of Y.

To continue the run, hit any key when requested to do so. Next, you are presented with three options for continuing the run. These are 1) determining specific points, 2) fitting another degree, 3) ending the program. Simply type 1, 2, or 3 to make your selection. A description of each choice now follows.

Option 1 allows you to see the value of Y that the current fit will produce for a given value of X. In this mode you are continually prompted to supply any value of X. The program then shows what the polynomial expression produces as the value for Y. Input 999 for an X value to leave this mode.

Option 2 allows you to fit another degree polynomial to the same data. Frequently, you will want to try successively higher values of D to improve the goodness of fit. Unless round-off errors occur, this will cause the percent goodness of fit to increase.

Option 3 simply terminates the program and with that we will terminate this explanation of how to use CURVE.

## SAMPLE PROBLEM AND RUN

*Problem*: An art investor is considering the purchase of Primo's masterpiece, "Frosted Fantasy." Since 1940, the painting has been for sale at auction seven times. Here is the painting's sales record from these auctions.

| Year | Price |
|------|-------|
| 1940 | $ 8000. |
| 1948 | $13000. |
| 1951 | $16000. |
| 1956 | $20000. |
| 1962 | $28000. |
| 1968 | $39000. |
| 1975 | $53000. |

The painting is going to be sold at auction in 1982. What price should the investor expect to have to pay to purchase the painting? If he resold it in 1985, how much profit should he expect to make?

*Solution*: The investor will try to get a polynomial function that expresses the value of the painting as a function of the year. This is suitable for CURVE. The year will be represented by the variable X, and the price is shown by the variable Y. To keep the magnitude of the numbers small, the years will be expressed as elapsed years since 1900, and the price will be in units of $1000. (thus a year of 40 represents 1940, a price of 8 represents $8000.)

**SAMPLE RUN**

```
- LEAST SQUARES CURVE FITTING -

ENTER A DATA PAIR IN RESPONSE
TO EACH QUESTION MARK.  EACH
PAIR IS AN X VALUE AND A Y
VALUE SEPARATED BY A COMMA.

WHEN ALL DATA IS ENTERED, TYPE
 999 , 999
AFTER THE LAST QUESTION MARK.

THE PROGRAM IS CURRENTLY SET
TO ACCEPT A MAXIMUM OF 500
DATA PAIRS.

X,Y=? 40,8
X,Y=? 48,13
X,Y=? 51,16
X,Y=? 56,20
X,Y=? 62,28
X,Y=? 68,39
X,Y=? 75,53
X,Y=? 999,999

 7 DATA PAIRS ENTERED

DEGREE OF POLYNOMIAL TO BE
FITTED? 1
```

```
X POWER              COEFFICIENT
   0                -48.2701204
   1                  1.28722711

GOODNESS OF FIT= .951214122

HIT ANY KEY TO CONTINUE

(A key is pressed)

CONTINUATION OPTIONS
  1) DETERMINE SPECIFIC POINTS
  2) FIT ANOTHER DEGREE
  3) END PROGRAM
WHAT NEXT? 2

DEGREE OF POLYNOMIAL TO BE
FITTED? 2

X POWER              COEFFICIENT
   0                 38.4753509
   1                 -1.83492108
   2                  .027034675

GOODNESS OF FIT= .998971767
                  .
                  .
    (continuation options displayed again)
                  .
                  .

WHAT NEXT? 1

ENTER 999 TO LEAVE THIS MODE

X=? 82
Y= 69.792977

X=? 85
Y= 77.8325858

X=? 999
```

.
.
(continuation options displayed again)
.
.

WHAT NEXT? <u>3</u>
OK

Initially, a first degree fit was tried and a goodness fit of
about 0.95 was obtained. The investor wanted to do better, so
he tried a second degree fit next. This had a very high goodness
of fit. He then asked for the extrapolation of his data to the
years 1982 and 1985. He found that he should expect to pay
about $69800 to buy the painting in 1982. Around an $8000
profit could be expected upon resale in 1985.

Of course, the investor did not make his decision solely on the
basis of this program. He used it only as one guide to his decision. There is never any guarantee that financial data will perform in the future as it has done in the past. Though CURVE is
probably as good a way as any, extrapolation of data can never
be a totally reliable process.

## PROGRAM LISTING

```
100 REM: CURVE - 16K
110 REM: (C) 1981, PHIL FELDMAN AND TOM
    RUGG
140 CLEAR 200
150 MX=500
160 EF=999
170 MD=5
200 DIM X(MX),Y(MX)
210 Q=MD+1:DIM A(Q,Q),R(Q),V(Q)
220 Q=MD*2:DIM P(Q)
300 CLS:PRINT"- LEAST SQUARES";
310 PRINT" CURVE FITTING -"
320 PRINT:PRINT"ENTER A DATA";
330 PRINT" PAIR IN RESPONSE
340 PRINT"TO EACH QUESTION";
350 PRINT" MARK.  EACH"
360 PRINT"PAIR IS AN X VALUE";
370 PRINT" AND A Y"
380 PRINT"VALUE SEPARATED BY";
390 PRINT" A COMMA.":PRINT
```

```
400 PRINT"WHEN ALL DATA IS";
410 PRINT" ENTERED, TYPE"
420 PRINT EF;",";EF
430 PRINT"AFTER THE LAST";
440 PRINT" QUESTION MARK."
450 PRINT:PRINT"THE PROGRAM IS";
460 PRINT" CURRENTLY SET"
470 PRINT"TO ACCEPT A MAXIMUM";
480 PRINT" OF";MX
490 PRINT"DATA PAIRS."
500 PRINT:J=0
510 J=J+1:INPUT"X,Y=";X(J),Y(J)
520 IF X(J)<>EF THEN 550
530 IF Y(J)<>EF THEN 550
540 J=J-1:GOTO 600
550 IF J<MX THEN 510
560 PRINT"** NO MORE DATA";
570 PRINT" ALLOWED **"
580 GOSUB 6000
600 NP=J:PRINT
610 IF NP>0 THEN 650
620 PRINT"** - FATAL ERROR - **"
630 PRINT"** NO DATA ENTERED **"
640 GOSUB 6000:STOP
650 PRINT NP;"DATA PAIRS";
660 PRINT" ENTERED"
700 PRINT:PRINT"DEGREE OF";
710 PRINT" POLYNOMIAL TO BE"
720 INPUT"FITTED";D:PRINT
730 IF D>=0 THEN 780
740 PRINT"** ERROR **"
750 PRINT"** DEGREE MUST BE";
760 PRINT" >= 0 **"
770 GOSUB 6000:GOTO 700
780 D=INT(D):IF D<NP THEN 820
790 PRINT"** ERROR **"
800 PRINT"** NOT ENOUGH DATA **"
810 GOSUB 6000:GOTO 700
820 D2=2*D:IF D<=MD THEN 860
830 PRINT"** ERROR **"
840 PRINT"** DEGREE TOO HIGH **"
850 GOSUB 6000:GOTO 700
860 N=D+1
900 FOR J=1 TO D2:P(J)=0
910 FOR K=1 TO NP:Q=1
```

```
920 FOR L=1 TO J:Q=Q*X(K):NEXT
930 P(J)=P(J)+Q:NEXT:NEXT
940 P(0)=NP:R(1)=0:FOR J=1 TO NP
950 R(1)=R(1)+Y(J):NEXT
960 IF N=1 THEN 1020
970 FOR J=2 TO N:R(J)=0
980 FOR K=1 TO NP:Q=1
990 FOR L=1 TO J-1
1000 Q=Q*X(K):NEXT
1010 R(J)=R(J)+Y(K)*Q:NEXT:NEXT
1020 FOR J=1 TO N:FOR K=1 TO N
1030 A(J,K)=P(J+K-2):NEXT:NEXT
1040 GOSUB 2000
1100 PRINT
1110 PRINT"X POWER",
1120 PRINT"COEFFICIENT"
1130 FOR J=1 TO N
1140 PRINT" ";J-1,V(J):NEXT
1150 Q=0:T=0:FOR J=1 TO NP
1160 Q=Q+Y(J):NEXT:M=Q/NP:G=0
1170 FOR J=1 TO NP:Q=0
1180 FOR K=1 TO N:Z=1
1190 K1=K-1:IF K1=0 THEN 1210
1200 FOR L=1 TO K1:Z=Z*X(J):NEXT
1210 Q=Q+V(K)*Z:NEXT
1220 T=T+(Y(J)-Q)*(Y(J)-Q)
1230 G=G+(Y(J)-M)*(Y(J)-M):NEXT
1240 IF G=0 THEN T=1:GOTO 1260
1250 T=1-T/G
1260 PRINT
1270 PRINT"GOODNESS OF FIT=";T
1280 PRINT:PRINT"HIT ANY KEY";
1290 PRINT" TO CONTINUE"
1300 Q$=INKEY$
1310 IF Q$="" THEN 1300
1400 PRINT
1410 PRINT"CONTINUATION OPTIONS"
1420 PRINT" 1) DETERMINE";
1430 PRINT" SPECIFIC POINTS"
1440 PRINT" 2) FIT ANOTHER";
1450 PRINT" DEGREE"
1460 PRINT" 3) END PROGRAM"
1470 INPUT"WHAT NEXT";Q
1480 Q=INT(Q):IF Q=3 THEN END
1490 IF Q=2 THEN 700
```

```
1500 IF Q<>1 THEN 1400
1600 PRINT:PRINT"ENTER";EF;
1610 PRINT"TO LEAVE THIS MODE"
1620 PRINT:INPUT"X=";XV
1630 IF XV=EF THEN 1400
1640 YV=V(1):IF N=1 THEN 1680
1650 FOR K=2 TO N
1660 Q=1:FOR L=1 TO K-1:Q=Q*XV
1670 NEXT:YV=YV+V(K)*Q:NEXT
1680 PRINT"Y=";YV:GOTO 1620
2000 IF N>1 THEN 2020
2010 V(1)=R(1)/A(1,1):RETURN
2020 FOR K=1 TO N-1:I=K+1
2030 L=K
2040 Q=ABS(A(I,K))-ABS(A(L,K))
2050 IF Q>0 THEN L=I
2060 IF I<N THEN I=I+1:GOTO 2040
2070 IF L=K THEN 2110
2080 FOR J=K TO N:Q=A(K,J)
2090 A(K,J)=A(L,J):A(L,J)=Q:NEXT
2100 Q=R(K):R(K)=R(L):R(L)=Q
2110 I=K+1
2120 Q=A(I,K)/A(K,K):A(I,K)=0
2130 FOR J=K+1 TO N
2140 A(I,J)=A(I,J)-Q*A(K,J):NEXT
2150 R(I)=R(I)-Q*R(K)
2160 IF I<N THEN I=I+1:GOTO 2120
2170 NEXT
2180 V(N)=R(N)/A(N,N)
2190 FOR I=N-1 TO 1 STEP -1
2200 Q=0:FOR J=I+1 TO N
2210 Q=Q+A(I,J)*V(J)
2220 V(I)=(R(I)-Q)/A(I,I):NEXT
2230 NEXT:RETURN
6000 SOUND 8,8:RETURN
```

## EASY CHANGES

1. The program uses 999 as the flag number to terminate various input modes. This may cause a problem if your data include 999. You can easily change the flag number by modifying the value of EF in line 160 to any value not needed in your data. To use 10101, for example, make this change:

$$160 \ EF = 10101$$

2. A 16K machine, required to run this program, will allow you to use higher degree fits. To achieve up to tenth degree fits, set the value of MD appropriately:

$$170 \ MD = 10$$

However, it must be stressed that it can be unreliable to attempt high degree fits. Unless your data is well behaved (X and Y values close to 1), the program will often not produce accurate results if D is greater than 5 or so. This is because sums of powers of X and Y are calculated up to powers of 2*D. These various sums are several orders of magnitude different from each other. Errors result because of the numerous truncation and round-off operations involved in doing arithmetic with them. A practical limit for MD is 7.

## MAIN ROUTINES

| | |
|---|---|
| 140- 170 | Initializes constants. |
| 200- 220 | Dimensions arrays. |
| 300- 490 | Displays introductory messages. |
| 500- 660 | Gets X-Y input data from the user. |
| 700- 860 | Gets degree of polynomial from the user, determines if it is acceptable. |
| 900-1040 | Sets up equations for the simultaneous equation solver and calls it. |
| 1100-1310 | Calculates goodness of fit, displays all results. |
| 1400-1500 | Gets user's continuation option and branches to it. |
| 1600-1680 | Determines Y value corresponding to any X value. |
| 2000-2230 | Subroutine to solve simultaneous linear algebraic equations. |
| 6000 | Sound generating subroutine. |

## MAIN VARIABLES

| | |
|---|---|
| MX | Maximum number of data pairs allowed. |
| MD | Maximum degree allowed to fit. |
| EF | Ending flag value for data input and X point mode. |
| X,Y | Arrays of X and Y data points. |
| NP | Number of data pairs entered. |
| D | Degree of polynomial to fit. |
| D2 | 2*D, the maximum power sum to compute. |
| N | D + 1, number of simultaneous equations to solve. |

A,R,V      Arrays for simultaneous linear equation solver.
P          Array for holding sums of various powers of X.
I,J,K,L    Loop indices.
Q,G,Z,K1   Work variables.
M          Mean value of Y.
T          Goodness of fit.
XV         Specific X point to calculate Y for.
YV         Y value corresponding to XV.
Q$         User input string.

## SUGGESTED PROJECTS

1.  No provision for modifying the data is incorporated into the program. Often it would be nice to add, subtract, or modify parts of the data after some results are seen. Build in a capability to do this.

2.  You may desire other forms of output. A useful table for many applications might include the actual X values, calculated Y values, and/or percentage errors in Y.

3.  Sometimes certain points (or certain regions of points) are known to be more accurate than others. Then you would like to weight these points as being more important than others to be fit correctly. The least squares method can be modified to include such a weighting parameter with each data pair. Research this technique and incorporate it into the program. (Note: you can achieve some weighting with the current program by entering important points two or more times. There is a certain danger in this, however. You must only ask for a solution with D less than the number of *unique* data points. A division by zero error may result otherwise.)

4.  Often you wish to try successively higher degree polynomials until a certain minimum goodness of fit is obtained. Modify the program to accept a minimally satisfactory goodness of fit from the user. Then have the program automatically try various polynomial fits until it finds the lowest degree fit, if any, with a satisfactory goodness of fit.

# DIFFEQN

## PURPOSE

Differential equations express functions by giving the rate of change of one variable with respect to another. This type of relation occurs regularly in almost all the physical sciences. The solution of these equations is necessary in many practical engineering problems.

For many such equations, a closed form (or exact analytical expression) solution can be obtained. However, for just as many, no such "simple" solution exists. The equation must then be solved numerically, usually by a computer program such as this.

There are many types and classes of differential equations. This program solves those of a simple type; namely, first order, ordinary differential equations. This means the equation to be solved can be written in the form

$$\frac{dY}{dX} = (\text{any function of } X, Y)$$

Here, X is the independent variable and Y is the dependent variable. The equation expresses the derivative (or rate of change) of Y with respect to X. The right-hand-side is an expression which may involve X and/or Y.

To use the program, you must supply it with the differential equation to be solved. The procedure to do this is explained in the "How To Use It" section.

A technique known as the "fourth-order, Runge-Kutta" method is used to solve the equation. Space limitations prevent any detailed explanation of it here. However, it is discussed well in the numerical analysis books referenced in the bibliography.

## HOW TO USE IT

The first thing you must do is enter the differential equation into the program. This must be done at line 3000. Currently this line contains a REM statement which you must replace. The form of line 3000 should be:

3000 D = (your function of X,Y)

D represents dY/dX. GOSUBs are made to line 3000 with X and Y set to their current values. Thus, when each RETURN is made, D will be set to the appropriate value of dY/dX for that given X and Y. If necessary, you may use the lines between 3000 and 3999 to complete the definition of D. Line 3999 already contains a RETURN statement so you do not need to add another one.

The program begins by warning you that you should have already entered the equation at line 3000. You acknowledge that this has been done by hitting the C key to continue.

Now the various initial conditions are input. You are prompted for them one at a time. They consist of: the initial values of X and Y, the stepsize interval in X at which to display the output, and the final value of X.

With the input phase completed, the program initializes things to begin the output. A question mark will be displayed in the lower left of the screen, telling you the program is waiting for you to hit any key to begin the output.

The two-column output is displayed at each interval of the stepsize until the final value of X is reached. Output may temporarily be halted at any time by simply hitting any key. This will stop the display until you hit any key to resume the output. The output may be started and stopped as often as desired, thus enabling you to leisurely view intermediate results before they scroll off the screen.

## SAMPLE PROBLEM AND RUN

*Problem*: A body, originally at rest, is subjected to a force of 2000 dynes. Its initial mass is 200 grams. However, while it moves, it loses mass at the rate of 1 gram/sec. There is also an air resistance equal to twice its velocity retarding its movement. The differential equation expressing this motion is:

$$\frac{dY}{dX} = \frac{(2000 - 2Y)}{(200 - X)} \quad \text{where } Y = \text{velocity (cm./sec.)}$$
$$X = \text{time (sec.)}$$

Find the velocity of the body every 10 seconds up through two minutes. Also, plot this velocity as a function of time.

*Solution and Sample Run*: The solution and sample run are illustrated in the accompanying photographs.

```
    DIFFERENTIAL EQUATION SOLVER
---------------------------------
    THE EQUATION MUST BE DEFINED
AT LINE 3000.  THE FORM IS
3000 D=(YOUR FUNCTION OF X,Y)
WHERE D=DY/DX.
    IF THIS HAS BEEN DONE, HIT
THE "C" KEY TO CONTINUE.
    IF NOT, HIT ANY OTHER KEY.
THEN ENTER LINE 3000 AND RE-RUN
THE PROGRAM.
---------------------------------
OK
3000 D=(2000-2*Y)/(200-X)
RUN
```

The operator hits a key to exit from the program. Then he enters the differential equation into line 3000. He types RUN to restart the program.

```
DIFFERENTIAL EQUATION SOLVER
------------------------------------
    THE EQUATION MUST BE DEFINED
AT LINE 3000.    THE FORM IS
3000 D=(YOUR FUNCTION OF X,Y)
WHERE D=DY/DX.
    IF THIS HAS BEEN DONE, HIT
THE "C" KEY TO CONTINUE.
    IF NOT, HIT ANY OTHER KEY.
THEN ENTER LINE 3000 AND RE-RUN
THE PROGRAM.
------------------------------------
INITIAL VALUE OF X?
```

The operator has hit the "C" key. The program responds by beginning the input phase.

```
------------------------------------
INITIAL VALUE OF X? 0
INITIAL VALUE OF Y? 0
STEPSIZE IN X? 10
FINAL VALUE OF X? 120
------------------------------------
    THE FOLLOWING OUTPUT CAN BE
HALTED BY HITTING ANY KEY.    IT
CAN THEN BE RESUMED BY HITTING
ANY KEY.    THIS MAY BE REPEATED.
    WHEN THE QUESTION MARK (?)
APPEARS, HIT ANY KEY TO BEGIN
THE OUTPUT.
------------------------------------
    X                         Y
?
```

The operator has completed the input. The program signals with a question mark that it is waiting for him to hit any key. It will not continue the run until he does so.

```
     X                        Y
     0                        0
     10                       97.4999135
     20                       189.999821
     30                       277.49972
     40                       359.999609
     50                       437.499483
     60                       509.999337
     70                       577.499165
     80                       639.998955
     90                       697.498692
     100                      749.998352
     110                      797.497896
     120                      839.997256
     OK
```

The operator hits a key and the program responds with the tabulated output. X is time in seconds and Y is velocity in cm./sec.

## PROGRAM LISTING

```
100 REM: DIFFEQN
110 REM: (C) 1981, PHIL FELDMAN AND TOM
    RUGG
150 CLEAR 100
200 CLS:PRINT" DIFFERENTIAL ";
210 PRINT"EQUATION SOLVER"
220 GOSUB 2500:PRINT
230 PRINT"  THE EQUATION MUST ";
240 PRINT"BE DEFINED"
250 PRINT"AT LINE 3000.  THE ";
260 PRINT"FORM IS"
270 PRINT"3000 D=(YOUR ";
280 PRINT"FUNCTION OF X,Y)"
290 PRINT"WHERE D=DY/DX."
300 PRINT"  IF THIS HAS BEEN ";
310 PRINT"DONE, HIT"
320 PRINT"THE 'C' KEY TO ";
330 PRINT"CONTINUE."
340 PRINT"  IF NOT, HIT ANY ";
350 PRINT"OTHER KEY."
```

```
360 PRINT"THEN ENTER LINE 3000";
370 PRINT" AND RE-RUN"
380 PRINT"THE PROGRAM."
390 GOSUB 2500:PRINT
400 R$=INKEY$:IF R$="" THEN 400
410 IF R$<>"C" THEN END
500 INPUT"INITIAL VALUE OF X";XX
510 INPUT"INITIAL VALUE OF Y";YY
520 Y=YY:X=XX:GOSUB 3000
530 INPUT"STEPSIZE IN X";DX
540 INPUT"FINAL VALUE OF X";XF
600 GOSUB 2500:PRINT
610 PRINT"  THE FOLLOWING ";
620 PRINT"OUTPUT CAN BE"
630 PRINT"HALTED BY HITTING ";
640 PRINT"ANY KEY.  IT"
650 PRINT"CAN THEN BE RESUMED ";
660 PRINT"BY HITTING"
670 PRINT"ANY KEY.  THIS MAY ";
680 PRINT"BE REPEATED."
690 PRINT"  WHEN THE QUESTION ";
700 PRINT"MARK (?)"
710 PRINT"APPEARS, HIT ANY ";
720 PRINT"KEY TO BEGIN"
730 PRINT"THE OUTPUT."
740 GOSUB 2500:PRINT
800 PRINT" X"," Y":PRINT"?";
810 R$=INKEY$:IF R$="" THEN 810
820 PRINT CHR$(8);CHR$(32);
830 PRINT CHR$(8);
900 PRINT XX,YY:GOSUB 1600
910 Q=XX+DX
920 IF Q>XF+1.E-5 THEN END
930 X=XX:Y=YY:GOSUB 3000:K0=D
940 X=XX+DX/2:Y=YY+K0*DX/2
950 GOSUB 3000:K1=D:Y=YY+K1*DX/2
960 GOSUB 3000:K2=D:X=XX+DX
970 Y=YY+K2*DX:GOSUB 3000:K3=D
980 DY=DX*(K0+2*K1+2*K2+K3)/6
990 YY=YY+DY:XX=XX+DX:GOTO 900
1600 R$=INKEY$
1610 IF R$="" THEN RETURN
1620 R$=INKEY$
1630 IF R$="" THEN 1620
```

```
1640 RETURN
2500 FOR J=1 TO 30:PRINT"-";
2510 NEXT:RETURN
2900 REM
2910 REM *** DEFINE THE
2920 REM *** DIFFERENTIAL EQTN.
2930 REM *** IN LINES 3000-3999
2940 REM
2950 REM *** MAKE LINE 3000
2960 REM *** THE FIRST LINE OF
2970 REM *** THE DEFINITION
2980 REM
3000 REM D=(THE FUNCTION OF X,Y)
3999 RETURN
```

## EASY CHANGES

1. If you have already entered the differential equation and
   wish to skip the introductory output, add this line:

   190 GOTO 500

   This will immediately begin the input dialog.
2. If you wish to use negative stepsizes, line 920 must be
   changed to:

   920 IF Q < XF − 1.E − 5 THEN END

## MAIN ROUTINES

200- 390 Displays initial messages.
400- 540 Gets user's inputs.
600- 740 Displays additional messages.
800- 830 Initializes output display.
900- 990 Computes each step.
1600-1640 Stops and starts output.
2500-2510 Subroutine to display a dashed line.
3000-3999 User supplied routine to define D.

## MAIN VARIABLES

| | |
|---|---|
| D | Value of $dY/dX$. |
| X,Y | Values of X,Y on current step. |
| XX,YY | Values of X,Y on last step. |
| DX | Stepsize in X. |
| XF | Final value of X. |

| K0,K1, | Runge-Kutta coefficients. |
| K2,K3 | |
| R$ | User entered string. |
| Q | Work variable. |
| J | Loop index. |

## SUGGESTED PROJECTS

1. Modify the program to display the output in graphical form.
2. The value of dY/dX as a function of X is often a useful quantity to know. Modify the program to add it to the columnar display.
3. The inherent error in the calculation depends on the stepsize chosen. Most cases should be run with different stepsizes to insure the errors are not large. If the answers do not change much, you can be reasonably certain that your solutions are accurate. Better yet, techniques exist to vary the stepsize during the calculation to insure the error is sufficiently small during each step. Research these methods and incorporate them into the program.
4. The program can be easily broadened to solve a set of coupled, first order, differential equations simultaneously. This would greatly increase the types of problems that could be solved. Research this procedure and expand the program to handle it.

# GRAPH

## PURPOSE

Is a picture worth a thousand words? In the case of mathematical functions, the answer is often "yes." A picture, i.e. a graph, enables you to see the important behavior of a function quickly and accurately. Trends, minima, maxima, etc. become easy and convenient to determine.

GRAPH produces a two-dimensional color plot of a function that you supply. The function must be in the form $Y = $ (any function of X). The independent variable X will be plotted along the abscissa (horizontal axis). The dependent variable Y will be plotted along the ordinate (vertical axis). You have complete control over the scaling that is used on the X and Y axes.

## HOW TO USE IT

Before running the program, you must enter into it the function to be plotted. This is done as a subroutine beginning at line 5000. It must define Y as a function of X. The subroutine will be called with X set to various values. It must then set the variable Y to the correct corresponding value. The subroutine may be as simple or as complex as necessary to define the function. It can take one line or several hundred lines. Line 5999 is already set as a RETURN statement, so you need not add another one.

Having entered this subroutine, you are ready to run the program. The program begins by warning you that it assumes the function has already been entered at line 5000. It will then ask you for the domain of X, i.e. the lowest and highest values of X that you wish to have plotted. Values can be positive or negative as long as the highest value is actually larger than the lowest one.

Now you must choose the scale for Y. To do this intelligently, you probably need to know the minimum and maximum values of Y over the domain of X selected. The program finds these values and displays them for you. You must then choose the minimum and maximum values you wish to have on the Y scale. Again, any two values are acceptable as long as the maximum scale value of Y is larger than the minimum scale value of Y.

The program will now display the plot of your function. Each axis is twenty characters long, with the origin defined as the minimum scale values of both X and Y. Ten tick marks appear on each axis. The locations of the lower, middle, and upper values on each scale are displayed appropriately.

The graph axes and tick marks are drawn in red. The function is plotted in buff.

If a value for Y should be off-scale, a special orange colored point is displayed at the appropriate value of X. If the actual value of Y is too large, it is plotted just above the maximum Y value. If this actual value of Y is too small, it is plotted just below the Y axis.

After the plot is drawn, the program will tell you to hit any key to continue. When you do so, information about the plot scaling is provided. For both X and Y, you are given the low, mid, and upper values on each axis.

You now have the option of hitting G to draw the graph again or any other key to terminate the program.

GRAPH                                                     261

**SAMPLE RUN**

```
OK
5000 Y=SIN(X)
RUN
```

After loading the program, the operator enters line 5000 to request the graph Y = SIN(X). RUN is typed to begin the program.

```
••••••••••• WARNING •••••••••••
 •     THE SUBROUTINE AT LINES    •
 •    5000-5999 IS ASSUMED TO     •
 • DEFINE Y AS A FUNCTION OF X •
 ••••••••••••••••••••••••••••••••••

LOWEST VALUE OF X? 0
HIGHEST VALUE OF X? 6.28

OVER THIS RANGE OF X
   MINIMUM Y =-.999997146
   MAXIMUM Y = .999999683

CHOOSE Y SCALE
MIN Y SCALE VALUE? -1
MAX Y SCALE VALUE? 1
```

The input dialog transpires. The operator asks that the domain of X be 0-6.28. The program responds by showing the maximum and minimum value of Y over this domain. The operator chooses an appropriate scale for the Y axis.

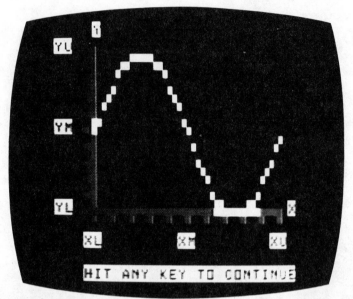

The graph is displayed as requested. The program waits for the operator to hit any key to continue.

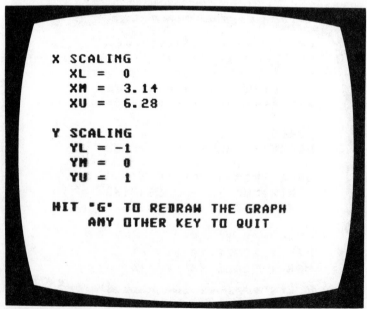

Relevant scaling information is shown. By pressing "G", the operator can see the graph again.

GRAPH 263

## PROGRAM LISTING

```
100 REM: GRAPH
110 REM: (C) 1981, PHIL FELDMAN AND TOM
    RUGG
140 CLEAR 50
150 CA=4:CG=5:CS=8
160 A$="*"
200 CLS:PRINT@11,"G R A P H"
210 PRINT:GOSUB 2000:PRINT
220 PRINT
230 INPUT"LOWEST VALUE OF X";XL
240 INPUT"HIGHEST VALUE OF X";XU
250 IF XU>XL THEN 280
260 PRINT:PRINT"- BAD X RANGE -"
270 GOTO 220
280 GOSUB 300:GOSUB 500
290 GOSUB 700:GOSUB 1000:CLS:END
300 DX=(XU-XL)/40:X=XL
310 GOSUB 5000:MN=Y:MX=Y
320 FOR J=1 TO 40
330 X=XL+DX*J:GOSUB 5000
340 IF Y>MX THEN MX=Y
350 IF Y<MN THEN MN=Y
360 NEXT:PRINT
370 PRINT"OVER THIS RANGE OF X"
380 PRINT"  MINIMUM Y =";MN
390 PRINT"  MAXIMUM Y =";MX
400 PRINT:PRINT"CHOOSE Y SCALE"
410 INPUT"MIN Y SCALE VALUE";YL
420 INPUT"MAX Y SCALE VALUE";YU
430 IF YU>YL THEN RETURN
440 PRINT:PRINT"- BAD Y SCALE -"
450 PRINT:GOTO 370
500 XA=10:YA=23:CLS0
510 FOR J=10 TO 50:SET(J,YA,CA)
520 NEXT:FOR J=3 TO 23
530 SET(XA,J,CA):SET(9,J,CA)
540 NEXT:FOR J=10 TO 50 STEP 4
550 SET(J,24,CA):SET(J-1,24,CA)
560 NEXT:FOR J=3 TO 23 STEP 2
570 SET(8,J,CA):SET(7,J,CA):NEXT
580 PRINT@420,"XL";
590 PRINT@430,"XM";
600 PRINT@440,"XU";
```

```
610 PRINT@353,"YL";
620 PRINT@193,"YM";
630 PRINT@33,"YU";
640 PRINT@5,"Y";
650 PRINT@378,"X";:RETURN
700 DX=(XU-XL)/40:DY=(YU-YL)/20
710 FOR J=0 TO 40:X=XL+DX*J
720 XP=10+J:GOSUB 900
730 IF F=0 THEN SET(XP,YP,CG)
740 IF F=1 THEN SET(XP,24,CS)
750 IF F=2 THEN SET(XP,2,CS)
760 NEXT:PRINT@484,"HIT ANY ";
770 PRINT@492,"KEY TO CONTINUE";
780 Q$=INKEY$:IF Q$="" THEN 780
790 XM=(XL+XU)/2:YM=(YL+YU)/2
800 RETURN
900 GOSUB 5000:V=(Y-YL)/DY
910 IF Y<YL THEN F=1:RETURN
920 IF Y>YU THEN F=2:RETURN
930 F=0:YP=23-INT(V):RETURN
1000 CLS:PRINT:PRINT"X SCALING"
1010 PRINT"   XL = ";XL
1020 PRINT"   XM = ";XM
1030 PRINT"   XU = ";XU
1040 PRINT:PRINT"Y SCALING"
1050 PRINT"   YL = ";YL
1060 PRINT"   YM = ";YM
1070 PRINT"   YU = ";YU:PRINT
1080 PRINT"HIT 'G' TO REDRAW";
1090 PRINT" THE GRAPH"
1100 PRINT"    ANY OTHER KEY";
1110 PRINT" TO QUIT"
1120 Q$=INKEY$
1130 IF Q$="" THEN 1120
1140 IF Q$<>"G" THEN RETURN
1150 GOSUB 500:GOSUB 700:RETURN
2000 PRINT@76,"WARNING"
2010 PRINT@100,"THE SUBROUTINE"
2020 PRINT@115,"AT LINES"
2030 PRINT@132,"5000-5999 IS"
2040 PRINT@145,"ASSUMED TO"
2050 PRINT@162,"DEFINE Y AS A"
2060 PRINT@176,"FUNCTION OF X"
2070 FOR J=64 TO 74:PRINT@J,A$;
```

GRAPH                                                   265

```
2080 NEXT:FOR J=84 TO 94
2090 PRINT@J,A$;:NEXT
2100 FOR J=96 TO 160 STEP 32
2110 PRINT@J,A$;:PRINT@J+30,A$;
2120 NEXT:FOR J=192 TO 222
2130 PRINT@J,A$;:NEXT:RETURN
4990 REM
5000 REM ** Y=F(X) GOES HERE **
5999 RETURN
```

## EASY CHANGES

1. You may want the program to self-scale the Y axis for you. That is, you want it to use the minimum and maximum Y values that it finds as the limits on the Y axis. This can be accomplished by adding the following lines:

   363 IF MX < = MN THEN 370
   365 YU = MX:YL = MN:RETURN

2. Do you sometimes forget to enter the subroutine at line 5000 despite the introductory warning? As is, the program will plot the straight line Y = 0 if you do this. If you want a more drastic reaction to prevent this, change line 5000 to read

   5000 Y = 1/0

   Now, if you don't enter the actual subroutine desired, the program will stop and print the following message after you enter the X scaling values.

   ?/0 ERROR IN 5000

3. The colors used for the axes, function, and off-axis points are controlled by the variables CA, CG, and CS respectively. These are set in line 150. You can change any or all of these colors should you desire. For example, to get blue axes, cyan function, and yellow off-scale points, change line 150 to:

   150 CA = 3:CG = 6:CS = 2

   Consult your manual for the numerical values required to achieve the desired colors.

## MAIN ROUTINES

140- 160 Initializes constants.
200- 210 Displays introductory warning.

## MAIN VARIABLES

| | |
|---|---|
| XL,XM, XU | Lower, middle, upper scale values of X. |
| YL,YM, YU | Lower, middle, upper scale values of Y. |
| DX,DY | Scale increments of X,Y. |
| X,Y | Current values of X,Y. |
| XP,YP | Plot position of X,Y point. |
| A$ | Message string. |
| F | Special plot character flag (1 = Y too low, 2 = Y too high). |
| V | Value of X or Y in scale units. |
| MN,MX | Minimum, maximum values of Y. |
| Q$ | User reply string. |
| J | Loop index. |
| CA | Color code for axes and tick marks. |
| CG | Color code for function. |
| CS | Color code for off-scale points. |

## SUGGESTED PROJECTS

1. Determine and display the values of X at which the minimum values of Y occur.
2. After the graph is plotted, allow the user to obtain the exact value of Y for any given X.

# INTEGRATE

## PURPOSE AND DEFINITION

The need to evaluate integrals occurs frequently in much scientific and mathematical work. This program will numerically integrate a function that you supply using a technique known as Simpson's rule. It will continue to grind out successive approximations of the integral until you are satisfied with the accuracy of the solution.

Mathematical integration will probably be a familiar term to those who have studied some higher mathematics. It is a fundamental subject of second-year calculus. The integral of a function between the limits $x = l$ (lower limit) and $x = u$ (upper limit) represents the area under its curve; i.e. the shaded area in Figure 1.

We may approximate the integral by first dividing up the area into rectangular strips or segments. We can get a good estimate of the total integral by summing the areas of these segments by using a parabolic fit across the top. For those who understand some mathematical theory, Simpson's rule may be expressed as

$$\int_{x=l}^{x=u} f(x)dx \cong \frac{\Delta}{3} \left\{ f(l) + f(u) + 4 \sum_{j=1}^{N/2} f[l + \Delta(2j - 1)] + 2 \sum_{j=1}^{(N-2)/2} f[l + 2\Delta j] \right\}$$

Here N is the number of segments into which the total interval is divided. N is 4 in the diagram.

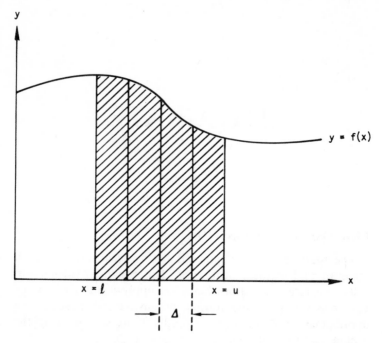

**Figure 1.** The Integral of f(x)

For a good discussion of the numerical evaluation of integrals see: McCracken, Dorn, *Numerical Methods and Fortran Programming*, New York, Wiley, 1964, pp. 160. Don't let the word "Fortran" scare you away. The discussions in the book are independent of programming language with only some program examples written in Fortran.

## HOW TO USE IT

The program begins with a warning! This is to remind you that you should have already entered the subroutine to evaluate Y as a function of X. This subroutine must start at line 7000. More about it shortly.

You will then be asked to provide the lower and upper limits of the integration domain. Any numerical values are acceptable. It is not even necessary that the lower limit of X be smaller than the upper one.

The program will now begin displaying its numerical evaluations of the integral. The number of segments used in the calculation continually doubles. This causes the accuracy of the integral to increase at the expense of additional computation time. For most functions, you should see the value of the integral converging quickly to a constant (or near constant) value. This, of course, will be the best numerical evaluation of the integral at hand.

When you are satisfied with the accuracy of the solution, you must hit the **BREAK** key to terminate the program. If not, the program will run forever (assuming you can pay the electric bills). The amount of computation is approximately doubled each step. This means it will take the computer about the same amount of time to compute the next step that it took to compute *all* the previous steps. Thus, it will soon be taking the Color Computer hours, days, and weeks to compute steps. Eventually, round-off errors begin degrading the results, causing a nice, constant, converged solution to change. However, the high precision of the computer's floating point arithmetic will postpone this for quite a while. You will probably lose patience before seeing it.

The function to be integrated can be as simple or as complicated as you desire. It may take one line or a few hundred lines of code. In any case, the subroutine to express it must start at line 7000. This subroutine will be continually called with the variable X set. When it returns, it should have set the variable Y to the corresponding value of the function for the given X. The subroutine must be able to evaluate the function at any value of X between the lower and upper bounds of the integration domain.

If your function consists of experimental data at discrete values of X, you must do something to enable the subroutine to evaluate the function at intermediate values of X. We recommend one of two approaches. First, you could write the subroutine to linearly interpolate the value of Y between the appropriate values of X. This will involve searching your data table for the pair of experimental X values that bound the value of X where the function is to be evaluated. Secondly, the program CURVE presented elsewhere in this section can produce an approximate polynomial expression to fit your experimental data. This expression can then be easily entered as the subroutine at line 7000.

By the way, Simpson's rule is *exact* for any polynomial of degree 3 or less. This means that if the function can be written in the form

$$Y = A*X*X*X + B*X*X + C*X + D$$

where A, B, C, D are constants, the program will calculate the integral exactly even with only two segments.

## SAMPLE RUN

The sample run illustrates the following integration

$$\int_{x=0}^{x=1} \frac{4}{1+x^2}\, dx$$

This integral has the theoretical value of $\pi$ (pi) as the correct answer! Pi, as you may know, has the value 3.1415926535.... Before the run is started, the above function is entered at line 7000.

```
OK
7000 Y=4/(1+X*X)
RUN
```

The integrand function is entered at line 7000 and RUN is typed to start the program.

```
      INTEGRAL BY SIMPSON'S RULE

      ┌─────────────────────────────────┐
      │            WARNING!             │
      │                                 │
      │    THE SUBROUTINE AT LINES      │
      │                                 │
      │   7000-7999 IS ASSUMED TO       │
      │                                 │
      │  DEFINE Y AS A FUNCTION OF,X    │
      └─────────────────────────────────┘

      LOWER LIMIT OF X? 0
      UPPER LIMIT OF X? 1
```

The upper and lower bounds of the integration are input as requested.

```
   # SEGMENTS            INTEGRAL
   2                     3.13333334
   4                     3.14156863
   8                     3.1415925
   16                    3.14159265
   32                    3.14159266
   64                    3.14159266
   128                   3.14159266
   256                   3.14159266
   512                   3.14159266
   1024                  3.14159266

   BREAK IN 660
   OK
```

The results are computed up to 1024 segments. Then the BREAK key
is pressed to terminate the calculation.

## PROGRAM LISTING

```
100 REM: INTEGRATE
110 REM: (C) 1981, PHIL FELDMAN
150 CLEAR 200
160 N=2
200 CLS
210 C$=CHR$(191)
220 PRINT"  INTEGRAL BY SIMPSON'S RULE"
230 PRINT:GOSUB 400:GOSUB 420
240 PRINT TAB(11);"WARNING!";
250 GOSUB 430:GOSUB 440
260 GOSUB 420
270 PRINT"  THE SUBROUTINE AT";
280 PRINT" LINES";:GOSUB 430
290 GOSUB 440:GOSUB 420
300 PRINT"  7000-7999 IS";
310 PRINT" ASSUMED TO";
320 GOSUB 430:GOSUB 440
330 GOSUB 420:PRINT" DEFINE Y";
340 PRINT" AS A FUNCTION OF X";
350 GOSUB 430:GOSUB 440
360 GOSUB 400:PRINT:GOTO 500
400 FOR J=1 TO 32
410 PRINT C$;:NEXT:RETURN
420 PRINT C$;:RETURN
430 PRINT TAB(31);C$;:RETURN
440 GOSUB 420:GOSUB 430:RETURN
500 INPUT"LOWER LIMIT OF X";L
510 INPUT"UPPER LIMIT OF X";U
550 PRINT
560 PRINT"# SEGMENTS","INTEGRAL"
600 DX=(U-L)/N:T=0
610 X=L:GOSUB 7000:T=T+Y
620 X=U:GOSUB 7000:T=T+Y
650 M=N/2:Z=0
660 FOR J=1 TO M
670 X=L+DX*(2*J-1):GOSUB 7000
680 Z=Z+Y:NEXT:T=T+4*Z
700 M=M-1:IF M=0 THEN 800
710 Z=0:FOR J=1 TO M
720 X=L+DX*2*J:GOSUB 7000:Z=Z+Y
730 NEXT:T=T+2*Z
800 A=DX*T/3
810 PRINT N,A
```

```
820 N=N*2
830 GOTO 600
6960 REM
6970 REM *** ENTER SUBROUTINE
6980 REM *** AT LINE 7000
6990 REM
7000 REM ** Y=F(X) GOES HERE **
7999 RETURN
```

## EASY CHANGES

1.  You might want the program to stop calculation after the integral has been evaluated for a given number of segments. Adding the following line will cause the program to stop after the integral is evaluated for a number of segments greater than or equal to 100.

    **815 IF N > = 100 THEN END**

    Of course, you may use any value you wish instead of 100.

2.  Perhaps you would like to see the number of segments change at a different rate during the course of the calculation. This can be done by modifying line 820. To increase the rate of change, try

    **820 N = N*4**

    to change it at a constant (and slower) rate, try

    **820 N = N + 50**

    Be sure, however, that the value of N is always even.

3.  You can experiment with the border used around the introductory warning by changing the CHR$ argument used in line 210. This might be particularly desirable if you are using a black and white TV. Values from 128-255 will produce various color combinations. Values from 96-127 will produce reverse video characters. To get a pleasing asterisk border, which looks good on a black and white set, try

    **210 C$ = CHR$(42)**

## MAIN ROUTINES

150- 160  Initializes constants.
200- 360  Displays introductory messages and warning.
400- 440  Graphics display subroutines.
500- 510  Gets integration limits from operator.
550- 560  Displays column headings.

600- 620  Computes integral contribution from end points.
650- 680  Adds contribution from one summation.
700- 730  Adds contribution from other summation.
800- 830  Completes integral calculation and displays it. Increases number of segments and restarts calculation.
7000-7999  Operator supplied subroutine to evaluate f(x).

## MAIN VARIABLES

| | |
|---|---|
| N | Number of segments. |
| J | Loop index. |
| L,U | Lower, Upper integration limit of x. |
| DX | Width of one segment. |
| T | Partial result of integral. |
| M | Number of summations. |
| Z | Subtotal of summations. |
| A | Value of integral. |
| X | Current value of x. |
| Y | Current value of the function $y = f(x)$. |
| C$ | String used in messages. |

## SUGGESTED PROJECTS

1. Research other similar techniques for numerical integration such as the simpler trapezoid rule. Then compute the integral with this new method. Compare how the two methods converge toward the (hopefully) correct answer.

# SIMEQN

**PURPOSE**

This program solves a set of simultaneous linear algebraic equations. This type of problem often arises in scientific and numerical work. Algebra students encounter them regularly— many "word" problems can be solved by constructing the proper set of simultaneous equations.

A Color Computer with 4K of memory can handle up to twelve equations in twelve unknowns. This should prove more than sufficient for any practical application. A 16K system can handle many more if, somehow, this should ever be necessary.

The equations to be solved can be written mathematically as follows:

$$A_{11}X_1 + A_{12}X_2 + \ldots + A_{1N}X_N = R_1$$
$$A_{21}X_1 + A_{22}X_2 + \ldots + A_{2N}X_N = R_2$$
$$\cdot \qquad \cdot \qquad \qquad \cdot \qquad \cdot$$
$$\cdot \qquad \cdot \qquad \qquad \cdot \qquad \cdot$$
$$\cdot \qquad \cdot \qquad \qquad \cdot \qquad \cdot$$
$$A_{N1}X_1 + A_{N2}X_2 + \ldots + A_{NN}X_N = R_N$$

N is the number of equations and thus the number of unknowns also. The unknowns are denoted $X_1$ through $X_N$.

Each equation contains a coefficient multiplier for each unknown and a right-hand-side term. These coefficients (the A matrix) and the right-hand-sides ($R_1$ through $R_N$) must be constants—positive, negative, or zero. The A matrix is denoted with doubled subscripts. The first subscript is the equation number and the second one is the unknown that the coefficient multiplies.

## HOW TO USE IT

The program will prompt you for all necessary inputs. First, it asks how many equations (and thus how many unknowns) comprise your set. This number must be at least 1. If it is too large, an OM or BS error will immediately result.

Next, you must enter the coefficients and right-hand-sides for each equation. The program will request these one at a time, continually indicating which term it is expecting next.

Once it has all your inputs, the program begins calculating the solution. This may take a little while if the value of N is high. The program ends by displaying the answers. These, of course, are the values of each of the unknowns, $X_1$ through $X_N$.

If you are interested, the numerical technique used to solve the equations is known as Gaussian elimination. Row interchange to achieve pivotal condensation is employed. (This keeps maximum significance in the numbers.) Then back substitution is used to arrive at the final results. This technique is much simpler than it sounds and is described well in the numerical analysis books referenced in the bibliography.

### SAMPLE PROBLEM AND RUN

*Problem*: A painter has a large supply of three different colors of paint: dark green, light green, and pure blue. The dark green is 30% blue pigment, 20% yellow pigment, and the rest base. The light green is 10% blue pigment, 35% yellow pigment, and the rest base. The pure blue is 90% blue pigment, no yellow pigment, and the rest base. The painter, however, needs a medium green to be composed of 25% blue pigment, 25% yellow pigment, and the rest base. In what percentages should he mix his three paints to achieve this mixture?

*Solution*: Let $X_1 =$ percent of dark green to use,
$X_2 =$ percent of light green to use,
$X_3 =$ percent of pure blue to use.

The problem leads to these three simultaneous equations to solve:

$$0.3\,X_1 + 0.1\ \ X_2 + 0.9\,X_3 = 0.25$$
$$0.2\,X_1 + 0.35\,X_2 \qquad\quad = 0.25$$
$$X_1 + \qquad X_2 + \qquad X_3 = 1.0$$

The first equation expresses the amount of blue pigment in the mixture. The second equation is for the yellow pigment. The third equation states that the mixture is composed entirely of the three given paints. (Note that all percentages are expressed as numbers from 0-1.) The problem leads to the following use of SIMEQN.

**SAMPLE RUN**

```
     A SIMULTANEOUS LINEAR EQUATION
               SOLVER

  NUMBER OF EQUATIONS? 3

  THE 3 UNKNOWNS WILL BE DENOTED
  X1 THROUGH X3
  _____

  ENTER VALUES FOR EQUATION 1

  COEFFICIENT OF X1? .3
  COEFFICIENT OF X2? .1
  COEFFICIENT OF X3? .9
  RIGHT HAND SIDE? .25
```

The operator chooses to solve a set of three simultaneous equations and then enters the coefficients for the first equation.

```
------------------------------------
ENTER VALUES FOR EQUATION 2

COEFFICIENT OF X1? .2
COEFFICIENT OF X2? .35
COEFFICIENT OF X3? 0
RIGHT HAND SIDE? .25

------------------------------------
ENTER VALUES FOR EQUATION 3

COEFFICIENT OF X1? 1
COEFFICIENT OF X2? 1
COEFFICIENT OF X3? 1
RIGHT HAND SIDE? 1
```

The coefficients for the remaining two equations are entered.

```
------------------------------------
ENTER VALUES FOR EQUATION 3

COEFFICIENT OF X1? 1
COEFFICIENT OF X2? 1
COEFFICIENT OF X3? 1
RIGHT HAND SIDE? 1

------------------------------------
THE SOLUTION IS

   X1= .55
   X2= .4
   X3= .05
OK
```

The computer provides the solution. The painter should use a mixture
of 55% dark green, 40% light green, and 5% pure blue.

## PROGRAM LISTING

```
100 REM: SIMEQN
110 REM: (C) 1981, PHIL FELDMAN AND TOM
    RUGG
150 CLEAR 100
200 CLS
210 PRINT@1,"A SIMULTANEOUS"
220 PRINT@16,"LINEAR EQUATION"
230 PRINT@45,"SOLVER"
240 PRINT
250 INPUT"NUMBER OF EQUATIONS";N
260 IF N>0 THEN 400
270 PRINT:PRINT"** ERROR! **
280 PRINT"THERE MUST BE AT ";
290 PRINT"LEAST 1":GOSUB 6000
300 GOTO 240
400 DIM A(N,N),R(N),V(N)
410 PRINT
420 PRINT"THE";N;"UNKNOWNS";
430 PRINT" WILL BE DENOTED"
440 PRINT"X1 THROUGH X";
450 PRINT MID$(STR$(N),2)
460 GOSUB 900:FOR J=1 TO N
470 PRINT"ENTER VALUES FOR";
480 PRINT" EQUATION";J
490 PRINT:FOR K=1 TO N
500 PRINT"COEFFICIENT OF X";
510 PRINT MID$(STR$(K),2);
520 INPUT A(J,K):NEXT
530 INPUT"RIGHT HAND SIDE";R(J)
540 GOSUB 900:NEXT
550 GOSUB 2000
600 PRINT"THE SOLUTION IS"
610 PRINT:FOR J=1 TO N
620 PRINT"  X";MID$(STR$(J),2);
630 PRINT"=";V(J)
640 NEXT:END
900 PRINT:FOR L=1 TO 31
910 PRINT"-";:NEXT:PRINT:RETURN
2000 IF N>1 THEN 2020
2010 V(1)=R(1)/A(1,1):RETURN
2020 FOR K=1 TO N-1:I=K+1
2030 L=K
2040 Q=ABS(A(I,K))-ABS(A(L,K))
```

```
2050 IF Q>0 THEN L=I
2060 IF I<N THEN I=I+1:GOTO 2040
2070 IF L=K THEN 2110
2080 FOR J=K TO N:Q=A(K,J)
2090 A(K,J)=A(L,J):A(L,J)=Q:NEXT
2100 Q=R(K):R(K)=R(L):R(L)=Q
2110 I=K+1
2120 Q=A(I,K)/A(K,K):A(I,K)=0
2130 FOR J=K+1 TO N
2140 A(I,J)=A(I,J)-Q*A(K,J):NEXT
2150 R(I)=R(I)-Q*R(K)
2160 IF I<N THEN I=I+1:GOTO 2120
2170 NEXT
2180 V(N)=R(N)/A(N,N)
2190 FOR I=N-1 TO 1 STEP -1
2200 Q=0:FOR J=I+1 TO N
2210 Q=Q+A(I,J)*V(J)
2220 V(I)=(R(I)-Q)/A(I,I):NEXT
2230 NEXT:RETURN
6000 SOUND 8,8:RETURN
```

## EASY CHANGES

You may be surprised sometime to see the program fail completely and display this message:

### ?/0 ERROR IN 2180

This means your input coefficients (the A array) were ill-conditioned and no solution was possible. This can arise from a variety of causes; e.g. if one equation is an exact multiple of another, or if *every* coefficient of one particular unknown is zero. If you would like the program to print a diagnostic message in these cases add these lines.

```
2172 IF A(N,N)< >0 THEN 2180
2174 PRINT "BAD INPUT – ";
2176 PRINT "NO SOLUTION POSSIBLE"
2178 GOSUB 6000: STOP
```

## MAIN ROUTINES

200- 240 Clears screen and displays program title.
250- 550 Gets input from user and calculates the solution.
600- 640 Displays the solution.
900- 910 Subroutine to space and separate the output.

2000-2230  Subroutine to calculate the solution; consisting of
           the following parts:
2000-2010  Forms solution if N = 1.
2020-2170  Gaussian elimination.
2030-2110  Interchanges rows to achieve pivotal condensation.
2180-2230  Back substitution.
6000       Sound generation subroutine.

## MAIN VARIABLES

I,J,K,L   Loop indices and subscripts.
N         Number of equations (thus number of unknowns
          also).
A         Doubly dimensioned array of the coefficients.
R         Array of right-hand-sides.
V         Array of the solution.
Q         Work variable.

## SUGGESTED PROJECTS

1. The program modifies the A and R arrays while computing
   the answer. This means the original input cannot be displayed after it is input. Modify the program to save the information and enable the user to retrieve it after the solution
   is given.

2. Currently, a mistake in typing input cannot be corrected
   once the **ENTER** key is pressed after typing a number.
   Modify the program to allow correcting previous input.

# STATS

## PURPOSE

Ever think of yourself as a statistic? Many times we lament at how we have become just numbers in various computer memories, or we simply moan at our insurance premiums. To most people, the word "statistics" carries a negative connotation. To invoke statistics is almost to be deceitful, or at least dehumanizing. But really, we all use statistical ideas regularly. When we speak of things like "she was average height" or the "hottest weather in years," we are making observations in statistical terms. It is difficult not to encounter statistics in our lives, and this book is no exception.

Of course, when used properly, statistics can be a powerful, analytical tool. STATS analyzes a set of numerical data that you provide. It will compile your list, order it sequentially, and/or determine several statistical parameters which describe it.

This should prove useful in a wide variety of applications. Teachers might determine grades by analyzing a set of test scores. A businessman might determine marketing strategy by studying a list of sales to clients. Little leaguers always like to pore over the current batting and pitching averages. You can probably think of many other applications.

## HOW TO USE IT

First, your data list must be entered. The program will prompt you for each value with a question mark. Two special inputs, *END and *BACK, may be used at any time during this data input phase. To signal the end of data, input the four character string, *END, in response to the (last) question mark. You must, of course, enter at least one data value.

If you discover that you have made a mistake, the five character string, *BACK, can be used to back up the input process. This will cause the program to re-prompt you for the previous entry. By successive uses of *BACK you can return to any previous position.

With the input completed, the program enters a command mode. You have four options to continue the run:

1) List the data in the order input
2) List the data in ranking order
3) Display statistical parameters
4) End the program

Simply input the number 1, 2, 3, or 4 to indicate your choice. If one of the first three is selected, the program will perform the selected function and return to this command mode to allow another choice. This will continue until you choose 4 to terminate the run. A description of the various options now follows.

Options 1 and 2 provide lists of the data. Option 1 does it in the original input order while option 2 sorts the data from highest value to lowest.

The lists are started by hitting any key when told to do so. Either list may be temporarily halted by hitting any key while the list is being displayed. This allows you to leisurely view data that might otherwise start scrolling off the screen. Simply hit any key to resume the display. This starting and stopping can be repeated as often as desired. When the display is completed, you must again hit a key to re-enter the command mode.

Option 3 produces a statistical analysis of your data. Various statistical parameters are calculated and displayed. The following is an explanation of some that may not be familiar to you.

Three measures of location, or central tendency, are provided. These are indicators of an "average" value. The *mean* is the sum of the values divided by the number of values. If the values are arranged in order from highest to lowest, the *median* is the middle value if the number of values is odd. If it is even, the median is the number halfway between the two middle values. The *midrange* is the number halfway between the largest and smallest values.

These measures of location give information about the average value of the data. However, they give no idea of how the data is dispersed or spread out around this "average." For that we need "measures of dispersion" or as they are sometimes called, "measures of variation." The simplest of these is the *range* which is just the difference between the highest and lowest data values. Two other closely related measures of dispersion are given: the *variance* and the *standard deviation*. The variance is defined as:

$$VA = \frac{\sum_{i=1}^{N} (V_i - M)^2}{N-1}$$

Here N is the number of values, $V_i$ is value i, M is the mean value. The standard deviation is simply the square root of the variance. We do not have space to detail a lengthy discussion of their theoretical use. For this refer to the bibliography. Basically, however, the smaller the standard deviation, the more all the data tends to be clustered close to the mean value.

One word of warning — the first time option 2 or 3 is selected, the program must take some time to sort the data into numerical order. The time this requires depends upon how many items are on the list and how badly they are out of sequence. Average times are fifteen seconds for twenty-five items, about one minute for fifty items, about four minutes for a hundred items. The Color Computer will pause while this is occurring, so don't think it has hung up or fallen asleep! If you have several items on your list, this is the perfect chance to rob your refrigerator, make a quick phone call, or whatever.

**SAMPLE RUN**

```
                  S T A T S

    ENTER A DATA VALUE AFTER EACH
QUESTION MARK.

    IF YOU MAKE A MISTAKE, TYPE
*BACK  TO RE-ENTER THE LAST
DATUM.

    WHEN THE LIST IS ENTERED, TYPE
*END   TO TERMINATE THE INPUT.

VALUE # 1 ?
```

The program prompts the operator to begin entering the input data values.

```
        WHEN THE LIST IS ENTERED, TYPE
    *END   TO TERMINATE THE INPUT.

    VALUE # 1 ? 98
    VALUE # 2 ? 76
    VALUE # 3 ? 81.5
    VALUE # 4 ? 97.5
    VALUE # 5 ? 69
    VALUE # 6 ? *END

    CONTINUATION OPTIONS
      1) LIST DATA IN ORIGINAL ORDER
      2) LIST DATA IN RANKING ORDER
      3) DISPLAY STATS
      4) END PROGRAM
    WHAT NEXT? 2
```

The operator completes entering the scores of those who took a programming aptitude test. The actual test was given to many people, but for demonstration purposes, only five scores are used here. The special string, *END, is used to signal the end of the data. The operator then requests that the list be sorted into numerical order.

```
        WHILE THE LIST IS DISPLAYING,
    YOU CAN HIT ANY KEY TO CAUSE A
    TEMPORARY HALT. THE DISPLAY WILL
    RESUME WHEN YOU HIT ANOTHER KEY.

    HIT ANY KEY TO START

        #                VALUE
        1                98
        2                97.5
        3                81.5
        4                76
        5                69

    HIT ANY KEY TO CONTINUE
```

The operator hits a key to start the display and is then shown the data list in ranking order. The program waits for the pressing of a key to continue.

```
    NUMBER OF VALUES= 5
     5 POSITIVE, 0 NEGATIVE, 0 ZERO
    MIN VALUE= 69
    MAX VALUE= 98
    RANGE= 29
    SUM OF VALUES= 422

    MEAN= 84.4
    MEDIAN= 81.5
    MID-RANGE= 83.5

    STD. DEVIATION= 12.9682304
    VARIANCE= 168.174999

    HIT ANY KEY TO CONTINUE
```

Later in the run, the operator selects continuation option 3. This calculates and displays the various statistical quantities.

## PROGRAM LISTING

```
100 REM: STATS - 16K
110 REM: (C) 1981, PHIL FELDMAN AND TOM
    RUGG
140 CLEAR 50
150 B$="*BACK":E$="*END"
160 MX=100
170 DIM V(MX),Z(MX)
180 Z(0)=0
200 CLS:PRINT@12,"S T A T S"
210 PRINT:PRINT"  ENTER A DATA";
220 PRINT" VALUE AFTER EACH";
230 PRINT" QUESTION MARK."
240 PRINT:PRINT"  IF YOU MAKE";
250 PRINT" A MISTAKE, TYPE"
260 PRINT B$;"  TO RE-ENTER";
270 PRINT" THE LAST"
280 PRINT"DATUM.":PRINT
290 PRINT"  WHEN THE LIST IS";
300 PRINT" ENTERED, TYPE";
310 PRINT E$;"  TO TERMINATE";
320 PRINT" THE INPUT.":PRINT
500 N=1
510 IF N<1 THEN N=1
520 PRINT"VALUE #";N;
530 INPUT R$:IF R$=E$ THEN 700
540 IF R$=B$ THEN N=N-1:GOTO 510
550 V(N)=VAL(R$)
560 IF N=MX THEN PRINT ELSE 600
570 PRINT"* NO MORE DATA";
580 PRINT" ALLOWED! *":N=N+1
590 GOSUB 3000:GOTO 700
600 N=N+1:GOTO 510
700 N=N-1
710 IF N=0 THEN PRINT ELSE 800
720 PRINT"* NO DATA - RUN";
730 PRINT" ABORTED *"
740 GOSUB 3000:END
800 PRINT
810 PRINT"CONTINUATION OPTIONS"
820 PRINT" 1) LIST DATA IN";
830 PRINT" ORIGINAL ORDER"
840 PRINT" 2) LIST DATA IN";
850 PRINT" RANKING ORDER"
```

```
860 PRINT" 3) DISPLAY STATS"
870 PRINT" 4) END PROGRAM"
880 INPUT"WHAT NEXT";R$
890 R=INT(VAL(R$))
900 IF R<1 OR R>4 THEN 800
910 IF R=4 THEN END
920 ON R GOSUB 1000,1200,1500
930 GOTO 800
1000 CLS:PRINT"THE ORIGINAL";
1010 PRINT" DATA ORDER":PRINT
1020 PRINT N;"TOTAL ENTRIES"
1030 PRINT:GOSUB 2000:PRINT
1040 PRINT" #","VALUE"
1050 FOR J=1 TO N:FOR K=1 TO 100
1060 NEXT:PRINT J,V(J)
1070 GOSUB 2500:NEXT:GOSUB 2900
1080 RETURN
1200 CLS:PRINT"THE DATA IN";
1210 PRINT" RANKING ORDER":PRINT
1220 PRINT N;"TOTAL ENTRIES"
1230 PRINT:GOSUB 2700:GOSUB 2000
1240 PRINT:PRINT" #","VALUE"
1250 FOR J=1 TO N:FOR K=1 TO 100
1260 NEXT:PRINT J,V(Z(J))
1270 GOSUB 2500:NEXT:GOSUB 2900
1280 RETURN
1500 CLS:NP=0:NN=0:NZ=0:SQ=0:W=0
1510 PRINT"STATISTICAL ANALYSIS"
1520 PRINT
1530 PRINT"NUMBER OF VALUES=";N
1540 FOR J=1 TO N:W=W+V(J)
1550 SQ=SQ+V(J)*V(J)
1560 IF V(J)>0 THEN NP=NP+1
1570 IF V(J)<0 THEN NN=NN+1
1580 IF V(J)=0 THEN NZ=NZ+1
1590 NEXT:M=W/N:VA=0
1600 IF N=1 THEN 1620
1610 VA=(SQ-N*M*M)/(N-1)
1620 SD=VA/3:IF VA=0 THEN 1650
1630 FOR J=1 TO 65
1640 SD=(SD+VA/SD)/2:NEXT
1650 PRINT NP;"POSITIVE,";
1660 PRINT NN;"NEGATIVE,";
1670 PRINT NZ;"ZERO"
1680 GOSUB 2700
```

```
1690 PRINT"MIN VALUE=";V(Z(N))
1700 PRINT"MAX VALUE=";V(Z(1))
1710 Q=V(Z(1))-V(Z(N))
1720 PRINT"RANGE=";Q
1730 PRINT"SUM OF VALUES=";W
1740 PRINT:PRINT"MEAN=";M
1750 Q=INT(N/2)+1:MD=V(Z(Q))
1760 IF N/2>INT(N/2) THEN 1780
1770 MD=(V(Z(Q))+V(Z(Q-1)))/2
1780 PRINT"MEDIAN=";MD
1790 Q=(V(Z(1))+V(Z(N)))/2
1800 PRINT"MID-RANGE=";Q:PRINT
1810 PRINT"STD. DEVIATION=";SD
1820 PRINT"VARIANCE=";VA
1830 GOSUB 2900:RETURN
2000 PRINT"  WHILE THE LIST IS";
2010 PRINT" DISPLAYING,"
2020 PRINT"YOU CAN HIT ANY KEY";
2030 PRINT" TO CAUSE A"
2040 PRINT"TEMPORARY HALT. THE";
2050 PRINT" DISPLAY WILL";
2060 PRINT"RESUME WHEN YOU HIT";
2070 PRINT" ANOTHER KEY.";:PRINT
2080 PRINT"HIT ANY KEY TO START"
2090 R$=INKEY$
2100 IF R$="" THEN 2090
2110 RETURN
2500 R$=INKEY$
2510 IF R$="" THEN RETURN
2520 R$=INKEY$
2530 IF R$="" THEN 2520
2540 RETURN
2700 IF Z(0)=1 THEN RETURN
2710 FOR J=1 TO N:Z(J)=J:NEXT
2720 IF N=1 THEN RETURN
2730 NM=N-1:FOR K=1 TO N
2740 FOR J=1 TO NM:N1=Z(J)
2750 N2=Z(J+1)
2760 IF V(N1)>V(N2) THEN 2780
2770 Z(J+1)=N1:Z(J)=N2
2780 NEXT:NEXT:Z(0)=1:RETURN
2900 PRINT
2910 PRINT"HIT ANY KEY";
2920 PRINT" TO CONTINUE";
```

```
2930 R$=INKEY$
2940 IF R$="" THEN 2930
2950 PRINT:RETURN
3000 SOUND 8,8:RETURN
```

## EASY CHANGES

1. The program arrays are currently dimensioned to allow a maximum of 100 data items. A 16K TRS-80 Color Computer, which is required to run this program, has enough storage for over 1000 data items. To achieve up to 1000 data items, make this change:

$$160 \text{ MX} = 1000$$

2. You may wish to change the special strings that signal termination of data input and/or the backing up of data input. These are controlled by the variables E$ and B$, respectively. They are set in line 150. If you wish to terminate the data with /DONE/ and to back up with /LAST/ for example, line 150 should be:

$$150 \text{ B\$} = \text{"/LAST/"}:\text{E\$} = \text{"/DONE/"}$$

3. You may wish to see your lists sorted from smallest value to largest value instead of the other way around, as done now. This can be accomplished by changing the "greater than" sign ($>$) in line 2760 to a "less than" sign ($<$). Thus:

$$2760 \text{ IF } V(N1) < V(N2) \text{ THEN } 2780$$

This will, however, cause a few funny things to happen to the statistics. The real minimum value will be displayed under the heading "maximum" and vice-versa. Also, the range will have its correct magnitude but with an erroneous minus sign in front. To cure these afflictions, make these changes also:

$$1690 \text{ PRINT "MIN VALUE} = \text{";}V(Z(1))$$
$$1700 \text{ PRINT "MAX VALUE} = \text{";}V(Z(N))$$
$$1710 \text{ Q} = V(Z(N)) - V(Z(1))$$

## MAIN ROUTINES

140- 180 Initializes constants and dimensioning.
200- 320 Displays messages.
500- 600 Gets data from the user.
700- 740 Checks that input contains at least one value.

 800- 930  Command mode—gets user's next option and does a GOSUB to it.
1000-1080  Subroutine to list data in the original order.
1200-1280  Subroutine to list data in ranking order.
1500-1830  Subroutine to calculate and display statistics.
2000-2110  Subroutine to display various messages.
2500-2540  Subroutine to allow user to temporarily start and stop display listing.
2700-2780  Subroutine to sort the list in ranking order.
2900-2950  Subroutine to detect if user has hit a key to continue.
3000       Sound generating subroutine.

## MAIN VARIABLES

| | |
|---|---|
| MX | Maximum number of data values allowed. |
| V(MX) | Array of the data values. |
| Z(MX) | Array of the sorting order. |
| N | Number of data values in current application. |
| B$ | Flag string to back up the input. |
| E$ | Flag string to signal end of the input. |
| R$ | User input string. |
| NM | $N-1$. |
| R | Continuation option. |
| NP | Number of positive values. |
| NN | Number of negative values. |
| NZ | Number of zero values. |
| W | Sum of the values. |
| SQ | Sum of the squares of the values. |
| M | Mean value. |
| MD | Median of the values. |
| VA | Variance. |
| SD | Standard deviation. |
| J,K | Loop indices. |
| N1,N2 | Possible data locations to interchange during sorting. |
| Q | Work variable. |

## SUGGESTED PROJECTS

1. The sorting algorithm used in the program is efficient only when the number of list items is fairly small—less than

twenty-five or so. This is because it does not do checking along the way to see when the list becomes fully sorted. If your lists tend to be longer than twenty-five items, you might wish to use another sorting algorithm more appropriate for longer lists. Try researching other sorts and incorporating them into the program. To get you started, try these changes:

```
2730  Q = 0: FOR J = 1 TO N - 1:N1 = Z(J)
2740  N2 = Z(J + 1)
2750  IF V(N1) > = V(N2) THEN 2780
2760  Z(J + 1) = N1:Z(J) = N2
2770  Q = 1
2780  NEXT:IF Q = 1 THEN 2730
2790  Z(0) = 1:RETURN
```

If your lists are short, this routine will probably be a little slower than the current one. However, for longer lists it will save proportionately more and more time.

2.  Many other statistical parameters exist to describe this kind of data. Research them and add some that might be useful to you. One such idea is classifying the data. This consists of dividing the range into a number of equal classes and then counting how many values fall into each class.

# Section 6

# Miscellaneous Programs

## INTRODUCTION TO MISCELLANEOUS PROGRAMS

These programs show how simple programs can do interesting things. Most of them have a mathematical flavor. They are short and, as such, would be useful for study for those just learning BASIC in particular or programming in general.

Monte Carlo simulation involves programming the computer to conduct an experiment. (It doesn't involve high-stakes gambling!) PI shows how this technique can be used to calculate an approximation to the famous mathematical constant pi.

PYTHAG will find all right triangles with integral side lengths. A clever algorithm is utilized to do this.

Have you ever looked around your classroom or club meeting and wondered if any two people had the same birthdate? BIRTHDAY will show you what the surprising odds are.

Very high precision arithmetic can be done on the Color Computer with the proper "know-how." POWERS will calculate the values of integers raised to various powers; not to the computer's standard nine digit precision, but up to 250 full digits of precision.

Your computer can play music! TUNE allows you to enter tunes into your computer in a simple, convenient manner. Then your computer will play them for you.

# BIRTHDAY

## PURPOSE

Suppose you are in a room full of people. What is the probability that two or more of these people have the same birthday? How many people have to be in the room before the probability becomes greater than 50 percent? We are talking only about the month and day of birth, not the year.

This is a fairly simple problem to solve, even without a computer. With a computer to help with the calculations, it becomes very easy. What makes the problem interesting is that the correct answer is nowhere near what most people immediately guess. Before reading further, what do you think? How many people have to be in the room before there is better than a 50-50 chance of birthday duplication? 50? 100? 200?

## HOW TO USE IT

When you RUN the program, it starts by displaying headings over two columns of numbers that will be shown. The left column is the number of people in the room, starting with one. The right column is the probability of birthday duplication.

For one person, of course, the probability is zero, since there is no one else with a possible duplicate birthday. For two people, the probability is simply the decimal equivalent of $\frac{1}{365}$ (note that we assume a 365 day year, and an equal likelihood that each person could have been born on any day of the year).

What is the probability of duplication when there are three people in the room? No, not just $\frac{2}{365}$. It's actually

$$1 - (\tfrac{364}{365} \text{ times } \tfrac{363}{365})$$

This is simply one minus the probability of *no* duplicate birthdays.

The probability for four people is

$$1 - (\tfrac{364}{365} \text{ times } \tfrac{363}{365} \text{ times } \tfrac{362}{365})$$

The calculation continues like this, adding a new term for each additional person in the room. You will find that the result (probability of duplication) exceeds .50 surprisingly fast.

The program continues with the calculation until there are 60 people in the room. You will have to **BREAK** the program long before that to see the point where the probability first exceeds 50 percent. You can also press the "at sign" key while holding **SHIFT** down to make the computer pause.

## SAMPLE RUN

```
NO. OF          PROB. OF 2 OR MORE
PEOPLE          WITH SAME BIRTHDAY
  1             0
  2             2.7397261E-03
  3             8.20416585E-03
  4             .0163559124
  5             .0271355736
  6             .0404624834
  .
  .
  .
(etc.)
```

## PROGRAM LISTING

```
100 REM: BIRTHDAY
110 REM: (C) 1981, TOM RUGG AND PHIL
    FELDMAN
120 CLEAR 200:CLS
130 PRINT"NO. OF     PROB. OF 2 OR MORE"
140 PRINT"PEOPLE     WITH SAME BIRTHDAY"
150 Q=1
160 FOR N=1 TO 60
170 PRINT N;TAB(12);1-Q
180 Q=Q*(365-N)/365
190 NEXT N
200 END
```

## EASY CHANGES

Change the constant value of 60 at the end of line 160 to alter the range of the number of people in the calculation. For example, change it to 100 and watch how fast the probability approaches 1.

## MAIN ROUTINES

120-140   Displays headings.
150       Initializes Q to 1.
160-190   Calculates probability of no duplication, then displays probability of duplication.

## MAIN VARIABLES

N         Number of people in the room.
Q         Probability of no duplication of birthdays.

## SUGGESTED PROJECTS

Modify the program to allow for leap years in the calculation, instead of assuming 365 days per year.

# PI

## PURPOSE AND DISCUSSION

The Greek letter pi, $\pi$, represents probably the most famous constant in mathematical history. It occurs regularly in many different areas of mathematics. It is best known as the constant appearing in several geometric relationships involving the circle. The circumference of a circle of radius r is $2\pi r$, while the area enclosed by the circle is $\pi r^2$.

Being a transcendental number, pi cannot be expressed exactly by any number of decimal digits. To nine significant digits, its value is 3.14159265. Over many centuries, man has devised many different methods to calculate pi.

This program uses a valuable, modern technique known as computer simulation. The name "simulation" is rather self-explanatory; the computer performs an experiment for us. This is often desirable for many different reasons. The experiment may be cheaper, less dangerous, or more accurate to run on a computer. It may even be impossible to do in "real life." Usually, however, the reason is that the speed of the computer allows the simulation to be performed many times faster than actually conducting the real experiment.

This program simulates the results of throwing darts at a specially constructed dartboard. Consider Figure 1 which shows the peculiar square dartboard involved. The curved arc, outlining the shaded area, is that of a circle with the center in the lower left hand corner. The sides of the square, and thus the radius of the circle, are considered to have a length of 1.

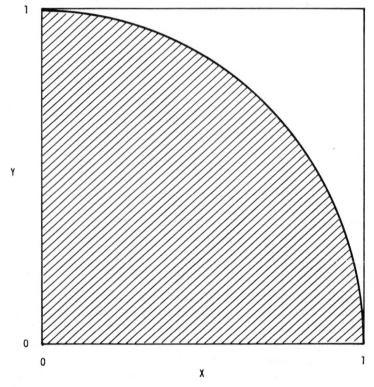

**Figure 1.** The PI Dartboard

Suppose we were able to throw darts at this square target in such a way that each dart had an equal chance of landing anywhere within the square. A certain percentage of darts would result in "hits," i.e. land in the shaded area. The expected value of this percentage is simply the area of the shaded part divided by the area of the entire square.

The area of the shaded part is one fourth of the area the entire circle would enclose if the arc were continued to completely form the circle. Recall the area of a circle is $\pi r^2$ where r is the radius. In our case, $r = 1$, and the area of the entire circle would simply be $\pi$. The shaded area of the dartboard is one fourth of this entire circle and thus has an area of $\pi/4$. The area of the square is $s^2$, where s is the length of a side. On our dartboard, $s = 1$, and the area of the whole dartboard is 1.

Now the expected ratio of "hits" to darts thrown can be expressed

$$\text{RATIO} = \frac{\text{\# hits}}{\text{\# thrown}} = \frac{\text{shaded area}}{\text{entire area}} = \frac{\pi/4}{1} = \frac{\pi}{4}$$

So we now have an experimental way to approximate the value of $\pi$. We perform the experiment and compute the ratio of "hits" observed. We then multiply this number by 4 and we have calculated $\pi$ experimentally.

But instead of actually constructing the required dartboard and throwing real darts, we will let the Color Computer do the job. The program "throws" each dart by selecting a separate random number between 0 and 1 for the X and Y coordinates of each dart. This is accomplished by using the built-in RND function of Basic. A "dart" is in the shaded area if $X^2 + Y^2 < 1$ for it.

So the program grinds away, continually throwing darts and determining the ratio of "hits." This ratio is multiplied by 4 to arrive at an empirical approximation to $\pi$.

**HOW TO USE IT**

The program requires only one input from you. This is the "sample size for printing," i.e. how many darts it should throw before printing its current results. Any value of one or higher is acceptable.

After you input this number, the program will commence the simulation and display its results. A cumulative total of "hits," darts thrown, and the current approximation to $\pi$ will be displayed for each multiple of the sample size.

This will continue until you press the **BREAK** key. When you are satisfied with the total number of darts thrown, press the **BREAK** key to terminate the program execution.

**SAMPLE RUN**

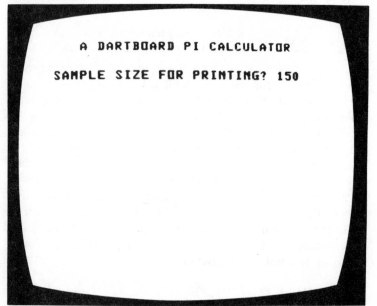

The operator selects 150 for the printing sample size.

```
         A DARTBOARD PI CALCULATOR

    ♦ HITS    ♦ THROWN       PI
      118       150      3.14666667
      241       300      3.21333333
      356       450      3.16444445
      472       600      3.14666667
      594       750      3.168
      717       900      3.18666667
      833      1050      3.17333333
      945      1200      3.15
     1057      1350      3.13185185

  BREAK IN 520
  OK
```

After 1350 darts are "thrown," the BREAK key is pressed to terminate the run.

## PROGRAM LISTING

```
100 REM: PI
110 REM: (C) 1981, PHIL FELDMAN AND TOM
    RUGG
140 CLEAR 200
160 T=0:TH=0
300 GOSUB 600
310 PRINT"SAMPLE SIZE FOR PRINTING? ";
320 Q=Q+1:A$=INKEY$
330 IF A$="" THEN 320
340 IF ASC(A$)=13 THEN 360
350 PRINT A$;:R$=R$+A$:GOTO 320
360 PRINT:NP=VAL(R$):NP=INT(NP)
370 IF NP<1 THEN 300
380 Q=RND(-Q):GOSUB 600
390 PRINT"# HITS";TAB(9);
400 PRINT"# THROWN";TAB(23);
410 PRINT"PI"
420 GOSUB 500:TH=TH+NH:T=T+NP
430 P=4*TH/T
440 PRINT TAB(1);TH;TAB(10);T;
450 PRINT TAB(19);P
460 GOTO 420
500 NH=0:FOR J=1 TO NP
510 X=RND(0):Y=RND(0)
520 IF (X*X+Y*Y)<1 THEN NH=NH+1
530 NEXT:RETURN
600 CLS:PRINT TAB(3);
610 PRINT"A DARTBOARD PI CALCULATOR"
620 PRINT:RETURN
```

## EASY CHANGES

1. If you want the program to always use a fixed sample size, change line 310 to read

   310 NP = 150:GOTO 370

   Of course, the value of 150 given here may be changed to whatever you wish.

2. If you want the program to stop by itself after a certain number of darts have been thrown, add the following two lines:

   375 INPUT"TOTAL # DARTS TO THROW";ND
   455 IF T> =ND THEN END

This will ask the operator how many total darts should be thrown, and then terminate the program when they have been thrown.

## MAIN ROUTINES

| | |
|---|---|
| 140-160 | Initializes constants. |
| 300-410 | Gets operator input, displays column headings. |
| 420-460 | Calculates and displays results. |
| 500-530 | Throws NP darts and records number of "hits." |
| 600-620 | Clears screen and displays program title. |

## MAIN VARIABLES

| | |
|---|---|
| T | Total darts thrown. |
| TH | Total "hits." |
| NP | Sample size for printing. |
| NH | Number of hits in one group of NP darts. |
| P | Calculated value of pi. |
| A$,R$ | Temporary string variables. |
| Q | Work variable. |
| X,Y | Random-valued coordinates of a dart. |
| J | Loop index. |

## SUGGESTED PROJECTS

1. Calculate the percentage error in the program's calculation of pi and display it with the other results. You will need to define a variable, say PI, which is set to the value of pi. Then the percentage error, PE, can be calculated as:

$$PE = 100*ABS(P - PI)/PI$$

2. The accuracy of this simulation is highly dependent on the quality of the computer's random number generator. Try researching different algorithms for pseudo random number generation. Then try incorporating them into the program. Change line 510 to use the new algorithm(s). This can actually be used as a test of the various random number generators. Gruenberger's book, referenced in the bibliography, contains good material on various pseudo random number generators.

# POWERS

## PURPOSE

By now you have probably learned that the Color Computer keeps track of nine significant digits when dealing with numbers. For integers less than one billion (1,000,000,000), the Color Computer can retain the precise value of the number. But for larger integers the Color Computer only keeps track of the most significant (leftmost) nine digits, plus the exponent. This means, of course, that there is no way you can use the computer to deal with precise integers greater than one billion, right?

Wrong.

This program calculates either factorials or successive powers of an integer, and can display precise results that are up to 250 digits long. By using a "multiple-precision arithmetic" technique, this program can tell you *exactly* what 973 to the 47th power is, for example.

## HOW TO USE IT

The program first asks you how many digits long you want the largest number to be. This can be any integer from 1 to 250. So, for example, if you enter 40, you will get answers up to forty digits long.

Next you are asked for the value of N. If you respond with a value of 1, you are requesting to be shown all the factorials that will fit in the number of digits you specified. First you will get one factorial, then two factorial, and so on. In case you have

forgotten, three factorial is 3 times 2 times 1, or 6. Four factorial is 4 times 3 times 2 times 1, or 24.

If you enter an N in the range from 2 through 100,000, you
are requesting the successive powers of that number up to the
limit of digits you specified. So, if you provide an N of 23, you
will get 23 to the first power, then 23 squared, then 23 cubed,
and so on.

Finally, after it has displayed the largest number that will fit
within the number of digits you entered, the program starts
over. The larger the number of digits you ask for, the longer it
will take the program to calculate each number. If you enter
zero, the program ends.

**SAMPLE RUN**

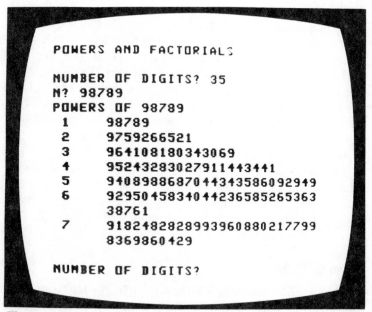

```
POWERS AND FACTORIALS

NUMBER OF DIGITS? 35
N? 98789
POWERS OF 98789
  1     98789
  2     9759266521
  3     964108180343069
  4     95243283027911443441
  5     9408988687044343586092949
  6     9295045834044236585265363
        38761
  7     9182482828993960880217799
        8369860429

NUMBER OF DIGITS?
```

The operator wants answers up to 35 digits long in the calculations of
the powers of 98789. The program calculates numbers up to $98789^7$
and then asks for the number of digits again (in preparation for the
next calculation the operator requests).

## PROGRAM LISTING

```
100 REM: POWERS
110 REM: (C) 1981, TOM RUGG AND PHIL
    FELDMAN
120 CLS:CLEAR 50
130 PRINT"POWERS AND FACTORIALS"
140 PRINT
150 L=250
160 DIM N(L+5)
170 INPUT"NUMBER OF DIGITS";M
180 M=INT(M):IF M>L THEN 170
185 IF M<1 THEN END
190 INPUT"N";N
200 N=INT(N)
210 IF N<1 OR N>100000 THEN 190
220 F=0:IF N=1 THEN F=1
230 IF F=1 THEN PRINT"FACTORIALS"
240 IF F=0 THEN PRINT"POWERS OF";N
250 T=10:K=1:N(0)=N
260 FOR J=0 TO M
270 IF N(J)<T THEN 300
280 Q=INT(N(J)/T):W=N(J)-Q*T
290 N(J)=W:N(J+1)=N(J+1)+Q
300 NEXT
310 J=M+1
320 IF N(J)=0 THEN J=J-1:GOTO 320
330 IF J>=M THEN 500
340 D=0:PRINT K;TAB(6);
350 N$=STR$(N(J)):N$=RIGHT$(N$,1)
360 D=D+1
370 IF D>25 THEN D=1:PRINT:PRINT TAB(6);
380 PRINT N$;:J=J-1
390 IF J>=0 THEN 350
400 N=N+F
410 K=K+1:PRINT
420 FOR J=0 TO M:N(J)=N(J)*N:NEXT
430 GOTO 260
500 FOR J=1 TO L+5:N(J)=0:NEXT
510 M=0:N=0:PRINT:GOTO 170
```

## EASY CHANGES

1. To change the program so that it always uses, say, fifty digit numbers, remove lines 170 and 180, and insert this line:

   170 M = 50

2. To clear the screen before the output begins being displayed, insert this line:

   215 CLS

3. If 250 digits isn't enough for you, you can go higher. For 500 digits, make this change:

   150 L = 500

   You need a 16K computer to go over 300 digits or so.

## MAIN ROUTINES

| | |
|---|---|
| 120-160 | Displays title. Sets up array for calculations. |
| 170-240 | Asks for number of digits and N. Checks validity of responses. Displays heading. |
| 250 | Initializes variables for calculations. |
| 260-300 | Performs "carrying" in N array so each element has a value no larger than 9. |
| 310-320 | Scans backwards through N array for first non-zero element. |
| 330 | Checks to see if this value would be larger than the number of digits requested. |
| 340-390 | Displays counter and number. Goes to second line if necessary. |
| 400-410 | Prepares to multiply by N to get next number. |
| 420-430 | Multiplies each digit in N array by N. Goes back to line 260. |
| 500-510 | Zeroes out N array in preparation for next request. Goes back to 170. |

## MAIN VARIABLES

| | |
|---|---|
| N | Array in which calculations are made. |
| M | Number of digits of precision requested by operator. |
| N | Starting value. If 1, factorials. If greater than 1, powers of N. |
| F | Set to zero if powers, 1 if factorials. |

T           Constant value of 10.
K           Counter of current power or factorial.
J           Subscript variable.
Q,W         Temporary variables used in reducing each integer
            position in the N array to a value from 0 to 9.
D           Number of digits displayed so far on the current line
            (maximum is 25).
N$          String variable used to convert each digit into dis-
            playable format.

## SUGGESTED PROJECTS

1. Determine the largest N that could be used without errors
   entering into the calculation (because of intermediate results
   exceeding one billion), then modify line 210 to permit values
   that large to be entered.
2. Create a series of subroutines that can add, subtract, multiply, divide, and exchange numbers in two arrays, using a
   technique like the one used here. Then you can perform
   high precision calculations by means of a series of GOSUB
   statements.

# PYTHAG

## PURPOSE

Remember the Pythagorean Theorem? It says that the sum of the squares of the two legs of a right triangle is equal to the square of the hypotenuse. Expressed as a formula, it is $a^2 + b^2 = c^2$. The most commonly remembered example of this is the 3-4-5 right triangle ($3^2 + 4^2 = 5^2$). Of course, there are an infinite number of other right triangles.

This program displays integer values of a, b, and c that result in right triangles.

## HOW TO USE IT

To use this program, all you need to do is RUN it and watch the "Pythagorean triplets" (sets of values for a, b, and c) come out. The program displays thirteen sets of values on each screen, and then waits for you to press any key (except **BREAK**) before it continues with the next thirteen. It will go on indefinitely until you press the **BREAK** key.

The left-hand column shows the count of the number of sets of triplets produced, and the other three columns are the values of a, b, and c.

The sequence in which the triplets are produced is not too obvious, so we will explain how the numbers are generated.

It has been proved that the following technique will generate all *primitive* Pythagorean triplets. ("Primitive" means that no set is an exact multiple of another.) If you have two positive integers called R and S such that:

1. R is greater than S,
2. R and S are of opposite parity (one is odd and the other is even), and
3. R and S are relatively prime (they have no common integer divisors except 1),

then a, b, and c can be found as follows:

$$a = R^2 - S^2$$
$$b = 2RS$$
$$c = R^2 + S^2$$

The program starts with a value of 2 for R. It generates all possible S values for that R (starting at R − 1 and then decreasing) and then adds one to R and continues. So, the first set of triplets is created when R is 2 and S is 1, the second set when R is 3 and S is 2, and so on.

**SAMPLE RUN**

```
PYTHAGOREAN TRIPLETS
COUNT    -A-      -B-      -C-
  1       3        4        5
  2       5       12       13
  3       7       24       25
  4      15        8       17
  5       9       40       41
  6      21       20       29
  7      11       60       61
  8      35       12       37
  9      13       84       85
 10      33       56       65
 11      45       28       53
 12      15      112      113
 13      39       80       89
PRESS A KEY TO GO ON
```

The program shows the first screen of Pythagorean triplets.

## PROGRAM LISTING

```
100 REM: PYTHAG
110 REM: (C) 1981, TOM RUGG AND PHIL
    FELDMAN
120 CLEAR 50
130 R=2:K=1:D=0
150 GOSUB 350
180 S=R-1
190 A=R*R-S*S
200 B=2*R*S
210 C=R*R+S*S
220 PRINT K;TAB(7);A;TAB(14);
225 PRINT B;TAB(21);C
230 K=K+1:D=D+1:GOTO 400
240 S=S-2
245 IF S<=0 THEN R=R+1:GOTO 180
250 S1=S
255 B1=R
260 N=INT(B1/S1)
270 R1=B1-S1*N
280 IF R1=0 THEN 300
290 B1=S1:S1=R1:GOTO 260
300 IF S1<>1 THEN 240
320 GOTO 190
350 CLS
360 PRINT"PYTHAGOREAN TRIPLETS"
370 PRINT"COUNT";TAB(7);"-A-";
380 PRINT TAB(14);"-B-";
390 PRINT TAB(21);"-C-":RETURN
400 IF D<13 THEN 240
410 PRINT"PRESS A KEY TO GO ON";
420 IF LEN(INKEY$)=0 THEN 420
430 GOSUB 350
440 D=0
460 GOTO 240
```

## EASY CHANGES

1. Alter the starting value of R in line 130. Instead of 2, try 50 or 100.
2. If you want, you can change the number of sets of triplets displayed on each screen. Change the 13 in line 400 to a 10,

for example. You probably won't want to try a value greater than 13, since that would cause the column headings to roll off the screen.

3.  To make the program continue without requiring you to press a key for the next screen of values, insert either of these lines:

$$405 \text{ GOTO } 430$$

or

$$405 \text{ GOTO } 440$$

The first will display headings for each screen. The second will only display the headings at the beginning of the run.

## MAIN ROUTINES

| | |
|---|---|
| 130 | Initializes variables. |
| 150 | Displays the title and column headings. |
| 180 | Calculates first value of S for current R value. |
| 190-210 | Calculates A, B, and C. |
| 220-230 | Displays one line of values. Adds to counters. |
| 240-245 | Calculates next S value. If no more, calculates next R value. |
| 250-300 | Determines if R and S are relatively prime. |
| 350-390 | Subroutine to display title and column headings. |
| 400-460 | Checks if screen is full yet. If so, waits for key to be pressed. |

## MAIN VARIABLES

| | |
|---|---|
| R,S | See explanation in "How To Use It." |
| K | Count of total number of sets displayed. |
| D | Count of number of sets displayed on one screen. |
| A,B,C | Lengths of the three sides of the triangle. |
| S1,B1, R1,N | Used in determining if R and S are relatively prime. |

## SUGGESTED PROJECTS

1.  In addition to displaying K, A, B, and C on each line, display R and S. You will have to squeeze the columns closer together.

2. Because this program uses integer values that get increasingly large, eventually some will exceed the Color Computer's integer capacity and produce incorrect results. Can you determine when this will be? Modify the program to stop when this occurs.

# TUNE

## PURPOSE

If you have Extended Color BASIC on your Color Computer, you can use the PLAY command to play music. But if you only have "regular" Color BASIC, you can't play a tune quite as easily. This program allows you to experiment with some simple computer tune-playing, whether you have Extended Color BASIC or not.

## HOW TO USE IT

As shown in the Program Listing, TUNE currently plays a familiar portion of the Blue Danube waltz. We'll explain how to enter other tunes in a moment.

When you RUN the program, it displays the title of the program at the top of the screen and immediately begins playing its tune. Of course, you have to be using a television with a speaker, and its volume control needs to be set loud enough for you to hear the music.

As each note is played, a graphics point (actually a small rectangle) is plotted on the TV screen, starting from the left and moving to the right. The vertical position of the point corresponds with the pitch of the note—high notes are near the top, and low notes near the bottom. No distinction is made between sharps, flats, and naturals during this display. For example, F sharp and F natural both have the same vertical position. If the tune has more than 64 notes, the display goes to the right edge of the screen and begins overlaying the notes at the left edge.

This graphics display gives you something to watch while the tune is being played, and for many tunes it clearly shows you the patterns and symmetry that make music enjoyable.

After you get tired of hearing the Blue Danube, you will undoubtedly want to enter some tunes of your own choosing. With only a little musical training, you can translate a simple piece of sheet music into the notation needed by this program. We may be crazy, but we think we can give you enough of an introduction to reading music in the next few paragraphs that you will be able to figure out how to understand simple musical notation and copy a tune into this program. For more details on reading music, refer to an introductory music text.

First, turn to Appendix A of your *Getting Started With Color BASIC* manual. The main thing to learn from Appendix A is the name for each musical note. We will refer to the lowest full octave (notes A through G, or tone numbers 58 through 147) as octave 1. The next one above that will be octave 2, and so on up to octave 4 (which stops at E, tone number 244). The lowest note is F of octave 0 (tone number 5). You may want to mark these octaves in pencil in your manual by drawing a line extending downwards between the G of one octave and the A of the next. Then write the octave number underneath the center of each octave. An octave is actually eight notes, such as A through A, but for our purposes here we will think of an octave as seven notes (A through G).

Each of the notes shown in Appendix A is a *quarter* note. A quarter note is represented by a solid black oval (note-head) with a "stick" (stem) attached. The most common notes in most music are whole notes, half notes, quarter notes, eighth notes, and sixteenth notes. The duration of each of these notes, relative to the others, is just as you would expect from their fraction-like names. For example, a quarter note lasts twice as long as an eighth note, but only half as long as a half note.

A half note looks like a hollow quarter note (i.e., an oval on a stick). A whole note is an oval with no stick. An eighth note looks like a quarter note with a flag on the stick, and a sixteenth note has two flags. If two eighth notes or sixteenth notes are next to each other, they are usually connected by one or two bars, respectively, rather than having individual flags.

A *chord* is several notes played simultaneously. It looks like a stack of ovals on one stick. Since our computer cannot play chords, we will have to simply play the top note on the stack when we encounter a chord. This is the simplest way to follow the melody like a one-finger piano player.

And now a word about sharps and flats. The white keys on a piano are the *natural* notes. The black keys are the *accidentals* (sharps and flats). On a musical score, sharps are indicated by the pound sign ("#"), and flats by a symbol that resembles a lower case "b." Naturals are assumed when neither the sharp or flat symbol is used. When a particular note is always sharp, for example, in a tune, this is indicated at the far left of the musical staff (the five parallel lines upon which the notes are drawn), rather than next to every occurrence of the note. This applies to any octave the note is played in. For example, if F sharp is indicated at the left of the staff, all F's are sharp, whether on that same line of the staff or not. When an F should be a natural instead of a sharp, the natural symbol is used next to the F. The natural symbol is drawn in various ways, but generally looks like a little rectangle.

With these fundamentals in mind, let's look at how we enter music into the TUNE program. The DATA statements that represent the tune to be played are located between lines 600 and 9990 of the program. To enter your own music, delete those lines so you can begin entering yours. Leave lines 600 and 9990 as they are, but delete all lines between them.

For each note of your tune, the computer needs to know two things: the note to be played and its duration. The DATA statements you enter after line 600 provide this information. Each entry you make is separated by commas, and can indicate either a duration, a note, or a rest.

The first thing you must provide is a duration. All subsequent notes will be played for this duration until you change it, to keep you from having to enter a duration indication for every note when many in a row are the same. The duration is specified by a number, indicating the number of time units to play the note. So, "1" indicates a note to be played for one time unit, "8" indicates eight time units, etc. These numbers must be integers. We know how long each type of note should be played in relation to the others (e.g., a whole note is twice as long as a half note), so we can choose whatever number of time units we find most convenient as a starting point. The best way to determine how many time units to assign to each type of note is to look for the shortest note in the tune. If it is an eighth note, then use 1 to indicate an eighth note, 2 for a quarter note, 4 for a half note, and 8 for a whole note.

Unfortunately, this scheme is complicated by something called a *dotted* note. A dotted note is shown by a dot immediately after the note, which indicates that note should be held for one and one-half times its normal length. For example, if a half note is being held for 4 time units, then a dotted half note would be held for 6 time units. This seems simple enough, but what if, as before, an eighth note is the shortest note in the tune, and there are also some dotted eighth notes? If the eighth note is held for one time unit, then the dotted eighth needs to be held for 1.5 time units. Our program doesn't allow fractional durations, so we need to double our time unit assignments. This way we can use 2 for an eighth note, 3 for a dotted eighth note, 4 for a quarter note, 6 for a dotted quarter note, 8 for a half note, etc.

Now that we know how to express the duration of each note, how do we say which note it is (i.e., its pitch)? This is done by entering two or three characters for each note, which have the following meanings. The first character says which note it is (A through G). The second character says which octave it is in (0 through 4, as explained earlier). The third character, if present, says if the note is a sharp or flat. The plus sign indicates a sharp, and any other character indicates a flat. Using a minus sign for a flat is recommended. If the third character is absent, the note is a natural (neither sharp nor flat).

One other type of entry is possible in the program. If the first character is an R, it means to *rest*, or make no sound. When this happens, the remaining one or two characters indicate the number of time units to rest. So R4, for example, means to rest for four time units, and R16 means to rest for 16 time units.

That covers all the rules. All you need to do is enter the DATA statements for your tune after line 600. It is generally a good idea to leave some space between your line numbers, in case you discover later that you need to add some more lines. Starting with line 610 or 620, and adding 10 or 20 for each new line number is a good approach.

To help you out, here is a short example. On page 52 of *Getting Started With Color BASIC* (first or second printing) you can find two bars of "Three Blind Mice." If we decide to assign one time unit to an eighth note, here are the DATA statements to use:

610  DATA 2,E1,D1,C1,R2
620  DATA G1,1,F1,F1,2,E1,R2

Note that we used a separate DATA statement for each *bar* (or *measure*, the space between two vertical lines on the staff), which helps keep things organized in case we have to go back to fix a mistake.

There is a great deal more about music that we cannot cover in this limited space, but we hope this introduction has been enough to get you going. Be sure to read the Easy Changes section of this chapter to see several useful modifications you can easily make.

**SAMPLE RUN**

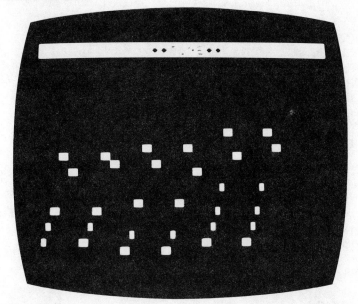

The program begins playing its tune and displaying a block for each note sounded.

## PROGRAM LISTING

```
100 REM: TUNE
110 REM: (C) 1981, TOM RUGG AND PHIL FELDMAN
120 CLEAR 200:GOSUB 350
200 READ T$:IF T$="X" THEN END
210 F$=LEFT$(T$,1)
220 IF F$>"G" THEN 400
230 IF F$<"A" THEN 300
240 J=ASC(F$)-63
250 J=J+7*(VAL(MID$(T$,2))-1)
255 SET(X,30-J,C)
260 X=X+1:IF X>63 THEN X=0
270 L=LEN(T$):IF L>2 THEN 320
280 SOUND N(J),D
290 GOTO 200
300 D=VAL(T$):IF D=0 THEN 460
310 D=T*D:GOTO 200
320 IF MID$(T$,3)<>"+" THEN 340
330 SOUND S(J),D:GOTO 200
340 SOUND S(J-1),D:GOTO 200
350 DIM N(27),S(27)
360 CLS(0):T=2:X=0:C=5
370 PRINT TAB(12);"**TUNE**"
380 FOR J=0 TO 27:READ N(J):NEXT
390 FOR J=0 TO 27:READ S(J):NEXT:RETURN
400 IF F$<>"R" THEN 460
410 L=VAL(MID$(T$,2))
420 IF L=0 THEN 460
430 L=T*L
440 FOR W=1 TO 30*L:NEXT
450 GOTO 200
460 PRINT T$;"**ILLEGAL**"
470 END
500 DATA 5,32,58,78,89,108
510 DATA 125,133,147,159,170,176
520 DATA 185,193,197,204,210,216
530 DATA 218,223,227,229,232,236
540 DATA 238,239,242,244
550 DATA 19,45,69,89,99,117
560 DATA 133,140,153,165,176,180
570 DATA 189,197,200,207,213,218
580 DATA 221,225,229,231,234,237
590 DATA 239,241,243,245
600 REM**TUNE FOLLOWS
```

```
620 DATA 2,D1,F1+,A2,4,A2,2,A3
630 DATA A3,R2,F2+,F2+,R2
640 DATA D1,D1,F1+,A2,4,A2,2,A3
650 DATA A3,R2,G2,G2
660 DATA R2,C1+,C1+,E1,B2,4,B2
670 DATA 2,B3,B3,R2,G2,G2,R2
690 DATA C1+,C1+,E1,B2,4,B2
700 DATA 2,B3,B3,R2,F2+,F2+,R2
710 DATA D1,D1,F1+,A2,4,D2
720 DATA 2,D3,D3,R2,A3,A3,R2
730 DATA D1,D1,F1+,A2,4,D2
740 DATA 2,D3,D3,R2,B3,B3,R2,E2,E2,G2
750 DATA 1,B3,R1,8,B3,2,G2+,A3,8,F3+
760 DATA 2,D3,F2+,4,F2+,2,E2,4,B3,2,A3
770 DATA D2,R1,1,D2,2,D2
9990 DATA X
9999 REM: BLUE DANUBE
```

## EASY CHANGES

1. To change the *tempo* (speed) of the tune, change the value of T in line 360. Larger values cause all the notes to be held longer, slowing down the tune. To experiment, it is easiest to change T by inserting line 365. For example, to make the tune go faster, insert:

$$365 \ T = 1$$

   To make it go slower, use:

$$365 \ T = 3 \quad \text{or} \quad 365 \ T = 4$$

2. Instead of having the graphics display overlay itself after 64 notes of a tune, you can make the screen go black before starting over at the left with this change:

$$260 \ X = X + 1 : IF \ X > 63 \ THEN \ X = 0 : CLS(0)$$

3. To display the DATA value for each note as the computer is playing the tune, insert:

$$205 \ PRINT \ T\$;",";$$

4. To eliminate the graphics display of each note, delete line 255.

5. If you would rather use the conventional musical symbol for a sharp instead of a plus sign, replace the plus symbol in line 320 with the "pound sign" ("#").

6. If you would rather use some color other than "buff" in the graphics display for each note, change the value of C in line

360. For example, to display blue instead of buff, set C
equal to 3.

7. To get a multicolored display as different notes of the scale
are played, insert:

$$245 \ C = J - 1$$

8. To display the title of the tune, insert line 375. For example:

375 PRINT TAB(10); "BLUE DANUBE"

9. To cause the program to ignore the tune in the DATA
statements and instead play random music in the key of C
until you press the BREAK key, make these changes:

200 T$ = CHR$(RND(7) + 64) + CHR$(RND(3) + 48)
205 D = RND(8)

## MAIN ROUTINES

| | |
|---|---|
| 120 | Calls subroutine to initialize variables and display title. |
| 200- 340 | Reads and interprets the next tune element. |
| 200 | Reads the next tune element. Checks for end. |
| 210- 230 | Examines first character; determines which type of entry it is. |
| 240- 250 | Determines which note is to be played, based on first 2 characters. |
| 255 | Displays graphics point based on note played. |
| 270- 290 | Determines if note is a natural. Plays it if so and goes back for next note. |
| 300- 310 | Processes numerical tune element (changes duration). |
| 320- 340 | Determines if non-natural note is sharp or flat. Plays it. |
| 350- 390 | Subroutine to initialize variables, display title, store tone numbers. |
| 400- 450 | Processes "rest" (silent) element. |
| 460- 470 | Displays message and ends program if an illegal element is found. |
| 500- 590 | DATA statements with values for N and S arrays. |
| 600-9989 | DATA statements with tune elements to be played. |
| 9990 | DATA statement indicating end of tune. |
| 9999 | Remark statement identifying the tune's title. |

## MAIN VARIABLES

| | |
|---|---|
| T$ | Tune element indicating note, duration, or rest. |
| F$ | First character of tune element. |
| J | Work, loop, and subscript variable. |
| X | Horizontal position of graphics point. |
| C | Color of graphics point. |
| L | Length of tune element; also, length of rest. |
| N | Array of natural notes. |
| D | Duration of note to be played. |
| T | Tempo indicator (how fast to play tune). |
| S | Array of sharp and flat notes. |
| W | Work variable to count time delay for a rest. |

## SUGGESTED PROJECTS

1. Revise the program to *compose* melodies, rather than simply play tunes that you enter. Use Easy Change #9 as your starting point, but insert statements to cause "organized" music to be played (with rhythm and harmony) instead of random music.
2. Draw a graphics piano keyboard on the video display, and indicate which key is being "played" as each note is sounded.
3. Draw a musical score on the video display and graphically draw each note as it is played.

# Appendix
# Memory Usage

Each of the programs in this book will fit in a TRS-80 Color Computer with 16K of RAM (user memory). All work with either (standard) Color BASIC or Extended Color BASIC.

The majority of the programs will also fit in a TRS-80 Color Computer with only 4K of RAM. Each program which will not fit in 4K has an indication somewhere in the chapter to tell you that 16K is required.

For your convenience, here is a list of all the programs that will *not* fit in 4K.

Applications: DECIDE, MILEAGE.
Educational: ARITHMETIC, METRIC.
Games: JOT, WARI.
Graphics: WALLOONS.
Mathematics: CURVE, STATS.

**NOTES FOR THE TRS-80 MC-10
MICRO COLOR COMPUTER**

The following 21 programs will all work as shown in the book on a 4K MC-10. No changes are needed.

| | | |
|---|---|---|
| Biorhythm | Vocab | Graph |
| Checkbook | Argo | Integrate |
| Loan | Decode | Simeqn |
| Quest/Exam | Kaleido | Birthday |
| Sortlist | Sparkle | PI |

| Metric | Squares | Powers |
|--------|---------|--------|
| Numbers | Diffeqn | Pythag |

In addition, the following 9 programs will work on a 4K MC-10 if changes are made as shown:

**ANNUAL:** Change each occurance of **PRINT#P**, (including the comma) to PRINT (without the **#P**, or **#P**). For example, change lines 190 and 200 to

190 PRINT "INTEREST RATE = ";R
200 PRINT

The following lines need this change: 190, 200, 210, 220, 230, 240, 280, 330, and 400.

**ARITHMETIC:** Change line 130 so it says

130 CLEAR 50

**HAMCODE:** Change the 12 in lines 320 and 560 to a 21. This will allow you to press **Control-Q** (L.DE.) to end options 1 and 3. The MC-10 has no equivalent to the **CLEAR** key on the Color Computer.

**TACHIST:** In lines 620 and 630, change the 8 to 16. This prevents phrases at the maximum speed from being invisible once in a while.

**GROAN:** Make the changes shown in Easy Change 5 to make the program small enough to fit into 4K of memory. However, there's no need to delete lines 100-110, 310, and 340-350. Also, you will probably want to change line 2750, as mentioned in Easy Change 3, to:

2750 FOR K = 1 TO 5000:NEXT:RETURN

**OBSTACLE:** Insert this line:

167 S = 16384

**ROADRACE:** In line 210, change the 1024 to 16384. Also, note that the car movement keys are the left and right arrow keys, which require the **CONTROL** key to be held down. To change the program to use different keys, see Easy Change 1. Note also that Easy Change 4 doesn't apply to the MC-10, and Easy Change 5 isn't needed to make the program fit into 4K.

**WARI:** In line 120, change the 200 to 50 to allow the program to fit into 4K.

**TUNE:** The tone and duration of the SOUND command are a little different on the MC-10. To get a better approximation of the correct sounds, make these additions and changes.

```
390 FOR J = 0 TO 27:READ S(J):NEXT
392 CF = .986
394 FOR J = 0 TO 27
396 N(J) = INT(CF*N(J) + .6)
397 S(J) = INT(CF*S(J) + .6)
398 NEXT:RETURN
440 FOR J = 1 TO 50*L:NEXT
```

In addition, the following 5 programs will work on an MC-10 with the 16K expansion module, but are too large to fit into 4K of memory:

DECIDE, JOT, WALLOONS, CURVE, STATS.

However, STATS will require these two lines to be changed:

```
560 IF N<>MX THEN 600
710 IF N<>0 THEN 800
```

That leaves these two, which will not work on an MC-10 because they use cassette data files, which are very much different on the MC-10:

MILEAGE, FLASHCARD.

# Bibliography

## BOOKS

Bell, R. C., *Board and Table Games From Many Civilizations*, Oxford University Press, London, 1969. (WARI)

Cohen, Daniel, *Biorhythms in Your Life*, Fawcett Publications, Greenwich, Connecticut, 1976. (BIORHYTHM)

Crow, E. L., David, F. A., and Maxfield, M. W., *Statistics Manual*, Dover Publications, New York, 1960. (STATS)

Croxton, F. E., Crowden, D. J., and Klein, S., *Applied General Statistics* (Third Edition), Prentice-Hall, Englewood Cliffs, N. J., 1967. (STATS)

Elson, Louis C., *Elson's Pocket Music Dictionary*, Oliver Ditson Company, Bryn Mawr, Pennsylvania, 1909. (TUNE)

Gruenberger, Fred J., and Jaffray, George, *Problems for Computer Solution*, John Wiley and Sons, New York, 1965. (BIRTHDAY, PI, SORTLIST)

Gruenberger, Fred J., and McCracken, Daniel D., *Introduction to Electronic Computers*, John Wiley and Sons, New York, 1961. (MILEAGE, PI, PYTHAG, WARI as Oware)

Hildebrand, F. B., *Introduction to Numerical Analysis*, McGraw-Hill, New York, 1956. (CURVE, DIFFEQN, INTEGRATE, SIMEQN)

Knuth, Donald E., *The Art of Computer Programming (Volume 3)*, Addison-Wesley, Reading, Massachusetts, 1973. (SORTLIST)

Kuo, S. S., *Computer Applications of Numerical Methods*, Addison-Wesley, Reading, Massachusetts, 1972. (CURVE, DIFFEQN, INTEGRATE, SIMEQN)

McCracken, Daniel D., and Dorn, W. S., *Numerical Methods And FORTRAN Programming*, John Wiley and Sons, New York, 1964. (CURVE, DIFFEQN, INTEGRATE, SIMEQN)

Orr, William I., *Radio Handbook* (19th Edition), Howard W. Sams & Co., Inc., Indianapolis, Indiana, 1972. (HAMCODE)

Radio Shack, *Getting Started With Color BASIC*, Tandy Corporation, Fort Worth, Texas, 1981.

Shefter, Harry, *Faster Reading Self-Taught*, Washington Square Press, New York, 1960. (TACHIST)

**PERIODICALS**

Feldman, Phil, and Rugg, Tom, "Pass the Buck," *Kilobaud*, July 1977, pp. 90-96. (DECIDE)

Fliegel, H. F., and Van Flandern, T. C., "A Machine Algorithm for Processing Calendar Dates," *Communications of the ACM*, October, 1968, P. 657. (BIORHYTHM)

# Errata Offer

All of the programs in this book have been tested carefully and are working correctly to the best of our knowledge. However, we take no responsibility for any losses which may be suffered as a result of errors or misuse. You must bear the responsibility of verifying each program's accuracy and applicability for your purposes.

If you want to get a copy of an errata sheet that lists corrections for any errors or ambiguities we have found to date, send one dollar ($1.00) and a self addressed stamped envelope (SASE) to the address below. Ask for errata for this book (by name). We hope we won't have any errors to tell you about, in which case we'll try to send you some other worthwhile information about the Color Computer.

If you think you've found an error, please let us know. If you want an answer, include a SASE.

Please keep in mind that the most likely cause of a program working incorrectly is a typing error. Please check your typing *very* carefully before you send us an irate note about an error in one of the programs.

Tom Rugg and Phil Feldman
Errata—TRS-80 Color Programs
P.O. Box 24815
Los Angeles, CA 90024